Unfree in Pales

# UNFREE IN PALESTINE

## Registration, Documentation and Movement Restriction

Nadia Abu-Zahra and Adah Kay

PLUTO PRESS

First published 2013 by Pluto Press
345 Archway Road, London N6 5AA
www.plutobooks.com

British Library Cataloguing in Publication Data
A catalogue record for this book is available from the British Library

ISBN   978 0 7453 2528 6    Hardback
ISBN   978 0 7453 2527 9    Paperback
ISBN   978 1 8496 4768 7    PDF eBook
ISBN   978 1 8496 4769 4    Kindle eBook
ISBN   978 1 8496 4767 0    EPUB eBook

Library of Congress Cataloging in Publication Data applied for

10   9   8   7   6   5   4   3   2   1

Designed and produced for Pluto Press by Chase Publishing Services Ltd
Typeset from disk by Stanford DTP Services, Northampton, England

# Contents

# Illustrations

# Acknowledgements

In memory: Tom Kay, Bahjat (Abu Sami) Abu Gharbiyyeh, Dr James Graff, Laila Bondugjie, Dr Peter Dodd, Arab Abdel-Hadi, Dr Tanya Reinhart, Mahmut Gokmen, and Sir Marrack Goulding. This book is the product of a highly successful and enjoyable "arranged marriage". We thank filmmaker and friend Peter Snowdon who introduced us at the start of our mainly virtual email/ Skype relationship.

We first met in 2005 – by email. Nadia was working on her thesis in Oxford, and Adah was in Ramallah doing interviews for a book on movement restrictions with two colleagues that Pluto had agreed to publish. Sadly that book fell through as, for personal reasons, Adah's two colleagues had to drop out. Then, after one of our few precious face-to-face meetings, Nadia suggested that we pool our resources and think about a book that in fact made more sense. We would start with the system of identity documentation and population registration that formed the obvious basis for all the other aspects of Israel's military occupation in Palestine – especially movement restrictions. In the process we decided to look at the whole system as a historical continuum from the late nineteenth century to the present and to locate it in a wider global context.

Fortunately Anne Beech at Pluto agreed to a new contract and we started the joint project in 2007. However, it has been a long birth punctuated by the death of Tom, Adah's husband, at the end of 2007, personal illness, and the birth of Nadia's first child.

Throughout we have felt supported and encouraged by the tremendous understanding and forbearance of Anne Beech and Will Viney at Pluto.

Many people helped us produce this book. We would like to thank Dr Ghassan Abdullah, Beatrix Campbell, and Richard Kuper for taking the time to review the text and provide tough and helpful feedback. We thank also those who kindly granted permission for use of their photographs and maps: Tom Kay, Zoriah (www. zoriah.com), Gustaf Hansson, the Deutsches Bundesarchiv, and *The Arab World Geographer* (AWG) (http://arabworldgeographer. metapress.com).

We are indebted to the following named interviewees who were so generous with their time, and those equal number of interviewees who wish to remain anonymous: Abu Ghaleb, Sharif Kanaana, Khalil Nahleh, Yusef Sawfat Odeh, Wasfiyye Ishrieh Abu Hassan, Riham Barghouti, Helen Murray, Jehan Helou, the staff at Al Amari Camp girls secondary school, Dr Mohammed Scaafi, Joan Jubran, Dr Jihad Mash'al, interviewees in Salfit, interviewees from Aida Camp Bethlehem, the staff at the NPA (National Plan for Children), Imm Ahmed, Hani Amer, Nazeeh Shalabi, Dr Rema Hammami, Hind Salameh, Anne Kindrachuk, Jan de Jong, and Drs Ilan Pappé, Eyal Benvenisti, Oren Yiftachel, and Sandy Kedar.

We are also grateful to all those individuals and organisations who helped with the logistics of fieldwork, and contributed their insights on the issues addressed in the book. Given the overlap with Nadia's doctoral research between 2004 and 2007, this book benefited from the financial support of a number of institutions, including the University of Oxford (St Antony's College Stahl Award and the Oxford Project for Peace Studies from the Cyril Foster Committee, Centre for International Studies, Department of Politics and International Relations), the Social Sciences and Humanities Research Council of Canada, the Palestinian American Research Centre, and the Canadian International Development Agency.

Adah would like to thank Cathy Cook and Adam Hanieh for early discussions and work on the initial book on movement restrictions, and Rana and Amahl Bishara for helping to arrange interviews. Also to my family and close friends both in London and Ramallah who encouraged me to keep going on a project that might have faltered at various points.

Nadia is grateful to Drs Dawn Chatty, Tony Lemon, Dan Brockington, Ghazi-Walid Falah, Rita Giacaman, and Geraldine Pratt for their insights and gentle nudges in the right direction when needed. To my family in Oxford who taught me the core principles in this book, and to friends who provided a roof over my head and good company, thank you. To those Swedes who conveyed more through film than is possible in a book. And to the Palestinians patient with my stumbling comprehension, I hope I have conveyed some of the realities with accuracy and respect.

A large number of academics, professionals, and organisers enabled the sharing of many ideas in this book with a broad audience, and they deserve more thanks than can fit here – in particular, Rosemary Tylka, Karen Abu Zayd, Jamal Jum'a, and Drs Elia Zureik, Jeanne Simonelli, Silvia Macchi, Cédric Parizot, Christopher

Harker, Naji Haraj, and Jane Caplan, who all believed in this from the beginning. Thanks also to those in Ottawa (graduating students as well as international human rights advocates) and in Toronto – especially Xing Pian Huang – for their support in the final days of preparation. Nothing would be complete without my loving husband, and nothing would have begun without my family – most of all, my incredible parents. This book is for you both.

# 1
# Introduction

*When I close my eyes, I still hear the crash of ocean waves, I still feel the warm sun on my face, and I still taste salt from the sea spray.*[1]

So wrote one of 27 passengers on the SS Dignity, one of several small sailing boats containing doctors, lawyers, teachers, and Nobel laureate Mairead Maguire. Calling themselves "the freedom riders of the twenty-first century", they were the first international vessels, in 2008, to enter the coast of Gaza in over 40 years.

Three years later, in the West Bank, six Palestinians stood at the 148 Bus stop near the Jewish colony of Migron, again, as "freedom riders". The bus is operated by Egged, an Israeli company edging into the global market, despite boycott efforts. It serves exclusive Jewish colonies, built on Palestinian land, but where Palestinians are forbidden to enter. After five buses sped by the Palestinians and their placards reading "freedom", "dignity", and "we shall overcome", a sixth bus pulled up, with a number of passengers already aboard. The Palestinians paid the fare and boarded. Israeli army and police vehicles surrounded the bus and boarded it when it stopped again. The settlers aboard the bus rushed off, including 54-year-old Haggai Segal from the colony of Ofra, once jailed for planting a car bomb that seriously wounded a Palestinian mayor.[2]

"This is our bus" said Maggie Amir, from the Jewish colony of Rimonim. "This is our land" said another passenger leaving the bus. Abraham, a 70-year old from the colony of Psagot, was more accommodating, "If they are good ... why not let them ride the bus?" A younger settler expressed irritation at the hold-up to her day, to which Palestinian activist Huwaida Arraf replied, "Your soldiers hold us up ten times longer than this, every day at checkpoints across the West Bank". Two policemen crowded over Huwaida's slight figure. Another policeman stood by, with two fully armed soldiers behind. Huwaida raised her eyebrows as they studied her ID.[3]

Another policeman asked for 38-year-old Badi' Dweik's ID. He had been seated a row away from bomber Haggai Segal. "I am not going to obey your discriminatory law" Badi' said in Arabic.[4] "So you are detained" replied the policeman, also in Arabic. "Fine. I am not moving" said Badi'. "Why don't you ask the settlers for a permit?" That was enough for the policeman, "I am the law, you are not the law".[5]

The freedom riders by sea and bus drew global attention to a system of movement restrictions that many considered unprecedented, despite powerful parallels to apartheid South Africa, the Jim Crow laws of the southern United States, and the internment of Japanese Canadians and Americans during the Second World War.[6] As of 2012, 101 different kinds of permits govern Palestinian movement.

> There are separate permits for worshipers who attend Friday prayers in Jerusalem and for clerics working at the site; for unspecified clergy and for church employees. Medical permits differentiate between physicians and ambulance drivers, and "medical emergency staff" ... There is a permit for escorting a patient in an ambulance and one for simply escorting a patient.
>
> There are separate permits for traveling to a wedding in the West Bank or traveling to a wedding in Israel, and also for going to Israel for a funeral, a work meeting, or a court hearing.[7]

In 2011 the Israeli Border police started to train young Jewish teenagers to carry M16s (5.56 mm calibre semi-automatic rifles) and hunt down Palestinian workers without movement permits. High-school student Reut enjoys the chase:

> I consider it a form of pleasure. It simply provides me with values, and I love the action.
>
> I like catching the Palestinian workers. [...] The point is to catch them and return them back where they belong.[8]

Another youth, Eran, described his feelings:

> It's a fun feeling – you are filled with adrenaline and energy during such operations. We also feel pride for protecting our home. For instance, one time we went to a construction site and found a few of them there. We saw them hiding and we caught them, took their identification cards, sat them down in the vehicle, and called our commander to come check them.[9]

The teenagers also stopped and searched buses.

These small vignettes, of freedom riders and teens with M16s, speak to many of the key issues for Palestinians and Israelis today: ideology and discourse, history and international relations, land, coexistence, and resistance.[10] Each of these subjects has its own, ever-expanding, library of key texts. What is particular to these vignettes, however, is the common theme of movement restriction.

## 1.1    FREEDOM AND UNFREEDOM IN PALESTINE

### "A History of the IDs"

By most accounts, movement restriction is one of the most pressing current problems in the West Bank and Gaza Strip, where identity documents, permits, and colour-coded license plates define who can go where, when, and for how long. If this book were to be translated to Arabic or Hebrew, it would probably have the simple title, "A History of the IDs", because of the weight of local meaning carried by the word "ID" (*hawiyya* in Arabic, or *teudat* in Hebrew). Palestinian poet Mahmoud Darwish in 1964 begins his oft-quoted poem on the ID:

*Sejjil! Ana 'Arabi. Wa raqam bitaaqati khamsoona elf.*
Register! I am an Arab. And my identity card number is fifty thousand.

The first word is addressed to an unknown administrator or registrar, and the challenge to register or "record me" is later followed with a detailed catalogue of indigeneity and rootedness, punctuated with:

*Fa hal tardheek manzilati?*
Are you satisfied with my status?

The last word, however, means both status and house, mocking the colonial presence. For Palestinians in the West Bank and Gaza Strip, and before them, for Palestinians displaced within the 1949 Armistice lines, the ID was an instrument of suppression, repression, and humiliation. It was a denial of rights and the condition on which these rights were temporarily restored at the whim of Israeli authorities.

The power of Darwish's poem is in the vivid explanation of all that the ID represents: population registration, denationalisation, and the stripping of all rights from the citizens of Palestine; a permit regime that makes all such rights subservient to Israeli state permission; the indignity of repeated ID checks in one's home, land, and movements from place to place; and the patient, split attitude toward the ID – acceptance of reliance on it, but rejection of its authority – until an opportunity arises to restore one's full rights.

Remarkably, although the separated pieces of the puzzle have all been painstakingly chronicled, and while this multifaceted history of movement restriction, identity documentation, and population registration and denationalisation is recognised as being the crux of the Palestinian problem, no single book-length document seems to draw the line from one phenomenon to the other in a continuous sweep.

Many publications on refugees, forced migration, and the right of return to their homes (as well as their rights *in situ*), cover only one piece of the puzzle: denationalisation. But there is little material describing the bureaucratic process of population registration.

In writing this book we have been able to draw on the extensive body of general and specialist literature on the bureaucracy of the occupation covering aspects such as the system of military rule and military courts, the secret services, the permit regime, the population registry, the Israeli high court, the Wall, collaboration, the role of architecture and planning, and so on. Other crucial sources include a range of specialist reports on the impact of movement restriction on: health and education; employment, agriculture, and the economy; and the family.[11]

We also acknowledge the important anthology by Abu-Laban, Lyon and Zureik which deals with movement restriction, identity documentation, and population registration viewed within a wider global context of evolving international trends in surveillance and control.[12]

These and other writings on Israeli bureaucracy emphasise the ubiquity of identity documents.[13] Darwish's "Register!" has not ceased to echo for the past five decades, during which:

> The permit regime functioned simultaneously as the scaffolding for many other forms of control and thus as part of the infrastructure of control, as well as a controlling apparatus in its own right.[14]

It is thus surprising that a chronological, cumulative account of registration, documentation, and movement restriction has not been written until now.

## Fresh Perspectives

Some would argue that a continuous history is misleading, and that the bureaucratic policies of the Zionist movement and Israel toward Palestinians are instead phases, perhaps oscillating between benevolence and open conquest, depending on the limits implied by Palestinian resistance and international norms and laws. Israeli policy has been conceived as being first survival (1948), then expansionism or colonisation (1967), and then separation (late 2000 onward).[15]

While most authors use the term "Zionist movement" comfortably for the period up to June 1948, after that point the term seems to drop out of use. This has become the unspoken consensus, despite the reality that the Zionist movement did not cease to exist, and that an increasing body of work views Zionist policy within the West Bank and Gaza as inseparable from analysis of Israeli society and politics today.[16]

In this book we focus on denationalisation rather than displacement or dispossession. Thus, instead of enumerating only the 850,000 refugees (or fewer, depending on which source you choose), we draw attention to the 1.4 million denationalised Palestinians. This figure, therefore, acknowledges the loss felt by Palestinians in the West Bank and Gaza Strip, numbering at least 400,000 in 1948, as well as that felt by Palestinians displaced within their homeland (at least 150,000 in 1948). The former group, for instance, numbers over four million today – excluding the millions living abroad in the diaspora without internationally recognised documents of state citizenship. Their loss (that is, their denationalisation) took place in 1948. It was not postponed until 1967 – the point at which most analysis of their interaction with the Zionist movement begins.

The focus on denationalisation, rather than solely dispossession, implicitly recognises the nationality and citizenship of Palestinians prior to 1948. Others imply that Palestinians have always been stateless, emphasising a history of "foreign rule". Yet, as international lawyer Henry Cattan points out, Palestinians were not stateless. International law professor John Quigley adds: they were passport-holding citizens of Palestine.[17]

## 1.2  SCANTILY-DOCUMENTED PASS SYSTEMS

This story is not unique: typically, movement restrictions are routinely unchronicled. In Canada for example, where indigenous peoples, the First Nations, were forced into reserves, very few publications exist on the pass system. Over 100 years after the pass system began, professor Frank Laurie Barron scoured the archives and found only brief mentions within half a dozen published accounts, amounting in total to less than 15 pages. Barron makes an important connection, however:

> The entire regime was fundamentally racist, but the aspect which particularly conjured up images of apartheid was the Indian pass system, applied in selected areas of the prairie west. Essentially, the pass system was a segregationist scheme which, without any legislative basis, required Indians to remain on their reserves unless they had a pass, duly signed by the Indian agent or farm instructor and specifying the purpose and duration of their absence.
>
> It is also relevant to note that in 1902 a commission from South Africa visited western Canada to study the pass system as a method of social control.[18]

Even if Canadians were not documenting the history and mechanisms of their pass system, South Africans involved in the construction of apartheid were keen to learn from it. This history placed Canada in an awkward position in the 1980s when it proclaimed opposition to South African apartheid. The same light-touch treatment of the pass system recurred in South Africa. Few concentrated on the detailed mechanisms and effects of the pass system. As with Palestine, many scholars writing about apartheid South Africa consider the pass system as inseparable from issues of ideology, land, violence, economy, and international relations.

Although these links are indeed important, they can obscure some equally important links between population registration, identity documentation, and movement restriction. Specifically: registration is linked to denationalisation, or the stripping of citizenship; consequently identity documentation in the absence of citizenship can enable blacklisting, coercion, and collaboration; and movement restriction in turn (and in tandem) then forces a limiting of options, horizons, and futures, which can lead to further displacement.

To fully understand this final step, the history of the pass system needs to be seen from beginning to end. We therefore aim for this kind of continuous approach, first in an international context in this chapter, and then later in the book for the case of Palestine.

## Registration and Denationalisation

> Only under conditions of pure freedom to come and go, irrespective
> of who or what a person is, would a passport constitute nothing
> but a restriction. Once the genie of the state's authority to identify
> persons and authorize their movements is out of the bottle, it is
> hard to get him back in.[19]

Population registries, identity documents, and restrictions on
movement have been tools of states and empires for centuries,
associated with nation-building, and with discrimination and
dispossession. In Australia, when ID cards were proposed in 1987,
a campaign of opposition likened it to a "ball and chain". In the
US, one writer nicknamed an ID "a licence to live", highlighting
an extraordinary property of ID cards: their potential to replace
people's rights and freedoms with a series of "permissions". The
stripping of civil rights, services, shelter, secure employment,
citizenship, and identity can be seen as a form of displacement
while staying in place.[20]

Activities that were once possible become forbidden: living
in one's own home, travelling to a nearby town to see relatives,
developing property, providing or pursuing employment, driving
one's own vehicle, practicing one's own profession, marrying and
raising children. Each of these becomes subject to a permit system.
Any activity carried out without prior permission and registration
is seen as a violation.

Indeed, the removal of citizenship, or denationalisation, has been
called "bureaucratic ethnic cleansing". Post-Revolutionary France,
at times, referred to and treated its peasantry or anyone opposing
the government as "foreigners", and then exported this internal
hierarchy to its colonies, such as Egypt. Under apartheid in South
Africa, "legal and administrative rights to remain in the town did
not exempt people from police harassment and arrest in the course
of raids and random checks". Today in Thailand, some highland
peoples are considered citizens, while others are not, based mainly
on ethnicity or income.[21]

Denationalisation was used to discourage Communism in the US.
Fascist Italy, in the late 1920s, withdrew passports from suspected
anti-fascists, and restricted emigration for much of the population.
Nazi-issued identity cards in Holland (and the corresponding
population registry) served to enforce the numerous bans on Jews,
such as travelling without a permit, entering the residential areas of

non-Jews, and moving during hours of curfew. They also enabled dispossession of land and assets, and deportation.

Less well known is the British census of Iraq (1919–20), conducted as part of its efforts to quell resistance. When asked to name their "origin" for the census, "many Arab Shi'is from the southern provinces chose 'Iranian' in the mistaken belief that this would get them out of military conscription and maybe other state obligations". This designation on *shahadat al-jinsiyyah* (IDs) resulted in waves of deportations in 1969, 1971, and 1977–90.[22]

## Documentation: Blacklists

Identity documentation constructs, rather than reflects, reality. It does more than simply invade privacy, which to date has been a principal reason for opposition to identity cards. Beyond privacy issues, many people do not object to centralised public records linked to their driving licence, passport, TV licence, car tax, hospital records, etc.[23]

States use identity documentation to monitor and exclude on ethnic, national, racial, economic, religious, ideological or medical grounds. Identity documents have been referred to as "social sorting" or "serialisation": dividing individuals into state-enforced categories or "replicable plurals". The "war on terror" has been used to justify the targeting of minorities and political opponents around the world from Mauritius to India, Zimbabwe, Uzbekistan, and beyond.[24]

> Djibouti, too, has received substantial US aid in the context of the war on terror, and its benefactor appears to have turned a blind eye to the expulsion, in early October 2003, of 100,000 residents (about 15 per cent of its population). Djibouti authorities described the foreign-born residents as possible terrorists and a "threat to the peace and security of the country".[25]

The increasing use of surveillance technologies has been brought about through legislation like the US Patriot Act of 2001.[26]

But discrimination based on IDs pre-dates the "war on terror". Colonial Indonesia instituted "special punchings" on IDs for "'subversives' and 'traitors'". European officials use IDs to distinguish religious affiliation and ethnic origin. In its most extreme form, markings on identity documentation can be a contributing factor to genocide. In Rwanda, French-made identity cards stated ethnicity, later considered a key factor in the genocide that took place.[27]

Sociologists describe how groups are separated by markers (like prescribed ethnicity) and "sorted" into new groups on this basis. They explain how workers are controlled through surveillance in their workplaces and outside them.[28] Categories imposed on people help to divide them and thus weaken resistance.

In 1940s Holland, the Nazi administration completed a population registry, issued identity cards, and then specially marked the identity cards of Jews.

*Figure 1.1*   A Nazi checkpoint in Kraków, Poland. Jews were forced to rely on the ID system that blacklisted and targeted them. In the year 1941, movement into and out of the Polish neighbourhood of Podgórze was restricted to four entrances, guarded from the outside by Polish and German armed forces, and on the inside by Jewish police. Internal matters were administered by the Jewish Council (Judenrat) set up by the Gestapo. Jews required permits to leave the area. A register of the Jewish population, identity documents, and stop-and-search procedures monitored movement. (Reproduced under the Creative Commons License from the Deutsches Bundesarchiv [German Federal Archive])

Researchers writing on the Nazi use of IDs concluded that the National Socialists were able to commit their "destructive activities" through an extensive administrative apparatus – "the use of raw numbers, punch cards, statistical expertise, and identification cards".[29]

Identity documents, combined with stop-and-search powers for various authorities (police, security guards, etc.), enable coercion.

Israeli police, for instance, stop those who they think are Arabs in West Jerusalem and routinely demand to see their IDs.[30]

Police who are given powers to demand ID invariably have consequent powers to detain people who do not have the card, or who cannot prove their identity. Even in such advanced countries as Germany, the power to hold such people for up to 24 hours is enshrined in law. The question of who is targeted for ID checks is left largely to the discretion of police.[31]

### Documentation: Coercion and Collaboration

The retention of identity documents – or the threat to do so – is listed by the International Labour Organisation (ILO) as one of the routes to forced labour. The "effective prohibition on international labour mobility" makes identity documentation "an economic endowment of unequal value".[32] Document retention is still observed in the transition economies of eastern and south-eastern Europe, among migrant workers from China, the Transcaucasus, and central Asia, as well as in the agriculture and mines of central Asia.

In an ILO survey covering 101 Tajik male migrant workers in the Russian construction industry, all respondents claimed that they had been repeatedly under pressure from law enforcement agencies. A worker without a residence permit always faces the threat of deportation. This has led to the emergence of a criminal business that blackmails and harasses these workers in order to extort money.[33]

A document can become so valuable that the issuing agency and its representatives have power over the individual.

A Privacy International survey of ID cards found claims of police abuse by way of the cards in virtually all countries. Most involved people being arbitrarily detained after failure to produce their card. Others involved beatings of juveniles or minorities. There were even instances of wholesale discrimination on the basis of data set out on the cards.[34]

Document retention can make people "easy prey for corrupt law enforcement officers", as documented by a 2005 International Labour Organisation survey:

For violating residency regulations, police require migrants to hand over their passport, which can then only be retrieved for a fee. Failing this, the passport is handed over to the intermediary, who then forces the worker to pay for its return.[35]

Such infractions can then have a domino effect: breaking the rules invokes fines; fines mean indebtedness; and indebtedness is a key factor behind severe labour exploitation.

The difficulty of even re-entering one's own state without a passport "explains the panic that grips international travellers abroad when they discover that they have lost their passport in some distant land" – the result is that "a lifeline has been cut, and the traveller is adrift in a world in which states have monopolized the authority to grant passage".[36] To anyone, anywhere in the world, the threat of statelessness can be "brandished as a weapon":

Any state ... [however repressive] is preferable to none at all. This is what all gradations of the shattering personal experience of statelessness and reversible citizenship brandished ... as a weapon ... eventually proves.[37]

Combining the movement-related and non-movement permissions into one document gives even greater influence to those who have stop-and-search capabilities. In Turkey for example, recruiters and employers have withheld the documents of women employed from the Republic of Moldova. Recruiters and employers would "deceive them, keep their identity documents and restrict their freedom of movement". Meanwhile in Russia, "documents were withdrawn, and wages left unpaid"; passports were held by employers in over one-fifth of all cases, leaving workers vulnerable to coercion, physical abuse, and movement restriction.[38]

The selective issuing and withholding of permissions acts as a system of reward and punishment, which enables manipulation and coercion. As Slater argues, "often absent in investigations of movements and mobilizations has been the continuing impact of ... invasive discourses of control and re-ordering".[39] Mounting resistance while an exploitative system of rewards and punishment is still in place means that collaboration is a constant threat. Such a system of rewards and punishment was instituted under the Nazi regime in Holland over a period of eight years, 1933–41:

The censuses of 1933 and 1939 were not the only registrations undertaken by the regime. "The Labor book" (1935), the "Health Pedigree Book" (1936), the "Duty to Register" (1938), the "Volkskartei" ("registry of the populace") (1939), and finally the "Personal Identification Number" (1944) *provided a bureaucratic foundation for a graded system of rewards and punishment* [emphasis added].[40]

Even the act of issuing permissions was itself considered a reward, and elicited cooperation from among the targeted population. Permits were issued by the "Jewish Council, Joodsche Raad ... consisting of 20 members, including rabbis, lawyers and middle class business men". In 1941, it was "given authority over all Jewish organizations" and "quickly became the unwitting tool of the German destruction machinery, actually delivering the Jews directly to the German deportation trains".[41]

### Movement Restriction and Induced Transfer

Nowadays, the use of internal passports to control movement within state boundaries bespeaks illegitimate, authoritarian governments lording it over subdued or terrorized populations ... It may be a state's principal means for discriminating among its subjects.[42]

Internal passports are now past history for many regions and states, such as: feudal Europe; the Nazi regime; China; post-Revolutionary France; the former Soviet Union; apartheid South Africa; colonial Egypt; the North American internment camps of the Japanese; and the former Yugoslavia. In these and other instances, prohibitions on movement made life so intolerable that they generated an impetus to leave. Post-Revolutionary Russia provides perhaps the most powerful illustration: in 1922, following a three-year period of mass emigration during civil war and famine, the Soviet government banned further departure. During the emergence of the international refugee regime between the two world wars, in places where people most required mobility for survival they were forbidden from moving.[43]

There is no shortage of earlier examples. Over 200 years ago France passed a measure issuing passports specific to cantons, and threatening up to a year of detention for not having a passport. In retrospect, "if the government had had the teeth to make this measure bite, it would have turned France into a gigantic prison in which the cantons constituted the individual cells". In 1830 in colonial Egypt, a government ordinance restricted Egyptian villagers from travelling across district boundaries, making them "inmates of their own villages". An 1852 text records that "it was scarcely possible for a *fellah* [farmer] to pass from one village to another without a written passport". The apparent goal was conscription, and to prevent soldiers from deserting the army. But all Egyptians were confined, regulated, and supervised; all were inspected (*taftish*) or instructed by officials. As Egyptians were cramped into ever more crowded quarters, the cities of colonists were kept spacious and open. The compulsory military service of French rule in Egypt and the compulsory labour situations of today have in common the restriction of movement and the use of identity documentation for the purpose of manipulating and exploiting ordinary people.[44]

Today states continue to use identity documentation and movement restrictions to gain resources such as territory, taxes, labour, and military service.[45] In the process, they can make life unbearable.

> Characteristics of today's compulsory labour situations include restrictions on freedom of movement, removal of identity documents, and threats of denouncing to immigration authorities any migrants who complain about substandard living and working conditions.[46]

In the US a driver's licence renewal can trigger a check on immigration status, police can search vehicles at internal checkpoints, and employers can be punished for employing individuals without the required documents. Since 1990, US municipalities have shouldered the responsibility of checking individuals' identity documents. Looking outside North America and Western Europe, checkpoints can be found in the Congo, Somalia, the Sudan, Egypt, India, Indonesia, Sri Lanka, and across the former Soviet Union. In Uzbekistan, for example, internal checkpoints simply changed hands – the old Soviet style of governing continued, just with a new government. Internal checkpoints became stricter, not softer, and the boundaries with other states became more pronounced.[47]

Post-Revolutionary Russia, colonial Egypt, and today's exploitative labour conditions are not the only examples of restricting departure and catalysing the wish to leave.

Spatial segregation has long been a means of perpetuating social hierarchy. Slaves, women, religious minorities and racial minorities have been literally kept in their place by explicit and informal control over movement and settlement.

The mechanisms of control include formal and informal ghettos, military detention centers, forced resettlement, concentration camps, and private discrimination and violence.[48]

In 1996, Max van der Stoel, then UN Special Rapporteur of the Commission on Human Rights, wrote of how permission to travel was denied by the Iraqi state to former detainees and persons with "suspected oppositional opinions".[49] Sometimes family members of these excluded persons were also denied permits. The process was – and continues to be – arbitrary:

[Iraqis abroad] find themselves taping their passports to their bodies or forever feeling inside their jackets and peering into handbags; no Iraqi will ever leave impossible-to-get official papers in a hotel room ... In a world of nation-states, even the privileged few who travel abroad are perpetually reminded of the existence of this wasteland [of statelessness] into which they can be dumped.[50]

Iraqi permits to travel (exit visas) require "certificates of nationality, a security clearance, certification from the Ministry of Defence stating that they have regulated their situation concerning military service, identity cards, certificates of residence and the government food ration card".[51] Exit visas cost 40,000 dinars in 1994, raised to 400,000 (US$800) in 1995. Bribes raised the price of obtaining each document.

An Iraqi woman, Sabah, describes the process in 2007:

The places where you renew your papers are very risky, they are scary. Most of them are by main roads, the queue of people is visible to everyone. The line begins at 6 am and there are no guards to protect you.[52]

It took her two days to obtain a new ID. After this, she obtained a passport application form, and waited until the day the Baghdad passport office processed her region.

We went at our allotted time but it was incredibly crowded, the police were outside, Hummers were passing by and there was random shooting. Young men were jumping over the walls to get to the passport office. We didn't think we had any hope of getting in. I turned to my husband and told him: "There's no way we can get a passport in such madness".

Others paid intermediaries, up to US$800 in the mid-1990s. According to ratios cited by former UN Special Rapporteur Max van der Stoel in 1994, this was the equivalent to 15 years' salary for an average civil servant in 1994 – before the two decades of inflation that have happened since. Yet intermediaries are unreliable: in 2007 an Iraqi who paid for four passports was given three; another Iraqi was given a passport that he was told two days later was invalid. Sabah, who could not afford intermediaries, did not receive the G-passport for which she applied.

Forgive me, we are treated like animals, actually even animals are treated better. The police kick you with their shoes, only those who have money can get inside easily. If you don't have money, you are humiliated – it was so hard and in the end all I got was an S passport which is useless.

The restrictions on departure combine with the production of the desire to leave. As of 2007, two million Iraqis had left or been driven out of Iraq.[53]

In addition to laws specifically outlining the right to movement, other laws outlaw the obstruction of this right. The International Convention on the Suppression and Punishment of the Crime of Apartheid of 1973 declares illegal the "deliberate creation of conditions preventing [a people's] full development" by denying them "basic human rights and freedoms, including the right to freedom of movement".[54]

### Resistance

Resistance and political activity take many forms that challenge our preconceptions as to what constitutes activism or struggle. A search for dignity is too often sidelined from the field of "politics" and sometimes interpreted as "disempowerment" rather than resistance.[55]

Much of the Western discussion of social movements has proceeded as if such phenomena have never surfaced in the societies of the South.[56]

As the process of documenting identity is imbued with inequalities, subtle forms of opposition often pass unnoticed. In India, census takers and development workers adopted the trappings or markings of superior status, driving in jeeps with official license plates. But people still resisted from within the system by walking away, using the census as an occasion to complain, asking for compensation for providing information, asking for surveyors' names, or asking to be listed as "below poverty line" to receive benefits. They avoided "being literally written into state registers" under the terms and conditions imposed upon them.[57]

When Nazi-issued identity cards (and their corresponding population registry) limited freedom of movement during the Second World War, some resisted by removing their "markings". They still operated within the system of permissions, but evaded being categorised in the ways the system imposed. An excerpt from one woman's testimony explains the marking of IDs, and efforts to avoid it:

I had many Jewish friends ... They would often ask me how to get a non-Jewish I.D. card. First, I had them give me a photograph. I put their fingerprint on the back of the photo, using a little machine I had which was made for this purpose. Then I would steal a passport of the appropriate age group, soak off the seal, put their picture in it, and seal it again. They looked good.

I usually stole passports from people I knew ... It was very inconvenient to have had your passport stolen: you had to go through a lot of misery to get a new one, but it was small potatoes compared to not having one at all, or worse, having one that had a "J" on it. There was no way to get that "J" off. It was large.[58]

Literally removing the marking was too difficult, but with manoeuvring, resistance within the system was still possible. Hence resistance within a system does not equate to acceptance.

The irony of identity documentation is that it forces people to recognise their own surrender of rights. In Peru, for example, as the Titicaca National Reserve was created on indigenous land, its inhabitants were forced to acknowledge their own dispossession in order to apply for state permission to remain. The Reserve was "decreed" in 1978, and harvesting of the local reed-like building material, *totora*, was prohibited without state permission. All adult men were required to undergo "qualification": registering as household heads and "listing their holdings of livestock and craft items".[59] The National Forestry Centre claimed it would not issue harvesting permits to "unqualified" communities (although this was not enforced). Beginning in 1980, permits were issued on an annual basis, only for specified areas, and on condition of payment. Communities were also compelled to present the "national identification documents" of several members, as well as a map of the requested areas.

> The peasants were troubled by these requirements, not only because of the fees that they would have to pay if they obtained contracts, and the fines that would be imposed if they did not, but also because the law challenged one of the fundamental principles of the social and political life of peasant communities: their right to manage their territories.[60]

People worried not only about obtaining short-term permits, but also more importantly, about the principle of non-ownership implied.

To address exploitation at its roots requires addressing this early stripping of rights and the subsequent status that identity documentation creates – the hierarchy between the surveilled and the surveiller. Despite initial opposition to systematic oppression, identity documentation, and movement restrictions, this resistance is subdued as the prohibitions become more thoroughly enforced. In South African cities under apartheid, the adoption of "pass" laws was originally "greeted by demonstrations and protest meetings". Punishment used the same measures, and political organisation "was severely undermined by the extensive bannings and imprisonments of leaders". From 1916 until 1981, 17.5 million people were detained for contravening "pass" law regulations. The pass laws became a chief means of suppressing resistance.[61]

As prohibitions were more tightly enforced, the pass became a necessity to obtain the basics of life. Pass laws continued until 1986.[62]

This is the meaning of the "genie in the bottle" of identity documentation and movement restrictions. While resistance to blanket prohibitions is high at first, eventually people are forced to comply: trying to live life without these permissions and returning to a situation of freedom becomes a tremendous challenge.

## 1.3   OVERVIEW OF THE BOOK

In our book we provide a continuous review of identity documentation and movement restrictions in Palestine from the 1800s to the present. Rather than looking solely at land and the discourse of security, we focus instead on population and how it is divided and affected using bureaucratic instruments.

The introduction in this chapter has explained what is meant by the terms "population registration", "identity documentation", and "movement restriction". It has drawn upon international examples to demonstrate the power that such tools can have, and what their impacts can be: denationalisation, discrimination, displacement, dispossession, coercion, collaboration, and death.

The next three chapters trace, from the Ottoman period to the present, the history of the census, the population registry, denationalisation, blacklists, coercion, and collaboration. The fifth chapter then explains how movement restrictions on millions of people became possible. Chapters 6 and 7 draw a connection between the population policies listed above and "induced transfer", that is, cultivating unbearable conditions that force Palestinians out of their homes and lands. The book therefore links today's displacement back to identity documentation processes from the 1930s onward.

In particular, Chapters 6 and 7 look at the impact of all these policies on two vital services: health and education. The health system, for example, is undermined through restricted access for patients, personnel, ambulances, and supplies, resulting in de-development and induced transfer. In parallel, the education system is undermined through restricted access for students and teachers, as well as the closure of and attacks on schools. This leads to the narrowing of horizons for the next generation, that is, de-development and induced transfer.

However, Palestinians resist. In the conclusion we show that, at the most basic level, Palestinians resist inducements to leave. Despite the de-development of all systems of support – health and education are two prominent examples – Palestinians for the most part resist the *effects* of movement restrictions. This takes an enormous toll, and the new definition of "normal" involves a level of adaptation that can be as harmful as it is necessary.

The second level of resistance is against the movement restrictions themselves: how people circumvent checkpoints. Finally there is resistance against the system's authority. This is virtually impossible, however, when the system is the only way to access health care, education, a family, income, and of course, mobility. This explains why Palestinians place so much emphasis on land. Land is not only a cultural and sacred heritage; it is also a source of independence, self-sustenance, and dignity. It opens the possibility of escaping the monopoly on rights held by the ID system.

Yet without the return of land or capital, the near-complete enforcement and reliance on IDs renders resistance (against having an ID) almost futile. Thus, while the key to resilience and coping has always lain with those who rely on the system, rejecting the system requires action and engagement from those who do not.

# 2
# Registration and Denationalisation

As the cogs and wheels of the Nazi machinery in the Second World War ground to a halt, international law was born. The registration and denationalisation that had occurred under the Nazi regime – already illegal – was denounced and prohibited in further international agreements. Never again, the world said, would discriminatory databases be built and used in ethnic cleansing. Never again would innocent victims be stripped of citizenship and the world's doors be replaced by "paper walls". International law, already forbidding denationalisation from the early 1900s, was strongly reinforced.[1]

This chapter chronicles the time from the 1400s to the present, following the trail of international legal instruments that emerged both prior to and in the wake of the Second World War. These include, among others, the Hague Regulations, the Covenant of the League of Nations, the Universal Declaration of Human Rights, the Fourth Geneva Convention, various United Nations Resolutions, the Convention Relating to the Status of Refugees, the International Convention on the Elimination of All Forms of Racial Discrimination, and the International Covenant on Civil and Political Rights.

These legal documents run parallel to another story – that of the largest denationalisation project in modern history. The United Nations High Commissioner for Refugees describes Palestine as "by far the most protracted and largest of all refugee problems in the world today".[2] In Palestine, the tools of the census, the population registry, and residence permits effectively denationalised a nation. It is one of the greatest ironies that, as nationalism faded in Europe, it waxed in the Zionist movement to Palestine, and as international law opposed denationalisation, denationalisation in Palestine rose ever higher.

The story begins outside Palestine, in Europe, where Zionist leaders were – as early as 1914 – already discursively erasing the Palestinian presence. Negating the existence of more than half a million Palestinians, Chaim Weizmann (later president of the World Zionist Congress) asserted:

> There is a country which happens to be called Palestine, a country without a people, and, on the other hand, there exists the Jewish people, and it has no country. What else is necessary, then, than to fit the gem into the ring, to unite this people with this country?[3]

This slogan of an empty Palestine is all the more remarkable when we look back at the census data available at the time. Today's "Israel State Archives" house the Ottoman collection of population registries for Palestine – no less than 460 volumes. Zionist movement members were actively involved in the British censuses. Not only did the Zionists *see* the Palestinians whose existence they denied; they made a science out of studying and counting them.

Today the Israeli state seeks to export their practices of documenting and restricting individuals, but it was not the first to invent and apply them in Palestine.[4] However, while previous censuses and population registries were used at worst for taxation and conscription, the censuses of 1948 and 1967 were used for denationalisation and dispossession. While previous censuses took into account protection for vulnerable or mobile persons, the censuses of 1948 and 1967 denied refugees' rights to their land, their nation, and freedom of movement.

In this chapter, we first look at these early censuses, as well as the relation between expulsion and the first census and population registry. Then we describe the Zionist attempt to assert authority – which initially encountered resistance, refusal, and appeals to international law – before returning to the themes of international law and denationalisation in Palestine.

## 2.1   THE CENSUS

### Early Palestine Censuses and Relevant International Law

The history of population registration in Palestine dates back to the Ottoman period when Palestinians of all faiths together with other Arabic and Turkish-speaking peoples were divided into self-sufficient territories. Regular censuses began in the 1400s, centuries before Western Europe developed its own systematic state population counts. After 400 years of censuses, population registries were established to record births, deaths, and migrations. Ottoman registries had difficulty catching up with the massive migration taking place at the time: about two million Muslims fled from Russian conscription, from forced settlement in barren areas, and from forced conversion. In a similar time-period, Russian Jews also migrated into the area, with the Ottoman open-door policy helping to increase the Jewish population in Palestine from 12,000–15,000 in 1868 to 23,000–27,000 in 1882.[5]

In a short time, the Ottoman registration process was propelled forward by the Ministry of Interior's General Population Administration (*Nüfus-u Umumi Idaresi*). The 1882–4 census was kept up to date through the registries, and included a person's formal name, the name used within the community (*künye*), father's name, address, age, religion, occupation, profession, electoral status, physical disabilities, and civil status. Those absent from the locality, foreigners, or "protected" people were also registered under special procedures. Administrators in the Ottoman period produced over 400 geographically indexed volumes of records between 1875 and 1918, all of which were taken and used by Zionist forces.[6]

In 1919, Palestine was recognised as an "independent nation" through Article 22 of the Covenant of the League of Nations. Meanwhile, encouraged by a letter from Scotsman Arthur Balfour that the Jews would be permitted "a national home" in Palestine, the Zionist movement took its own count of Jews in Palestine. However, Balfour's letter was never approved by the House of Commons or the House of Lords, and contradicted assurances and pledges found in the McMahon–Hussein Correspondence of 1915–18, in General Allenby's statements during the First World War, and in the Anglo–French Declaration of 1918. Palestinian writer Muhammad Yunis al-Husayni pointed out that a simple letter had no weight in international law, and that Britain had no right to give away a country to which it had no legal claim. Britain itself stated in 1939 that, "His Majesty's Government therefore now declare unequivocally that it is not part of their policy that Palestine should become a Jewish State".[7]

British armed forces had entered and occupied Palestine in 1917, and quickly conducted their first census. This revealed over three-quarters of a million Palestinians in the country in 1922, including a small minority of Jewish Palestinians concentrated in Jerusalem (34,431) and Jaffa (24,000).

As with the Ottoman population registry, the Zionist movement again had full access to the 1922 and 1931 censuses. Members, such as R. Musam, Pinhas Hamburger, and Roberto Bachi, were

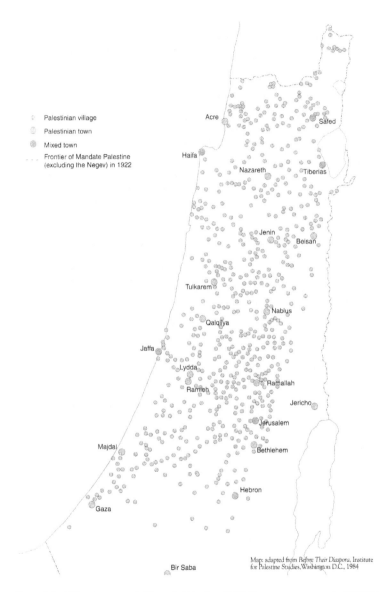

Figure 2.1   Cities, towns, and villages in Palestine, 1922. The census enumerated 757,182 Palestinians, although was later criticised for excluding many Palestinians in the south. According to the census administrators, 11 per cent of the enumerated population were Jews – generally an urban population in Jaffa and Jerusalem – including 7,844 people who had arrived that year, mostly from eastern Europe. (Reproduced with permission from *The Arab World Geographer* [AWG] http://arabworldgeographer.metapress.com)

incorporated into the British administration. For each of these individuals, their "statistical enterprise" was "deeply rooted in Zionist thought" – Bachi would later criticise the British censuses in Palestine for their equal treatment of different faith groups.[8]

As the British fought to maintain control over the indigenous population in Palestine, quelling revolts in the 1930s, they produced a battery of regulations that directly contravened the international law that had emerged during and after the Ottoman period. The great migrations and wars at the turn of the century had given rise to a system of international law that forbade states from rendering people stateless. The Hague Regulations, governing the status of refugees and of populations under military occupation, established the right of return to one's home, and the right to a "normal existence with a minimum of interference". In essence, they prohibited both expulsion and denationalisation. In 1945 the British brought out their series of numbered "regulations", including the "registration of inhabitants" and "possession and presentation of [an] identity certificate". Further regulations, numbered 108 and 112, sanctioned deportation. Recognising the implications at the time for Zionists entering Palestine, one lawyer – who would later become the Israeli Attorney General and Justice Minister – condemned the regulations as being worse than those of Nazi Germany.[9]

### Zionist Expulsion of Palestinians

The British were not the only power to overextend their jurisdiction. In what has been described as "an excess of jurisdiction", the United Nations, which had no sovereignty over Palestine or even any power to administer the country, decided on its partition. The date was set for May of 1948. The indigenous Palestinian population was nearing 1.4 million, and each of the proposed segments of the partition would contain a large portion of this population. Each segment was obliged to grant citizenship under the partition plan and according to international law, which prohibits denationalisation. The plan was announced six months in advance, in November 1947.[10]

A month after the announcement, in December 1947, the Zionist movement stepped up village incursions. In the city of Haifa, 75,000 Palestinians were subject to a terror campaign. Two hundred villages – some with populations of up to 5,000 people – were destroyed between March 30 and May 15, 1948; another 90 villages were ethnically cleansed a month later. Particularly affected were the 59,000 Bedouin expelled from the Naqab region in the south – all but two of the sub-tribes lost large numbers of their members. As

expulsions continued and the "legislative" machinery for denationalisation was set in motion, the rhetoric from the Zionist movement
stated exactly the opposite: the "Provisional State Council" promised
in May of 1948 to "uphold the full social and political equality of all
its [future state's] citizens, without distinction of religion, race, and
sex". Such language implied an automatic extension of citizenship,
as per international law. In reality, however, expulsions were at their
height, from the Bedouin tribes in the Naqab, which had lost 80 per
cent of their numbers, to the Greek Catholics in Galilee who had lost
nearly all their priests. Most political organisations "disappeared".[11]

Depending on where the Zionist forces were moving, Palestinians
moved from one village to another. Each Palestinian who managed
to remain in the area, and to survive, had to move three or four
times on average. A third of the villagers of Tarshiha moved to a
shelter village, then another, then back to the first. The same was
true of nearly half of the people in another two villages, Shafa
'Amr and Kabul. The rest either stayed in one shelter village, or fled
Palestine altogether (over 60 per cent of Tarshiha's population). The
loss of the majority of Palestinians – either in death or expulsion –
ricocheted through the groups of people who remained. They had
to live through the uncertainty of not knowing whether they would
be able to stay as time progressed.[12]

### Returnees and the Census Idea

The Zionist movement immediately drew upon resources from the
earlier period – their members who had participated in the British
census administration. By this time, they had also begun to use
censuses as a tool for Jewish conscription – a census was conducted
in Jerusalem in April and May of 1948 (as well as April 1947) to
augment the Jewish "People's Guard". Despite the offensives against
Palestinians in the first half of 1948, the indigenous population
resisted expulsion, and those who were temporarily displaced were
quick to return. By August of 1948 this had become a concern for
many in the military and political establishment. In the wake of
mass expulsions in 1947 and 1948, a Committee for Arab Affairs
took as its task the renewed expulsion of Palestinian returnees
and internal refugees and, to a lesser extent, Palestinians who had
remained throughout. The Committee's members included the same
intelligence members involved in the expulsions, now reincarnated
in positions in foreign affairs (Ya'acov Shimoni and Ezra Danin) and
"minority" and Arab affairs (Gad Machnes, Yehoshua Palmon, and
Bechor Shitrit). In order to identify returnees for future expulsion,

the Committee decided in the summer of 1948 to hold a census later that year.[13]

A 78-year-old woman from the Palestinian village of Tarshiha recalls how expelled Palestinians, upon hearing that a census would be conducted, doubled their efforts to return.[14] They were aware of the attempts to construe their expulsion as permanent. Despite their strongest efforts, however, even those inside Palestine were limited in their ability to be present for the census; some of the residents of the Upper Galilee, for instance, "were temporarily hospitalized, studying, or picking up their paychecks in Lebanon on the day of the registration".[15] Palestinians were convinced that their physical presence during the census would – as it had during the periods of British and Ottoman administration – continue the administrative recognition of their pre-established, longstanding legal ownership of their property.

Palestinian refugees also believed that their return prior to the census would lead to citizenship of whatever state was to encompass their property (be that state Zionist or otherwise). Palestinians of all faiths could trace their roots to Canaanites of 3000 BC, and had witnessed the granting of citizenship to newcomers under both the Ottoman and British administrations. The British administration, for instance, had granted citizenship to anyone who resided in Palestine for a mere two years, thus enabling 132,616 Jews to come – mainly from Poland, Germany, Romania, and Czechoslovakia – and enjoy equal rights with Palestinians.[16] For Palestinian refugees to have citizenship, including full and equal rights, was a given. In his September 1948 report, UN Mediator Count Folke Bernadotte recommended repatriation, and acknowledged that no new rights were being created: "It would be an offence against the principles of elemental justice if these innocent victims of the conflict were denied the right to return to their homes."[17]

The UN Mediator affirmed each refugee's "unconditional right ... to make a free choice [which] should be fully respected". But Palestinians risked death in order to return: "A number of people were killed as they tried to return. The Israeli soldiers would stop them and shoot them."[18]

The census was to be conducted under curfew, and by officials already responsible for expropriating Palestinian land and assets. This increased Palestinian wariness. On November 8, 1948, "military and security officers canvassed the entire population".[19] In areas where funds and Arabic-speaking military were lacking, however, the military government "reluctantly chose to hire local

Palestinians for the job"; today these Palestinian census officials help us to recall how Palestinians responded to the census:

> [A]fter passing a polygraph test [...] Ibrahim received a folder with a list of names of heads of households in each of the two villages. As he went from house to house to fill out the surveys, he was surprised at the number of people who were reluctant to provide complete and truthful answers to his questions. Many were suspicious of the government's intentions, fearing imprisonment and expulsion.[20]

Anyone who failed to provide the requisite information was threatened under Statistical Order number 31 of 1947 (a similar law was passed in 1951, and the 1947 order was revised in 1972). The census administrator, Roberto Bachi, mused in retrospect in 1992 that it could easily have been viewed as a "police operation".[21]

## 2.2   THE POPULATION REGISTRY

### The Discriminatory "Addendum"

While Palestinians were aware of the Zionist movement's potential (and in the end, actual) use of the census for denationalisation, dispossession, and expulsion, very little was disclosed by the movement publicly. Records and reports regarding Palestinians and their property remained classified, and Knesset (Israeli parliament) discussions on Palestinian landowners were closed; even the United Nations was denied access.[22] In the first meeting of the Committee for Arab Affairs, to plan the census, Ezra Danin (former intelligence member during the previous mass expulsions) objected to Palestinian freedom of movement and wished to make such freedom contingent upon Palestinians' provision of information. The aim was to "know how many families were separated and what property they owned". Only after "conducting this job", explained Danin, "will we be able to think of a system to allow these people to move".[23] Meanwhile, Palestinians were ignorant of such discussions, even when conducted by the newly formed government. The result was that Palestinians were forced to disclose details about their lives without knowing the plans being made for them and their property.

Incongruously, this information was needed less to physically dispossess Palestinians than to legitimate an already attained dispossession – by labelling Palestinians as "absent" and thus having "forfeited" their status, land, and possessions. Zionist officials claimed that the "greatest part" of Palestinian property "had already been seized" by squatters, army veterans, and organisations like the Jewish Agency and Jewish National Fund. In other words, the Palestinians had already been "transferred" off their land, so the information derived from the census simply cemented the transfer. As much as the census was about land, however, it was also about people. The Committee for Arab Affairs discussed the necessity of "identifying" remaining Palestinians, the number of returnees, and within that group, the number who had returned to their original homes. The Zionist movement was worried about "consanguinity across borders".[24]

In anticipation of Palestinian resistance to surveillance that was designed exclusively to learn about these returnees, the Committee decided to separate such questions from the generic ones.[25] The Minister of Minority Affairs (Bechor Shitrit, who was also the Minister of Police) explained:

We will prepare an additional questionnaire: a regular questionnaire for all residents, and a special form for [collecting information requested by] the Interior Minister, the Minority Affairs Ministry and the Military Governor.

While we fill in the regular form, we could add the details we are interested in to the second questionnaire without [Palestinians] noticing that we are asking additional questions.[26]

A general form was therefore devised for use among all census respondents, and for Palestinians only, a special two-part addendum was used to gather: (1) "Information on Absent Relatives"; and (2) "Information on Property of Family Members (Present or Absent)". The census was thus a crucial part of the effort to permanently exclude Palestinian refugees from returning; it defined the majority of Palestinians as "absent" and vulnerable to deportation if found; their property was to be seized and, according to the movement's new Minister of Finance, responsibility for its compensation would lie with neighbouring states.[27]

In addition, the constantly moving population of internal refugees presented similar challenges to those encountered by the Ottomans in the 1880s. The census takers refused to count anyone by proxy, unlike in the Ottoman census (or modern censuses around the world today). Thus individuals "could only be registered where they had been previously counted", and they could only receive an identification number if they had been counted. Census takers "carelessly bypassed" villages or, if they ran out of forms in a given village, did not complete the process.[28]

Between 13,000 and 15,000 Palestinians in the Naqab were excluded "secretly"; so too were 5,000 men and teenage boys interned in prisoner-of-war camps ("roughly 14 percent of all Palestinian males left in the country between the ages of 15 through 60"). Another 40,000 Palestinians were left out of the census, in the Upper Galilee villages taken by Zionist forces one week before the census. In addition, 31,000 Palestinians in the Little Triangle were not counted, as their lands were later annexed through an armistice with Jordan. The final group to be forcibly denationalised later were the 500,000 Palestinians who previously had free access to all of Palestine, but who had been shut out through partition and Zionist forces, in what became the Gaza Strip and West Bank. Thus, of the more than 1.4 million Palestinians, only about 69,000 were counted in the Zionist census of November 1948.[29]

### The Universal Declaration of Human Rights, and Resolution 194

In September 1948, UN Mediator Count Folke Bernadotte had affirmed that return was to be guided by the individual choice of each refugee. On December 10, 1948, this principle was included in the Universal Declaration of Human Rights adopted in New York by the General Assembly of the United Nations. Article 13(2) of the Declaration decreed that "Everyone has the right to leave any country, including his own, and to return to his country". Meanwhile at the Israeli consulate in New York, Palestinians were applying for identification papers in order to return. Also in the same period the United Nations Secretariat began drafting a resolution to "confer upon the refugees as individuals the right of exercising a free choice as to their future".[30]

Thus, one day after the Universal Declaration of Human Rights was adopted, the United Nations General Assembly passed Resolution 194, demanding that the refugees be allowed to return. The resolution specified that Palestinians would return to their exact homes; the General Assembly rejected amendments that referred generally to "the areas from which they [the refugees] have come".[31]

In the latter part of 1948, before, during, and after the census, expelled Palestinians flooded back to their homes and lands. The Galilee area alone received some 3,000 to 4,000 returnees, despite – or perhaps because of – seeing "how impossible it immediately became ... to come back". In October 1948, officials in the Foreign Ministry wrote of a plan to deport returnees; toward the end of the census, this plan was carried out. Thousands "who had tried to return to their homes were expelled again" and their property taken.[32]

### Returnees Labelled As Criminals

While contravening international law by blocking return, Zionist forces labelled returnees and their supporters as criminals: Palestinians who remained were suspect of harbouring returnees, and the newly formed "Ministry of Interior" called the returnees "infiltrators", a crime punishable in practice by death.

> The *mutasalilin* – the sneakers or infiltrators – were people who tried to come back to their land from Lebanon. That name was first applied to people who tried to sneak back to the village and take some of the crops and foodstuff or money they left behind, and they might be killed.[33]

Yet, according to international law and the United Nations Secretariat, these returnees were meant to have their passage home both "ensured" and "protected".[34]

The act of ensuring safe passage was an obligation on both Zionist forces, and the recently formed United Nations Conciliation Commission for Palestine. Yet it was Palestinians who most fulfilled this obligation.

> Sometimes [returnees] would hide in certain areas of the village and as a child I would bring them food and water. They would ask me lots of questions about the village and about particular people.[35]

Thousands of people were divided from their immediate family members. Despite punishment of "fraternisers", villagers tried to help the returnees. The self-declared Israeli state asserted that Resolution 194 did not apply to mass groups and was reserved only for "nationals" of Israel, and that the resolution's use of "should" rather than "shall" rendered it non-binding. That resolution has never since been "annulled, repealed, diluted or overturned" and instead has been "reaffirmed annually by the United Nations". So powerful was the international sense of Palestinian rights that Israel's application for membership in the United Nations was refused in December of 1948.[36]

## Deportation of Returnees and Non-returnees Alike

Even when the permanent return to which they were entitled seemed out of reach, Palestinians maintained contact with their homes and lands.

> I remember some were members of rich families with lots of property and yet they would be sneaking across the border at night just to look at their property, like thieves in the darkness of the night. They came to pick up documents or belongings.[37]

Those who succeeded in staying were under constant threat of deportation. "The *mukhtar* [village leader] would inform on [the returnees] to the Israelis and they used to send them back."[38]

Israel justified expulsions by arguing that returnees did not conform to Resolution 194's stipulation of wishing to "live at peace with their neighbors".[39] Returnees were fully aware, however, of the laws and regulations implanted by the Zionist movement and were seeking return even as subjects of those regulations. "In the files of the Police Ministry in the State Archives, there are applications made by Arab inhabitants asking to be granted entrance visas for members of their families."[40]

Many were deported two or three times after repeatedly trying to return to their villages. Expulsions began as early as April 1948 and continued well after the 1949 Armistice agreements.[41]

Not only were returnees from outside Palestine deported; so too were Palestinians who had never left Palestine, and in some cases, who had never left their homes. The census was conducted in a way that omitted over 90,000 Palestinians, and therefore all those excluded from the census, and even some who were included in the census, were vulnerable to deportation.

In the village of Majd al-Kurum, for example, Zionist forces conducted a massacre in November of 1948. Half the village fled to the nearby forests, and the census takers came the next day. Two months later, 355 of the 506 villagers of Majd al-Kurum were expelled, some on the pretext of not being listed in the census count. Meanwhile, the village of al-Majdal was reduced from 10,000 to 2,700 Palestinians in 1948, three days before the census. For the subsequent year the military leader of the area, Yigal Allon, "demanded ... that the town be emptied of its Arabs" and a "Committee for Transferring Arabs" approved his request in February 1949. Every remaining Palestinian in al-Majdal was expelled to the Gaza Strip in the summer of 1950.[42]

Justification for expulsions relied on the British Emergency Regulations related to deportation (such as Regulation 112, prescribing expulsion and banishment on the whim of officials). But even regulations not explicitly about deportation were used; for example, the Foreign Travel Ordinance forbade the population from foreign travel, except with special permission. This was used to prevent the return of any Palestinians who could not demonstrate their departure had been pre-approved.[43]

### The Population Registry

To keep track of Palestinians on a continuous basis, a population registry was developed out of the 1948 census. The completed forms from the 1948 census comprise some 300 boxes now held under "reading restrictions" at the Israel State Archives. The material is organised geographically, just as the census was conducted geographically. This served in part to conceal discrimination. For instance, instead of explicitly labelling Jews as being either of European or Middle Eastern origin, their towns were labelled as being new or old: "veteran settlements" or "development towns". Meanwhile, Palestinian Bedouin villages and townships were (and still are) not even labelled as locations, but rather as "tribes", reflecting "a politically motivated bias to reduce, by means of census manipulation, the number of permanent Arab localities".[44]

Throughout Palestine, Israeli statisticians claimed that "localities ... don't have an organized system of addresses". Palestinians in outlying village settlements, or *khirba*, were registered under the name of the nearby village. This resulted in mass displacement, for example, in the 'Ara valley after 1949.[45]

Contrary to the reality of Palestinians residing in their villages, census takers listed them as belonging to distant urban centres. The villagers of Beit Jann, for instance, were told in 1948 to report to the "military government" in the city of 'Akka. They continued to reach their lands through the surrounding hills, despite "the difficulties encountered in obtaining entry permits ... [and] being in constant jeopardy of arrest in the event of their being caught".[46]

The arbitrary assignment of addresses and names took – and continues to take – many forms. Men and women, for example, may be given the addresses of their aging parents, rather than their own places of residence. Against Palestinian custom, in which married women retain their maiden names, the Registry lists them as having the surnames of their husbands.[47]

The Population Registry created upon completion of the 1948 census still exists today. It continues to keep records of persons excluded from the census;[48] their information is there, but their status remains that of outsiders, denationalised and exiled from their homes, lands, and homeland.

The Registration of Inhabitants Ordinance of 1949, modelled on the British Emergency Regulations, obliges every individual – upon reaching the age of 16 – to submit his or her personal information to be entered into the Population Registry. This information includes details such as occupation, place of work, and language spoken at home. The Registry also retains labels and characteristics such as race/ethnicity, religion, kinship relations (including the ID numbers of spouse and children), place of birth, dates of exit and entry, age, sex, address, and marital status. Registration of religious denomination is only mandatory for Muslims and Christians, to foster and maintain "divisions within the non-Jewish population".[49]

The Population Registry's listing for citizenship reflects an understanding, dating back to Ben Gurion, that citizenship was to provide "justice for the nation" rather than "justice for the individual". Jewish infants are listed as having Israeli citizenship, while Palestinians are listed as having "indefinite" citizenship, or in other words, statelessness.[50]

## 2.3   FEIGNING AUTHORITY

### The "Special" Census for Expulsion

The motives behind using the census as a step toward denationalisation were often repeated by Zionist leaders. At the beginning of 1949, for example, Yitzhak Ben-Tzvi, a close associate of Ben-Gurion, and Chaim Weizmann's successor as president in 1952, declared that "there are too many Arabs in the country".[51] Shortly after, census takers returned to the Galilee, where they had previously overlooked 40,000 Palestinians. Again, Palestinians sensed that being counted would lead to citizenship. Again, they were mistaken. Despite being interrogated for this second, Palestinians-only census, any returnees would later be denied their citizenship. This included "any individual who may have gone to Beirut or Bethlehem, or the Old City of Jerusalem for even a day's visit".[52] The goal of the census was to reduce, not increase, the Palestinian population. As stated in mid-1949 by Knesset member Shlomo Lavi, "the large number of Arabs in the country worries me [...]; there are now 170,000 Arabs in the country, including 22,000 school-age children".[53]

In Haifa, Palestinians tried unsuccessfully to register family members by proxy, as had been permitted by census takers in the Ottoman period. In the village of Jish, rather than attempt proxy registration those who had not been counted in the first census went voluntarily to the second set of census takers. Instead of citizenship, however, they received a warning from the military governor of the Eastern Galilee that if they did not leave immediately, they would be deported.[54]

Not only returnees were victim to this second census, which enumerated Palestinians in order to denationalise them. Expulsions were also conducted of Palestinians who had remained in their homes throughout 1948 and subsequent years. Zionist leaders acknowledged that "other Arabs who had not infiltrated the country were sometimes driven out as well".[55] The central Galilee villagers of Shafa 'Amr, for example, were inside their homes in May of 1948, but were told to leave because they were not given authorisation to live in their homes. In a letter to the villagers' lawyer in 1950, Yehoshua Palmon the Advisor on Arab Affairs wrote:

> Even if I accept your assumption that they have no other place to live, this would not necessarily lead to your conclusion that they are entitled to live [here]. People who were not approved by the authorities to remain in their village will be removed.[56]

In this and other statements, there was an admission of expelling people from villages, "some of which had not been abandoned", and deporting Palestinians "in order to make room".[57]

### Armistices and Temporary Permits

The states to which Palestinians were deported were simultaneously signing agreements with little regard to Palestinian rights. The first armistice agreement between Egypt and Israel was signed in February of 1949, then Lebanon in March, Jordan in April, and Syria in July. With stable international conditions undeniably established by the summer of 1949, the refugees should have been allowed to return according to UN General Assembly Resolution 194 of December 1948. Deportations were illegal throughout this period, and the prevention of return was tantamount to expulsion – also illegal. Yet all aspects continued: deportation, expulsion, and prevention of return. Yehoshua Palmon repeatedly urged that "every infiltrator" be expelled.[58]

In June 1949, Emmanuel Markovsky, a lieutenant-colonel in the Israeli army, reported to his superior, Elimelech Avner:

> Upon our entry into the area [the Little Triangle] and the proclamation of [Israel's] rule in it, we announced that we will not recognize the [internal] refugees as being entitled to reside in the area or any aid and benefit. We prohibited their employment in any work ... we banned organizing permanent aid for them. When we received authorization to transfer them across the border, the action was implemented in full within a week.[59]

Meanwhile, the Armistice agreements had direct consequences on families and villages about to be split in two through the lines drawn on maps.

The border decided at Rhodes was drawn quite arbitrarily. No respect was paid to village boundaries and many people were separated from their lands; the villages of Barta' and Beit Safafa were cut into two bits, leaving members of the same family on different sides of the barbed-wire fence and unable to communicate.[60]

The discourse emerging from key Zionist figures was in stark contrast to the reality of their own actions. Ben Gurion claimed that citizenship was "not cancelled" for Palestinians and that they indeed "received full citizenship". A memorandum sent in July 1949 to the United Nations Conciliation Commission for Palestine confirmed Israel's commitment to Palestinians' right to return to Palestine.[61]

As a final nod in the direction of international law, residence permits for Palestinians were created, including for those who had returned following expulsion. In July 1949, the temporary residence permit was invented to formalise Israel's control over Palestinians' ability to live in their homes and lands – giving them three to twelve months of respite before threatening expulsion. The permit could be renewed, exchanged for a permanent residence permit, or cancelled (meaning expulsion).[62]

The summer of 1949, therefore, brought about not only armistice agreements that divided Palestinians once again, but also the reality of temporary residence permits as a mechanism for extending control over Palestinians who had successfully eluded expulsion.

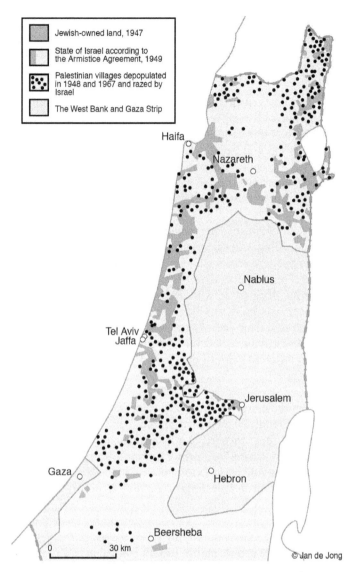

*Figure 2.2*  Villages from which Palestinians were expelled in 1948 (not shown are numerous depopulated Bedouin areas in the south). Palestinians in cities and towns were also expelled or forcibly relocated into assigned neighbourhoods or "ghettos". The Armistice lines of 1949 were decided upon by the Zionist movement, Egypt, Lebanon, Jordan, and Syria, and cut Palestinian villages in two. The Zionist movement proceeded to expropriate 93 per cent of Palestinian land within the Armistice lines subsequent to declaring the state of Israel, and to expel or keep out nearly 90 per cent of the Palestinian population. (Reproduced with permission from *The Arab World Geographer* [AWG] http://arabworldgeographer.metapress.com)

## The Fourth Geneva Convention

Yet the summer of 1949 also saw the establishment of some of the most remarkable legislation on expulsion and the right to return ever enacted. Article 49 of the Fourth Geneva Convention on Civilians declared that, "Individual or mass forcible transfers, as well as deportations of protected persons from occupied territory to the territory of the Occupying Power or to that of any other country, occupied or not, are prohibited, regardless of their motive".[63] It demanded immediate repatriation "to their *homes*" for *all* persons (including those temporarily evacuated during extreme necessity) following the cessation of "hostilities".

Article 147 called deportation and forcible population transfer "violations of humanitarian law of such egregious severity that they are required to be made subject to penal (criminal) sanctions by all other [...] states which have signed the Convention". Confirming the existing prohibition on denationalisation in customary international law, the Convention prohibited forcible expulsion in cases of non-international armed conflict. States may not "denounce" the Convention until after repatriating all those expelled, and the Convention remains in effect even after the cessation of hostilities – until all displaced persons are repatriated. Finally, "under the theory developed by the prosecutors at the [International Military Tribunal] in Nuremberg, deliberately blocking the right of return of persons forcibly expelled also falls well within the scope of a grave breach of the Fourth Geneva Convention".[64]

In November 1949, the legal advisor to the UN Economic Survey Mission, Paolo Contini, applied the prohibition on denationalisation to Palestine and Israeli attempts at denationalisation.

> It appears [...] that Arabs should be regarded as having the same citizenship status as Jews, both at the time of their displacement and upon their re-admission to Israeli territory. The temporary exodus from Israel of those refugees who will return legally to that country would not seem to change their citizenship status.[65]

According to international law, the mass denationalisation of Palestinians was illegal. The United Nations and states around the world had an obligation to uphold international law. But the Zionist leadership viewed international concern as "one of the primary obstacles" to its efforts.[66]

Each year from 1949 to 1954, between 10,000 and 15,000 Palestinians were documented as trying to return. Connections between Palestinians across the new Armistice lines remained strong despite the challenges. In the geographic spaces along the Armistice lines, Zionist forces formally adopted a free-fire policy in April 1949 (in the midst of signing four armistice agreements), killing between 2,700 and 5,000 people in the subsequent seven years.[67] "Because of the poverty and need, more and more people left the village and went to Lebanon and smuggled things in – they were called sneakers and would be shot on sight."[68]

By mid-December 1949, punishment intensified towards anyone who supported returnees or maintained connections across the new Armistice lines, including "fines, imprisonment, and exile for the offenders, and collective sieges and curfews for the communities in which returnees were found".[69] The small trading items brought in became excuses to mete out punishment.

> Mainly they smuggled tobacco and cigarette papers. There was a brand of papers called Shell Damascus and this became like gold dust "waraq al-Shaam". It became such a big crime to have these papers which weren't made in the country. If you had them you had to admit where they came from and so you must have cross-border connections. The Israelis criminalised things like cloth material, cigarette papers and traditional clothes.[70]

Frustrated with the continued strength of Palestinian ties and their persistent attempts at return, Israel pursued multiple tactics. In 1950, for instance, Foreign Minister Moshe Sharett would suggest that the United Nations establish a fund to integrate refugees into neighbouring countries. To drive the point home, Ambassador Abba Eban then explained that Israeli contributions to such a fund would preclude any individual claims to compensation (let alone rights to return).[71]

### Automatic Residency... For Jews Only

By this time, a mere year and a half after the most intensive mass expulsions, tens of thousands of Palestinians were still seeking recognition of their rights to their homes and lands. They applied for permanent residency, they submitted to the invasive exercise of the census, and they actively sought registration of their presence – an act which, unbeknownst to them, would later expedite their deportation and denationalisation.

To prevent Palestinians gaining the citizenship to which they were entitled under international law, and permanent residency, the Israeli army quickly began distributing temporary residence permits (which had been developed in July) in November 1949.[72] Recognising that the free-fire policy against returnees and the deportations were visible markers of oppression (especially in the wake of the Second World War), temporary permits were chosen as a more gradual and subtle means to achieve the same goals.

Meanwhile, Jewish immigration had been a priority for the Zionist movement, which granted itself the right to issue anyone from around the world "residency rights, social benefits, and state travel documents by virtue of claiming Judaism as his religion".[73] Yet it also considered that a more formal declaration of such individual rights (and the movement's right to grant those rights) was required. So in 1950, the "Law of Return" was developed to reify the existing policy. As explained nine years later, "the Law of Return does not discriminate against any racial group; it merely grants members of one group, the Jewish people, a privilege not granted to the members of any other group".[74] In particular, Palestinians were denied the citizenship of their own country that they had held a mere year and a half before.

As the Zionist movement debated (in July of 1950) what kind of "law" should be enacted to denationalise Palestinians, they referred to Palestinians still living in their homes as "foreigners" or, as one Palestinian historian put it, by the "absent pronoun 'they' rather than the present pronoun 'we'".[75] The discourse was borne out in practice. Tens of thousands of Palestinians were subjected to an arduous and arbitrary process of applying for permission to live *temporarily* in their homeland.

If they arrived between January and June 1949 but did not register themselves or obtain any paperwork whatsoever, the authorities were to expel them immediately unless there were "considerations which obliged" their ongoing residence.

If they entered the country after this date, they needed a cash bail and special approval from the Prime Minister in order to stay while the [Interministerial Committee comprised of representatives from the military government, Police, Foreign Ministry, intelligence (Shin Bet), and the Office of the Prime Minister's Advisor on Arab Affairs] ... evaluated their case.[76]

Unlike the privileged persons under the 1950 "Law of Return" who were automatically entitled to blue, permanent residence permits, Palestinians were the only group for whom the red "temporary residence permits" were reserved.

## Feigning Authority

Like the South Africans who rejected their passes, entire villages of Palestinians, notably in the western Galilee, rejected temporary residence permits. They were swiftly denied travel and employment permits.

In the Naqab, meanwhile, some 18,600 Bedouin had been registered but were not granted residence permits, on the urging of Yehoshua Palmon to "reduce as much as possible" the Palestinian population. The Palestinians in the Naqab, who had numbered 95,000 in 1948, and who had lost 59,000 people in the expulsions and attacks prior to 1949, were further reduced to only 13,000 by 1951. Crowded into confined areas like the First Nations of North America, using the euphemism of "relocation", they continued to be vulnerable to deportation; in 1953, the United Nations noted that 7,000 Arab Bedouin, approximately half of them from the 'Azazmeh tribe, had been forcibly expelled from the Naqab. The expulsions of the 1950s in the Naqab, as well as the expulsion of all 2,700 Palestinians in al-Majdal, were "directly facilitated" by the Israeli army's refusal to accept their residency rights.[77]

In this intermediate time period, 1948–52, the Zionist movement still had not attempted to openly contradict international law, using state law that denied citizenship to the indigenous people of Palestine. Thus, when a Tel Aviv district court was asked who should be a citizen, the judge replied using the prevailing view in public international law:

> So long as no law has been enacted providing otherwise, my view [based on the prevailing view in public international law] is that every individual who, on the date of the establishment of the State of Israel was resident in the territory which today constitutes the State of Israel, is also a national of Israel.
>
> Any other view must lead to the absurd result of a State without nationals – a phenomenon the existence of which has not yet been observed.[78]

Meanwhile, international law deepened its recognition of human rights for refugees, through the 1951 Convention Relating to the

Status of Refugees. As long as Palestinians were not receiving assistance from the United Nations Relief and Works Agency (established two years earlier), they fell under the mandate of the United Nations High Commissioner for Refugees (UNHCR). Moreover, since no agency existed for the protection of Palestinian refugees after the 1940s, the UNHCR was also to ensure the continuity of protection.[79]

Quick to respond, in 1952 Israel asked for – and was granted – responsibilities for assistance to the internally displaced Palestinians. Ever since, it has "refused to deal with the issue of internally displaced Palestinians as a 'refugee problem'", let alone a population entitled to citizenship of their own homeland.[80]

## 2.4   DENATIONALISATION

### Labelling Rights as Crimes

By 1952, the time had come to enact the golden rule that would denationalise Palestinians – the "Nationality Law". After two years of debate, the wording was finally agreed. Anyone falling outside the "Law of Return" was only to be an "Israel national" if s/he was "an inhabitant of Israel", and "was in Israel, or in an area which became Israel territory after the establishment of the State to the day of the coming into force of this Law, or entered Israel legally", including persons born "after the establishment of the State" to an "Israel national". Thus, a Palestinian needed to be recorded in the Population Registry by March of 1952, and to either have lived in Israel continuously since May 1948, or to have returned with the "permission" of the Zionist movement. All Palestinians who had lived in their own homes, but could not prove their presence for the four years up to 1952, were denationalised. No provision was made for citizenship through marriage, thus denationalising some family members but not others, with profound effect on the right to a family life.[81]

Palestinians who were denationalised had one last chance: to learn Hebrew and provide proof of residence for at least three years. But who could vouch for their story? This "different set of rules",[82] according to a small group of Arab and Jewish attorneys who campaigned against it, "marked the state's first legalization of 'racial discrimination'".[83] The discrimination deepened with clauses on citizenship revocation – jeopardising Palestinians only – that stripped citizenship if it was obtained "by the wrong committee", or if a Palestinian was outside the country for seven successive years. A third clause also threatened citizenship revocation for working "out of disloyalty to the state"; although in theory this could be used against Jews, in practice it was overwhelmingly used against Palestinians.[84]

A few months later, the "Entry into Israel Law" provided yet further "authorisation" for detention and deportation. After four years of expulsions, however, numerous Palestinians still remained. In January of 1953, a leading member of the Jewish National Fund, Yosef Nahmani, wrote, "Western Galilee has been occupied, but it has not been freed of its Arab population, as happened in other parts of the country". These 85,000 Palestinians (by his count) presented "a continual threat" to the "integrity of the state". Many were sheltered in Palestinian homes, despite being tracked, counted, and hunted. With a new rule in 1954 for the "Prevention of Infiltration", Palestinians needed only to be accused of having been temporarily absent – not even convicted of this "crime" – in order to be deported.[85]

And still, Palestinians remained. Divided villages continued to function as a "natural unit", so additional punishments were meted out:

> In one case, until the year 1955, a common *mukhtar* ruled both sides of the village Barta'a [...] as if it had remained one unit; the women of the village pumped water from the same well, and the men prayed together in the same mosque on Fridays. Finally, the *mukhtar* was arrested [...] and convicted of smuggling; villagers from both sides sent funds [...] to pay for his defence in court. Since then, the frontier seems to have deepened in meaning there.[86]

Indeed, the number of returnees struggling each year to go home fell from about 10,000 to 15,000, down to 4,500 from 1955 to 1956, and even fewer after that.[87]

Meanwhile even those with "legitimate" citizenship documents continued to be expelled. In 1959 Bedouin tribes were deported from their lands in the Naqab, a situation that was only reversed after the United Nations intervened. Others denationalised and expelled included those with registration certificates – who had been counted and registered in the census – residence permits, identity numbers, and identity cards. The vulnerability created by the temporary residence permits extended into the 1960s and beyond. Some estimate that, in addition to the expulsion of thousands of returnees, over 10,000 Palestinians were expelled in these early years.[88]

The number of Palestinians who struggled to live in or near their homes despite *in situ* denationalisation is not known. But amendments to the laws of 1949–52 (such as the replacement of the 1949 Registration of Inhabitants Ordinance by the 1965 Population Registry Law) indicate that at least several thousand Palestinians were in this situation for decades.[89] Despite these amendments, however, the majority of the Emergency Regulations remain in force today. They run counter to the advances in international law, such as the 1965 International Convention on the Elimination of All Forms of Racial Discrimination (CERD), and the 1966 International Covenant on Civil and Political Rights (ICCPR). The ICCPR, for instance, specifies that the right of entry to one's country is held by:

> nationals of a country who have been stripped of their nationality in violation of international law, [...] individuals whose country of nationality has been incorporated in or transferred to another entity, whose nationality is being denied them [... and] stateless persons arbitrarily deprived of the right to acquire the nationality of the country of [their long-term] residence.[90]

Both of these international legal documents, the CERD and ICCPR, prohibit discrimination and affirm the universal rights of entry and exit of one's country, for the first and subsequent generations of refugees.

While these and other international legal developments unfolded in the 1950s and 1960s, the rights they affirmed were labelled by the Israeli government as crimes. From 1948 to 1966, nearly 40 per cent of "convictions" by Israeli courts were for "political status offences": infringements of the laws for the Prevention of Infiltration, Entry into Israel, and Foreign Travel. As noted years later, these were the laws used to denationalise hundreds of thousands of Palestinians.[91]

### The 1967 Censuses

From 1948 to 1967, the Palestinian population almost doubled (through natural increase) from 1.4 million to 2.7 million. Roughly 300,000 were within the 1949 Armistice lines (including at least 30,000 returnees), between 975,000 and one million were in the West Bank, 400,000 were in the Gaza Strip, and a further one million were in Jordan. However, in a massive expulsion during August and September of 1967, the West Bank population was stripped by a third (to 600,000), and the Gaza Strip by an eighth (to 350,000), according to unofficial Israeli estimates.[92] Immediately, another census denationalised a vast swathe of the indigenous population. Once again, the census was taken under curfew, in "laboratory conditions ... in a closed area and on a separated population". As before, Palestinians not registered in the census were denationalised; as before, they were denied their status as nationals, refugees, or even deportees.[93] Not only were these denationalisation procedures "unique compared to census-taking in the Western world", they were also "unique" in the history of Palestine.[94]

In 1967, Military Order No. 5 declared the West Bank a closed military area; to this day, any Palestinian who wishes to leave must obtain a permit from the Israeli military to do so. In 1969, Military Order No. 297 was issued, entitled "Order concerning identity cards and Population Registration". Under this order, Palestinians in the West Bank and Gaza Strip were incorporated into the system of population surveillance that had been modelled and built up over the previous decades. A plan developed by Israel's deputy prime minister Yigal Allon in 1967 envisioned the colonisation of the West Bank "without granting citizenship to Palestinians living under Israeli control after 1967". The census and population registry were key tools in pursuing this objective.[95]

By September 1968, 400,000 Palestinians from the West Bank and Gaza had taken refuge in Jordan, and only 17,000 were ever allowed to return.[96] Meanwhile, from the summer of 1967 onward, "the Israeli estimate figures [of the Palestinian population] have been going down, indicating that depopulation continues".[97] Expulsions continued in the form of orders under the British Emergency Regulations of 1945, and under Military Order 329 (West Bank) and Military Order 290 (Gaza Strip) of 1969. Even Palestinians who had been born, or who had lived most of their lives, in the West Bank and Gaza Strip were vulnerable to expulsion.[98] And unlike the Palestinians within the 1949 Armistice lines, the Palestinians of the West Bank and Gaza Strip – including thousands of 1948 refugees – were all denationalised. They live without passports and constitute the largest, longest-standing denationalised population in the world.

## Population "Management"

For the Palestinians living in Israel – within the 1949 Armistice lines – permanent exile from their homes and lands remained a threat after 1967. The villagers of Kafr Bir'im, for example, whose lands were taken in autumn 1948, and whose homes were bombed in September 1953, began lobbying again in 1971. Despite election promises in the 1970s, the final verdict came in 1979: they would never be allowed to return to their lands.[99] On a larger scale, conscious efforts to displace and replace the Palestinian population were made under programs such as the "Judaization of the Galilee".

Some Palestinians waited decades for citizenship; when it came, it was citizenship of "the Jewish state" rather than recognition of their continued Palestine nationality. In 1980, Palestinians who had been registered in 1952 in the Population Registry finally received citizenship (the number of affected Palestinians, estimated in the tens of thousands, remains unknown). They did not, however, receive their lands and homes back.[100]

In 1981, the system of population control extended to the Palestinians in the Golan Heights, despite specific condemnation of this bureaucratic move by the United Nations (in 1981 and 2008).[101]

Expulsions continued into the 1980s and beyond.[102] The "mapping and management of the population" was an ongoing priority for Israeli politicians, think tanks, and statisticians.[103] The Israeli Central Bureau of Statistics expected "Jewish women to continue to produce enough children", despite worries that this would remain "much less than that" of Palestinians.[104] "The only way", surmised one analyst, "to change the demographic situation is through persuasion, that is to say, by talking up the need for a greater number of Jewish babies ... It is simply necessary to mount a campaign to encourage young Jews to marry other Jews and have children, more children at that."[105]

## Conclusion

Today (and as of the 1995 census) Israeli demographers consider themselves leaders in mapping computerised census data, and collecting such data through an "optical reading system".[106] While the information in the Population Registry is kept from the Palestinians it describes, much or all of it "can be seen on a screen by the lowest-ranking soldier at the most remote checkpoint in the West Bank or on the computers at the Erez [Gaza] crossing point".[107]

Over the course of decades, the Population Registry and its identity numbers have come to dominate Palestinian life. First and foremost, they served as the instruments of denationalisation for hundreds of thousands of Palestinians, with lasting effects to this day. Second, they centralised a series of bannings and permissions. Without an identity number listed in the Population Registry, a Palestinian is banned from residence, health services, employment, driving a vehicle, and uniting with family, amongst other rights. All personal affairs must also be registered via the identity number: marriage, tax payments, construction, commercial transactions, school matriculation examinations, birth certificates, and countless others. Without this number, without entry in the Registry, and without a series of permissions affixed to the identity number, a person can do none of these normal activities essential for everyday life.

Not only must individual Palestinians submit all their information for entry into the Registry, but (since 1994) Palestinians also serve as the first line of bureaucracy in the West Bank and Gaza Strip. They act as a conduit, passing on all information to be entered – into the very same Population Registry established in 1967, and modelled on the one established in the 1940s and 1950s.[108]

The legal principles that prohibit denationalisation – and its consequent subjectification and denial of basic human rights – continue to be reiterated and codified in bodies of international law. In 1999 the Articles on Nationality (of Natural Persons in Relation to the Succession of States) were drafted by the International Law Commission and adopted verbatim by the General Assembly. These reaffirm that "habitual residents" have a right to return to their homes, irrespective of why they were temporarily absent; they have the right to retain their status as nationals. Any state's nationality regulations that contradict and impede these rights may not receive international recognition (as per the 1930 Hague Convention on Certain Questions relating to Conflict of Nationality Laws).[109]

The great contradiction between rights under international law and realities under military rule continues to permeate Palestinian life. At no point did Palestinians legally cede their sovereignty. Neither the British, nor the United Nations, nor the Zionist movement had any claim to sovereignty; this always rested with the people of Palestine – the half a million people in 1914 that Chaim Weizmann pretended did not exist.[110] It continues to rest with the millions of Palestinians both inside Palestine and exiled as refugees.

It remains a great irony that after Palestinians took great risks to return and freely provide their confidential information to the census, they then experienced the same census and Population Registry being used to declare them dispossessed, denationalised, and due for deportation.

# 3
# Blacklists

While the Population Registry was critical to the denationalisation of the indigenous population of Palestine, identity documents became critical to enlisting the population's own participation in their oppression. Resistance to Zionism was high in the early years; to break this resistance required more than sheer, brute force. It required policies of divide and rule, and gradualism – affecting some people, then gradually others, then a few more categories of people, and so on. Blacklists were the first step in developing a gradualist approach.

The first part of this chapter provides an account of how, upon declaring their state, Zionist forces also seized documents from previous Palestine administrations regarding the Palestinian population, and used them to augment their already lengthy blacklists. The following decades, described in the second part of the chapter, would become landmarks in effecting institutionalised inequality through identity documents.

## 3.1 PAPER BLACKLISTS AND EXECUTIONS

### Blacklisting as "Reassurance"

Until 1937, blacklisting did not appear as a prominent strategy in the history of Palestine. And while identity documents did exist, they were not visible markers against blacklisted individuals until the 1980s. In the Ottoman period, Palestinians had four kinds of information certificates (*ilmuhaber*), registering birth, death, migration, and marriage.[1] Neither the Population Registry nor the certificates listed any measure of "hostility", "activism", or even a history of imprisonment for political reasons or otherwise. In essence, neither form of documentation constituted the basis for blacklisting.

The identity documents issued in Palestine under British administration were similarly free of threatening markings. First issued in 1926, Palestine passports corresponded to the Population Registry. Even British intelligence documents were less intent on blacklisting than on general descriptions of geography, ethnology, administration, and resources.[2]

In 1937, identity cards became part of the Palestine Order-in-Council (and were later absorbed as Article 143B in the 1945 Emergency Regulations). Although details of individual Palestinians' political activities began to be collected, such intelligence was not linked to the Population Registry or the identity cards. Nevertheless, Palestinian lawyers and intellectuals warned of British intentions in Palestine. Palestinian leaders refused to recognise the cards' authority, and called on Palestinians to disregard the British police orders to carry them.[3]

To lessen resistance, the identity cards and accompanying restrictions were presented as targeting some, not all, individuals in Palestine. In other words, not only was no attempt made to conceal their potential for blacklisting, but the fact that they could be used to blacklist individuals was even used as "reassurance". Even the Zionists protested, despite standing to benefit from British selective punishment of Palestinians through the Order-in-Council (and later Emergency Regulations):

> We are being reassured that the Regulations will be used only against criminals, not against the entire population, but so did the Nazi ruler in Oslo, Norway, reassure the population that no harm would come to any citizen who minded his own business.[4]

While only the British administration had the power at the time to force identity cards upon the population, the head of Zionist intelligence, Isar Harel, employed two individuals who eventually came to direct the blacklisting process: Syrian-born citrus-grove businessman (and former head of the Hagana's "Arab section") Ezra Danin, and Palestinian-born commando (with British forces) Yehoshua Palmon.[5] All three – Harel, Danin, and Palmon – were part of Ben-Gurion's inner circle (which also included intelligence officer Gad Machnes, as well as Head of the settlement department in the Jewish Agency Yossef Weitz, and six military leaders).

To create blacklists, Danin, Palmon, and Ya'acov Shimoni (who directed the supervision of collaborators) sought and collected information on individual Palestinians in about 1,200 villages.

By the 1930s, the project included information on each village such as: main income, sociopolitical composition, religious affiliation, homes of *mukhtars*, relation with other villages, and the ages of individual men who were between 16 and 50. Gradually further information was noted: number of cars, shop owners, members of workshops, and homes of artisans and their skills. In 1943 clans and their political affiliations were added, as well as social stratification (notables/peasants), and the names of civil servants. Finally, in 1945, details extended to the names of mosques and imams, "such characteristics as 'he is an ordinary man', and even precise accounts of the living rooms inside the homes of these dignitaries".[6]

## Blacklisting Against Jews

Blacklists were also created on Jews who criticised Zionism. In the early 1900s, a group of Zionists advocated coexistence; some of these individuals formed *Brit Shalom*, insisting on a binational state. Internationally, early Jewish nationalist ideas emerged that were neither colonial nor territorial, and some advocated communal enclaves where Jews were already living, rather than displacing others. Thus, many Jews – including in Palestine – continued to adopt and advocate assimilation, secularisation, or integration. Throughout the 1930s, resistance to exclusionary forms of Zionism persisted, as the influx of Zionists doubled their numbers in a five-year period (1931–6). Jewish opponents to Zionism in Palestine and elsewhere were accused of protecting their acquired social positions, and were carefully monitored.[7]

Meanwhile, the force and coercion of pre-1948 Zionism (ambushes, patrols, and raids) were less visible to the movement's members than the symbols of Jewish revival: immigration, construction, agriculture, industry, language acquisition, donor sponsorship, and "international struggle for [. . .] sovereignty". To many, Zionism was the embodiment of their cherished ideals of communal harmony, and the pursuit of these ideals often involved personal sacrifice rather than profit; that Zionism was also a colonial enterprise did not taint their good intentions.[8]

For some Zionists, however, especially among those seeking cultural renaissance or a renewed labourer class (rather than solely territory) – as well as religious, non-Zionist Jews – the colonial aspects became evident. Blacklists served to counter and target such individuals who resisted, or who made clear to the world what was taking place in Palestine. This culminated, perhaps at its height, in the assassination of the well-known journalist and professor, Jacob de Haan, by the Zionist military wing in 1924. It also manifested in harassment of Jews who employed Palestinians, defended Palestinian land ownership, or supported Palestinian indigenous rights; ultimately, suppression of Palestinians remained the chief outcome of blacklisting.[9]

## Marked for Death

A crucial element in blacklisting against Palestinians was the information collected on villages and individuals from the 1930s onward. These "Village Files" included a "hostility" index, measuring, for instance, the level of participation in the 1936 revolt (against British and Zionist colonisation of Palestine). Most of what we know about the "Village Files" and how they were used comes from the work of historian Ilan Pappé.[10] He describes how the "hostility" index contained a list of everyone involved in the revolt, as well as the families of Palestinians killed. The 1947 final update included lists of "wanted" persons in each village. Reasons for being on this list were broad and covered basic democratic participation in Palestinian politics. The label of involvement in the Palestinian national movement, for instance, could include entire villages. This movement dominated Palestinian politics during the 1920s and 1930s, and "the party's members went on to win national and municipal elections". Further reasons for blacklisting included travel to Lebanon, arrest by the British for "being a member of a national committee in the village", or participation in actions against British or Zionist forces.

The blacklists and village files were then converted, as part of "Plan C", into three aims: to kill, damage, or attack. The list of "potential human targets" included leaders, financial supporters, Palestinians who acted against Jews, and senior Palestinian officials in the Government of Palestine. Damage was to be done to transport and livelihoods, including water wells, mills, and other infrastructure. Attacks were to be launched against clubs, coffee houses, meeting places, and especially nearby villages before they could come to the assistance of their neighbours.

> His [Danin's] people were responsible for the procedures that were followed after a Palestinian village or neighbourhood had been occupied. This meant that, with the help of informants, they detected and identified men who [...] were usually executed on the spot. Danin quite often came to inspect these operations at first hand.[11]

During the occupation of Nazareth, for example, local intelligence officer Palti Sela searched the city from house to house with an informant, arresting anyone on a pre-prepared list of "undesirables".

Palmon, as Danin's second-in-command, "also took a great personal interest in implementing the policies of selection, interrogation and sometimes execution". In addition to executing those on blacklists, Danin and Palmon would also take captive "all men of 'military age', namely between ten and fifty" in numerous villages. About 8,000 people spent all of 1949 in prison camps.

> A common sight in rural Palestine in the wake of the cleansing operations were huge pens in which male villagers, ranging from children from the age of ten to older men up to the age of fifty, were being held.[12]

Strict instructions were given to pluck out individuals on the basis of religion:

> Prisoners: cars will be ready to transport the refugees (plitim) to points on the Lebanese and Syrian borders. POW camps will be built in Safad and Haifa, and a transit camp in Acre; all the Muslim inhabitants have to be moved out.[13]

A military leader (Moshe Carmel) responsible for carrying out such instructions observed:

> They abandon the villages of their birth and that of their ancestors and go into exile ... Women, children, babies, donkeys – everything moves, in silence and grief, northwards, without looking to right or left. Wife does not find her husband and child does not find his father.[14]

Carmel's reference to missing husbands and fathers is relevant; the absence of men was evident in the masses of refugees fleeing on foot. "Ragged women and children were conspicuously dominant in these human convoys: the young men were gone – executed, arrested or missing."[15]

### Stealing More Files

The feeling of being hunted was all-pervasive. On August 18, 1948, Moshe Sharett wrote to Chaim Weizmann, "we are equally determined to explore all possibilities of getting rid, once and for all, of the huge [Palestinian] Arab minority".[16] The "undesirables" were shot, captured, or expelled wherever they were found: in their own homes, in the homes of others, in places of sanctuary, or in the wooded areas, plains or caves nearby. "It was a severely cold winter", recounts survivor Sami Zahra of the village of Kafr Bir'im, "and I slept in a very old cave used as a tomb in the past and with many bones still there".[17]

Pappé notes that, "In the language of Israeli intelligence", Palestinians "were 'successfully shot at'". Killings were thus recorded, such as: "4 December 1948: 'successful shooting at Palestinians trying to return to the village of Blahmiyya and who attempted to retrieve their belongings'".[18] The blacklists of the Village Files were only the beginning of the systemic marking – and elimination – of Palestinians as "undesirable". After 1948, blacklisting of individuals and villages was found to be doubly "effective" given their "under-development", as they reeled from the attacks, dispossession, and forced impoverishment of the previous months.[19]

In the subsequent months, the significance of the blacklists would broaden in two ways. First, the reasons for being blacklisted would expand; and second, the consequences of blacklisting would engulf entire communities. The town of Beersheba, for instance, was targeted for "occupation, destruction and expulsion" because the deputy mayor, al-Hajj Salameh Ibn Said, and his brother had "both refused to collaborate". Search-and-arrest operations went by names such as "Operation Comb" or "Distillation" (ziquq). Orders were given "to find as many such 'suspicious Arabs' as possible, without actually bothering to define the nature of the suspicion".[20]

Once again, blacklists were pushed as "reassurance": those who "behaved" would have nothing to fear. But again, the mere presence and existence of a Palestinian was enough to cause his or her imprisonment and punishment. In the village of Majd al-Kurum, for instance, where Palestinian men and women had been lined up and shot in October 1948, Zionist forces "combed" the village time after time in the years 1949 to 1951, to detain and expel individuals without paper receipts (that is, receipts indicating their inclusion in the Population Registry).[21]

Behind these blacklists were the same individuals who had built the Village Files: Ezra Danin and Yossef Weitz continued to form "The Committee for Arab Affairs" (assembled in August 1948), and later a two-person specialised commission to continue evicting and dispossessing Palestinians from their land and property. The Committee's task was to reduce the Palestinian population quietly (without overt violent repression, and unfavourable international publicity); no more free-fire zone (on the perimeters of what would become the Armistice lines) in which to shoot Palestinians on sight. To meet this challenge, the less "drastic means" of blacklisting was again enlisted as a reassurance that only criminals, not the entire population, would face execution or expulsion.[22]

Thus, not only the Village Files, but also the demographic information collected by the British administration served a revived purpose. Taxation and land registration records – specifically pertaining to Muslim and Christian Palestinians – were demanded from, and for the most part given by, the departing British administrators. Israeli state archives today house demographic files from 1934 to 1948, regarding passports, visas, laissez-passer documents, and immigrant and entry registration. Such files had been in British possession and were subject to attack by the Jewish underground organisations. Some of these militants captured British vehicles, stole documents, and utilised the "agency of Jewish employees" in the British administration. The information gathered was then used in assaults on Palestinians who remained, both east and west of the 1949 Armistice Lines.[23]

## Expanding the Category of "Undesirables"

The data on Palestinians' personal lives was not the only "inheritance" from previous periods; once it declared a state, Israel adopted the rules and policies contained in the 1937 Palestine Order-in-Council and the 1945 Emergency Regulations. This included Article 143B on identity cards, forcing the population to submit to stop-and-search tactics on roads, in their homes, at their workplaces, and virtually anywhere an armed Israeli chose to stop them. The "undesirables", as they were called in correspondence between officials, were taken prisoner without charge or trial, or made to report several times a day to the nearest police station – which could be miles away from their homes or workplaces. Meanwhile, their villages could be denied electricity, refused permission to build essential structures such as schools, or to run public facilities like community centres.[24]

To get on a blacklist, Palestinians could "confess" in detention; they could sign a document written in Hebrew, potentially with a mistranslated Arabic version. Their "confession" could state their membership in the Communist Party, the Land Party (*el-Ard*), or even the Democratic Teachers List of the *Histadrut* (Zionist workers' union); all such blacklists were then circulated among officials. Since many Palestinians withstood torture, however, someone else's confession could suffice (or so decided the "courts" set up after 1948). Palestinians thus refrained from publicly expressing their political views and were "taught" the limits within which they were expected to remain.[25]

Palestinians were punished with blacklisting if they refused to act as informers, to sell land, or to vote for "this or that local chairman".[26] Teachers "were afraid to talk freely in class, to teach history the way they understood it, or to discuss political affairs".[27] Continuing well into the 1980s, lists were kept of Palestinian "high school and college graduates suspected of 'antigovernment activities'" whose blacklisting then blocked their employment in "government agencies [and] in privately owned Jewish establishments".[28]

The dilemma was that as it was impossible for Palestinians to undertake ordinary life tasks without permits from the Israeli military government, so they were forced to approach officials and thus have a file opened on themselves.[29] Permission was required not only for employment, but even simply to reside in one's home. Contrary to declared promises that Palestinians would be allowed to live in peace, they were repeatedly refused any form of documentation to verify these promises. Yehoshua Palmon, Danin's former second-in-command and now the "Prime Minister's Advisor on Arab Affairs", recommended to "reduce as much as possible the number of people with permanent residence".[30] The prerequisite for the right to property, employment or protection under the law was to become "generations of maternal Jewish descent".[31] Even when some 18,600 Bedouin had registered for identity documents, Palmon persuaded ID-granting officials to withhold IDs from all of them.[32]

Once a person's file was opened – in the process of requesting "permission" to live in one's home or to work – the potential for blacklisting made that person especially vulnerable. A blacklisted person could have a permit delayed, refused, or reduced in temporal or spatial validity, with restrictions on the time allowed for movement or the routes of travel. To continuously populate the blacklists, Israeli officials kept records of conversations in cafes, schools, buses, and private homes.[33]

Yet only a small fraction of blacklisting was due to voiced dissent; the vast majority of persons were blacklisted due to "status". Even "confessions" related to status:

> [T]he single most common charge against [Israeli officials] was that they forced several residents to sign documents which threatened either their own legal status or the status of others.

One woman, for example, watched Haggai [an assistant to Officer Avraham Yarkoni in the village of Dayr Hanna] beat her husband until she "confessed" to falsifying another woman's ID, and a male refugee living in the village was beaten until he initialed a statement that he and his family wished to be expelled.[34]

Blacklisting on the basis of status contradicted the previous "reassurance" that only dissidents would be targeted. Now that such claims rang hollow, the Israeli army were quick to find a new justification for blacklisting; to differentiate among Palestinians, they argued, was simply not "feasible" when it came to imprisonment, expulsion or execution.[35]

## 3.2   BLACKLISTS AS HIERARCHIES OF DISCRIMINATION

### Stamping Religion

When the Zionist movement declared itself a state in 1948, it promised to "maintain complete equality of social and political rights for all citizens, without distinction of creed, race or sex", and to "guarantee freedom of religion and conscience, of language, education and culture".[36] Yet this promise was not borne out in the documents issued regarding status:

> In Jewish communities, there were two steps: on the day of the census, families were counted and registered at home and immediately received "registration receipts," proof of having filled out the survey (required for everyone 18 years or older); they obtained their identity cards soon thereafter.
>
> By contrast, Arab families – whether in neighborhoods of mixed towns or in all-Arab localities – were required to complete four steps, each of which took place on a different day: first, to be counted in the census; second, to complete the registration survey; third, to obtain a registration receipt; and fourth, to receive their ID.[37]

During the census, while absent Palestinians were not counted, absent Jews – and even Jews who refused to participate based on faith-based opposition to Zionism – were counted in their own way: a list of their names was "forwarded to the government".[38]

For 18 years (1948–66), Palestinians were placed under military rule and controlled by a separate administration from Israeli Jews, for everything from education to statistics, land registration to the police, military, and intelligence.[39] Geographic segregation of the Palestinian population – one of the lasting outcomes of this 18-year confinement through military rule – ensured that such bureaucratic segregation could continue even after its official dissolution.

Continuing well past the 18 years, Palestinians who wished to marry other Palestinians from outside the Armistice lines (for example, from the "east" side of the same village) underwent different procedures to those who wished to marry Jews (from anywhere in the world). The prospective spouse could not travel home for at least five years, had to renounce his or her existing citizenship, and then apply for permission to remain – which could be rejected according to "undisclosed criteria set by the Population Registry".[40] There was no judicial appeal against rejections.

In addition to privileged treatment for all Jews, distinctions were also made for religious sects. In August 1949, Yehoshua Palmon received a letter from the military governor of the Eastern Galilee, asking: "what to do with the people who came who are not from the religious sects [`edot] getting special treatment ... so it can be clarified if the instructions are to expel everyone".[41] The Israeli state sought "forced segmentation of the population (Druze, Christian villages, townsfolk)" through the co-option of "positive elements".[42] Particularly in Galilee villages, "one of the first and thorniest issues to arise was the ambiguity surrounding the special treatment of certain Christian communities".[43]

The information on identity cards enabled discrimination in stop-and-search activities. "Israeli police are not blessed with special powers of perception", noted one researcher.[44] The cards explicitly labelled people, regardless of the person's own preference and self-identification. And invasive stop-and-search operations "fanned sectarian flames" even further.[45]

Before declaring an end to military rule in 1966 (although a "state of emergency" is still in effect), the Israeli state ensured that Palestinians would continue to be tied to their ID cards, by making the cards mandatory for all persons over 16. To facilitate the distinction of Palestinians, the new identity cards would carry religious identification instead of citizenship.[46]

The new ID cards gave full names of the carrier, parents, spouse, and children, as well as the person's address and age (and children's ages). Marital status was also listed, and distinguished between single, divorced, and widowed. Finally, and most crucially for discrimination in stop-and-search activities, the cards identified "nationality". This term has a peculiar interpretation, listing religion (for Jews, with additional categories like Samaritan or Hebrew), former citizenship for new immigrants (for example, Georgian, Russian, and another 100 or so options) and, among Palestinians, "confession": Druze, Abkhazi, Assyrian, or finally, "Arab" (combining Christians and Muslims). Thus, like the "nationality law" of 1952, the cards did not refer to any nationality defined by geographic borders. Instead, they reinforced the denial of Palestinian nationality.[47]

## Legal Apartheid

But the most powerful label remained, not the ID but rather its absence. The selective issuing of IDs was and has always been the key instrument in distinguishing some Palestinians from others – expelling some and not others. The town of Shafa 'Amr, for example, had IDs given to its Christian population while "the 465 Muslims in the group received other documents, which subjected them to ongoing, persistent harassment". They were kept hanging with the promise of IDs "on the way, but none came".[48]

The expulsion, denationalisation, and finally lack of identity cards in the West Bank and Gaza Strip, denied over a million Palestinians access to their homeland. This was sometimes as close as down the street; the villages along the Armistice lines were cut in half and villagers were prohibited from crossing the imaginary line on pain of death. Most Palestinians in the West Bank received Jordanian passports and identity cards. Palestinians, mostly refugees, in Gaza remained without passports, and only got Egyptian travel documents and identity cards.

The Israeli army, however, not only crossed the Armistice lines but also conducted multiple attacks on unarmed villagers. Using information gathered in the Village Files and from the departing British administration, incursions were made into the villages of Latrun, Falameh, Rantis, Qalqiliya, Khirbet al-Deir, Khirbet Rasm Nofal, Khirbet Beit Emin, Qatanna, Wadi Fukin, Idhna, and Surif.[49] In 1953, Israeli soldiers also buried alive over 40 people in the village of Qibya. Bullet-riddled doors and bodies were found among the remains of demolished homes, showing how villagers were "forced to remain inside until their homes were blown up over them".[50] South African-born Zionist leader Abba Eban – serving at the time as Vice President of the United Nations General Assembly – excused the Qibya massacre as "an unfortunate explosion of pent-up feelings".[51]

As Israeli expansion crept into the territory of the West Bank and Gaza Strip in 1967, one of the first steps taken was to acquire the intelligence archives of the previous administrations.[52] The next step was to ensure that all Palestinians once again submitted to the system of identity documentation, complete with labels. In addition to personal data, plus the all-important category of "nationality", the cards had special numbering, retained from the Population Registry, which marked the carrier's status. The first digits of an identity number indicate whether a Palestinian obtained his or her ID in East Jerusalem (08), the West Bank and Gaza Strip (09), or through gaining status via family reunification (086).[53]

Jewish colonists, meanwhile, were issued with identity cards that not only gave them freedom of movement, but also excluded them from applicable law and court jurisdiction in each of the territories.[54] Dividing a population on such a basis (that is, religion) for administrative purposes contravenes the Apartheid Convention and was thus dubbed "legal apartheid".[55] Colonists were exempt from the military orders issued in the West Bank, such as Military Order No. 297 of 1969, which compelled all Palestinian males to apply for an identity card at the age of 16, and which gave unlimited license for stop-and-search operations: IDs must be presented "upon the request of any soldier on duty or to any other soldier so authorised".[56] Failure to comply with the military order was punishable with up to one year's imprisonment – for Palestinians only. If children reach the age of 16 without their birth being registered in the Israeli Population Registry, they are not granted an ID card.[57]

Back on the other side of the Armistice lines, Israel decided to grant further "special treatment" to deepen sectarian divisions. In 1970, any individual whose identity card stated "Druze" as "nationality" was from that point on allowed to deal with the government departments ordinarily reserved for Jews.[58] All other Palestinians would continue to deal with their separate departments.

A year later, a Jewish Israeli petitioned the courts to change his label to "Israeli" rather than "Jew". He was refused, and branded a "separatist". The court stated that there was no such thing as an "Israeli nation separate from the Jewish people", thus excluding Palestinians as constituents. To this day, "neither political discourse nor formal Israeli identity documents mention an 'Israeli nationality' (leumiut yisrailit)".[59]

### Blacklists and War Crimes

Since the 1950s to the present, Israel continued to compile and use blacklists for Palestinians in Israel as well as in the West Bank and

Gaza Strip.[60] Indeed, until they are taken prisoner, most blacklisted Palestinians remain unaware of their inclusion on such lists. Blacklisting affected not only individuals, but also their families and communities. In the West Bank and Gaza Strip, military bulldozers demolished the homes of family and relatives of the blacklisted individuals.[61] Facing stiff opposition to this policy in Gaza, they went one step further: in 1971, the Israeli army pursued a policy of forced eviction. They proceeded "to break up the larger camps in Gaza, move the families that had lived in them into isolated regions of the Strip, and impose stricter and more brutal controls on the movement of peasants, workers, shopkeepers, students, and other inhabitants of the region".[62]

Nor were Palestinians with Israeli citizenship protected. In 1980, denationalisation was once again made a formal procedure for "a person who has done an act constituting a breach of allegiance to the State of Israel" – support for the leading Palestinian representative organisation at the time constituted such a breach. Personal information from the Population Registry was (and still is) regularly exploited – in later years via direct computer connection to the Registry – by various Israeli institutions and banks. All outgoing international telephone calls were tapped.[63]

A Palestinian could be sentenced to ten years in prison for "a march of ten or more people together; or the assembling for the purpose of marching together from one place to another for a political purpose; or for a matter which can be interpreted as a political matter whether or not they were in fact walking and whether or not they had congregated".[64] The arbitrariness and unaccountability of blacklisting was overt. More importantly, it explicitly contradicted international law, including the Geneva Convention Relative to the Treatment of Civilian Persons in Time of War.

Yet military courts upheld military actions: a Palestinian woman was put on "trial" for hanging a map of Palestine in her private office; a group of Palestinians were "convicted" for singing nationalist songs at a wedding.[65] Individuals on blacklists could be taken captive or "liquidated", through the agency of *musta'ribeen* (*mist'rivim* in Hebrew), or literally "those who are made [to appear] Arab".[66] International law institutions reminded Israel that their routine practices linked to blacklisting – imprisonment, torture, raids, collective punishment, expulsion, home demolition, and property confiscation – constituted war crimes.

The UN Human Rights Commission, using the Geneva Convention's provision that certain violations of humanitarian law are "grave breaches" meriting criminal punishment for perpetrators, found a number of Israel's practices during the uprising to constitute "war crimes."

It included physical and psychological torture of Palestinian detainees and their subjection to improper and inhuman treatment; the imposition of collective punishment on towns, villages, and camps; the administrative detention of thousands of Palestinians; the expulsion of Palestinian citizens; the confiscation of Palestinian property; and the raiding and demolition of Palestinian houses.[67]

### The Ultimate Police State

In 1986 Israel introduced magnetic ID cards as a prerequisite for anyone wishing to temporarily leave the West Bank or the Gaza Strip for employment across the Armistice lines. Only people who had passed the General Security Services (GSS) security screen could get a magnetic card. By 1987, any administrator in the institutions controlling the Palestinian population had access, "by pressing a key on a computer terminal", to blacklists of "hostiles" and collaborator lists of "positives". Using this carrot and stick approach, administrators could then draw upon these lists to make decisions on anything "from car licensing to water quotas, import permits and travel documents".[68] That year, Jerusalem's former Deputy Mayor and Chief Planning Officer Meron Benvenisti predicted the potential influence of blacklists.

The Data Bank might, however, develop into a sinister "big brother" control apparatus in the hands of an administration that already possess absolute power and is free of any checks and balances ...

The computerization project, if allowed to attain its stated goals, may prove to be a milestone in the institutionalization of the ultimate police state.[69]

Following his prediction, intelligence activities and thus blacklists increased in the 1980s and 1990s (especially after the Oslo Accords and colonists' further expansion in the West Bank and Gaza Strip), and into the turn of the millennium.[70]

The late 1980s brought about a number of changes in identity documentation. Palestinians in the West Bank, who were previously entitled to Jordanian passports, were from 1988 onward given only travel documents. Women and teenage girls (over 16), who had previously not been required to carry IDs at all times, were compelled to do so by Military Order No. 1232. And most ominously, former detainees – including those released without charge – were visibly blacklisted via the green covers to their IDs (Military Order 1269).[71]

In a green ID, the ID number remained unchanged, but the card expired after six months and required renewal. Green IDs prohibited travel across the Armistice lines, as well as to East Jerusalem; this compounded travel problems between the southern and northern West Bank, and made it impossible beyond the boundaries of either the West Bank or Gaza Strip, whichever area was ascribed to the ID-holder. Green IDs thus annulled chances to study, to seek medical treatment, to see or live with family, and to enjoy any aspect of daily life that required a modicum of movement.[72]

The green IDs represented the first separate and easily distinguishable cards to "mark" former detainees. Prior to 1989, certain Palestinians were blacklisted by marking their identity cards with special signs.[73] The visible marking of former detainees enabled harassment. One case among many documented by human rights groups involved a man who, with his wife and son in the car, was stopped on his way from the doctor's to the pharmacy, and asked for his identity card: "When I handed it to him, I saw the excitement on their faces and heard one of them saying, in Hebrew, "Yarok! Yarok!" which means green."[74]

He was taken to an isolated location and beaten and kicked for about seven minutes; his ID was then returned and he was told to leave.

The restrictions imposed on blacklisted Palestinians (green IDs) later, in the early 1990s, came to apply to all Palestinians in the West Bank and Gaza Strip.[75] Meanwhile, their first "passports", issued by the Palestinian Authority established via the Oslo Accords, were in fact merely travel documents, acting in much the same way as identity cards. Indeed, the "identity number" for each person was identical to that in the Population Registry. The Population Registry thus remained the pivotal element of the blacklisting process.

This meant that if Palestinians were marked as blacklisted using their ID number and ID card, the moment they needed to use their ID for a basic right, they would be vulnerable.

Palestinians had thus been made largely reliant on the system that was to target them throughout the latter half of the twentieth century. From 1967 to 2006, Israel detained and imprisoned – nearly all on political rather than criminal grounds – over 650,000

*Figure 3.1*   An Israeli checkpoint in Nablus, Palestine. Palestinians were forced to rely on the ID system that blacklisted and targeted them. In the year 2000, movement into and out of the Palestinian city of Nablus was restricted to four entrances, guarded from the outside by Israeli armed forces, and on the inside by Palestinian police. Internal matters were administered by the Palestinian Authority set up in the Oslo Accords with Israel. Palestinians required permits to leave the area. A register of the Palestinian population, identity documents, and stop-and-search procedures monitored movement. (Tom Kay)

Palestinians, that is, nearly one-fifth of the West Bank and Gaza Palestinian population, including hundreds of women and children.[76]

In the course of these arrests, identity cards were an additional factor. One of the first steps in each arrest was to demand the identity card, revealing to the army the private information of an individual and his or her family. Identity cards also marked Palestinians as non-Jews and thus even more vulnerable in the Israeli context. Israeli prisons and camps were known for their ill-treatment and torture of Palestinians, denial of access to lawyers and family members, prolonged interrogation sessions, use of collaborators to threaten detainees, and threats to family members.[77]

### Biometric Blacklists

In the new millennium very little changed – except for the worse – in the frequency and invasiveness of blacklisting. Minor changes to identity documents in 2002 removed the entry for "nationality", due to an internal debate on the definition of "Jew" as an entry. Israeli police opposed the removal of the "nationality" category, stating that it had been "helpful"; the entry thus remains in the Population Registry – widely accessible to officials – and Palestinians continue to face discrimination.[78] In 1999, human rights organisations – with a focus on Palestinians inside the Armistice lines – reported numerous counts (and ongoing court cases) of racism, hate speech, and rights violations regarding language, education, religion, land, women, housing, society, economy, and employment.[79]

In 2000, such discrimination manifested itself in hundreds of injuries and the killing of 13 Palestinians with Israeli citizenship. At least one of the dead, local doctors believed, could have been saved if Israeli ambulances had not refused to carry him to a hospital. Israeli police had shot him – unarmed – in the head, beside his left eye.[80]

Israeli institutions and banks continue to have open access to the Registry, despite a 2004 state court ruling, and despite a 2007 amendment to the 1965 rules that imposed the Population Registry in the first place. Military wire-tapping of private telephones also continues – despite officially ending in 2004, at least 1,128 wiretaps were conducted in 2006 alone.[81]

In 2003, the already stringent Israeli restrictions on marrying a Palestinian (or any "non-Jew") outside the Armistice lines were tightened to make such marriages impossible: "non-Jews would be ineligible for citizenship or possibly even residency", and so would any children from the marriage. As one couple, newly returned from their honeymoon on the eve of the new restrictions, put it: "We will learn to fear every knock on the door".[82] The new restrictions banned her from joining her husband, while existing restrictions banned him from entering her hometown of Bethlehem (unlike Jewish colonists who continued to have free access). Living together was thus to "live like fugitives". In 2005, Ariel Sharon explained the restrictions as targeted at Palestinians, who "have identification cards like us, the same licence plates, and [who] can't be stopped on the roadsides".[83]

In 2007, a new "Big Brother" Law was passed: providing Israeli police and six other authorities with unlimited access to private telephone information – who called whom, from where to where, when, and for how long, and all personal information entrusted to the service provider (address, payment details, and of course, ID number). In a separate development, new ID cards and passports were to have fingerprints, in addition to the usual photograph. A 2008 officially approved memorandum – translated two years later into "law" – explained how these documents and their biometric information would remain linked to a database, with open access to all armed officials and every level of government, down to the counter clerks. Rights to retain one's own biometric information – upheld internationally by institutions such as the European Court of Human Rights – were thus erased; failure to comply would be met with punishment of up to a year's imprisonment.[84]

As time went on, no place was safe for the hunted, the marked, the blacklisted. Between 2000 and 2011, the Israeli army assassinated 174 Palestinians, together with 254 bystanders.[85] It also killed 6,552 others, including well over 1,000 children, against whom the army discourse was little different from the language of blacklisting and executions. The killing of over 1,400 Palestinians in a three-week period during 2008 and 2009, for instance, was referred to as a "hunter-killer operation that involved scanning the entire Gaza area using [unmanned aerial vehicles]".[86] The agglomeration of Palestinian rights into a single number, used to blacklist some and dehumanise others, rendered them the ultimate victims of isolation and insecurity.

## Conclusion

Many perceive identity documents as symbols of entitlement and protection. But for Palestinians, identity numbers and cards mark them as less – not more – likely to have recourse to justice or state-protected human rights. Without the numbering of humans and the correspondingly colour-coded IDs, could the random imprisonments, extrajudicial killings, mass arrests, and other violations described in this chapter have taken place? Palestinians are in a bind and can little more rid themselves of their number and card than they could a tattoo or brand. Their ID numbers and cards represent the "permission" to hold rights that should otherwise be inalienable. When that number and card transform people into human targets, they are caught in a cage from which no escape can be found, nor is offered. Near-total surveillance is such that, after 10,000 Palestinians were taken captive *en masse* in 2002 and 2003, those released believed they "might never be able to go back home again".[87] Blacklisting creates indelible markings, which in turn facilitates gross violations of human rights.

Blacklisting is, by definition, a way of telling the majority that they are in the clear, as long as they do not interfere in the targeting of questionable individuals. Finally, since blacklisting is not a charge, it is rarely subject to due process, and holds no clear punishment, therefore the general public is encouraged to have a naïve optimism about the consequences.

Blacklisting may be a bureaucratic process – rather than a forceful, physical one – but insofar as it enables discrimination, bypasses due process, and facilitates a gradual decline in the rule of law and human rights, it is seriously problematic, as history illustrates. The president of the World Zionist Organisation, Chaim Weizmann, was once on a blacklist, developed by the Nazis in anticipation of an invasion of the United Kingdom. The list documented information on 2,820 persons who were to be arrested and questioned.[88]

It named key administrators in the universities of Bristol, London, and Oxford, 171 firms ranging from banks to the Western Union Telegraph Company; Masonic lodges, the Royal Institute of International Affairs and 389 societies including the Fabian Society, the Rotary International, the P.E.N. Club, the Oddfellows Society, the Society of Friends, the Y.M.C.A., the Church of England Committee for Non-Aryan Christians, the Society of Friends of the Soviet Union, the Maccabi World Union, and trade unions.[89]

Since the Nazis did not invade Britain, the blacklist was not activated. It is symbolic, however, of a strategy of gradualism, to pinpoint individuals and thus inhibit opposition and resistance.

# 4
# Coercion and Collaboration

In addition to gradualism by blacklisting, another form of gradualism was practiced which involved taking away all rights, and then selectively granting temporary "permissions", thereby creating a permanent atmosphere of insecurity. Thus an individual can never know for certain that "it is over", either for the best or for the worst. Residency was but one amongst many rights that was taken away and gradually, often temporarily but always selectively, restored.[1] Others included the right to own, access, and cultivate land, the rights to movement, employment, suffrage, and marriage, and the right to freedom from harassment, extortion, hunger, social isolation, detention, and deportation.[2] All such rights, and more, were labelled as crimes unless permitted by Israel. This led, of course, to a proliferation of "permits" from an assortment of "authorities". But eventually, the population registry, identity cards, and stop-and-search procedures became the strongest tools for implementing this gradualism.

The first section of this chapter describes how, building on Ottoman and British initiatives to distribute identity cards, Israel utilised a similar strategy: making ID cards mandatory to encourage Palestinians to provide information about themselves for the Population Registry (and by extension, for Israeli intelligence). Never before, however, had cards been so vital. Basic human functions and rights – to marry, live with one's children, earn a living, work on one's own land – were all taken away and "given" back at the behest of Israeli officials. As seen in the second section of this chapter, vast inequalities created on the basis of ascribed status – denationalised versus immediately naturalised – opened the door to extortion, theft, "acts of humiliation", and other forms of coercion.

Finally we describe how more and more Palestinians were enlisted into collaboration, bringing the system full circle: informants accused Palestinians of "misbehaving", blacklisted Palestinians were "removed", a weakened Palestinian polity was stripped of its leaders and intellectuals, votes were coerced, and political opposition was nipped in the bud. This cycle of blacklisting, coercion, and collaboration had little precedent in Palestine, and attracted little international awareness – let alone sanction.

## 4.1 WITHHOLDING RIGHTS AS COERCION

### Cards as Impetus for Registration

When identity cards were introduced in the late Ottoman period in the 1880s – and in effect represented "permission" for a plethora of rights – the population not only accepted them but actively sought entry in the population registry. The first identity cards were given only to a portion of the population represented in the Ottoman government. After the Crimean war, ID cards (*tezkere-i osmaniye*) were introduced in one province (*vilayet*), representing a quarter of the potential card-receiving population in the 1860s. Preparations were made to print and distribute five million cards, with another 15 million anticipated. The proposed use of the cards was for registration of changes in an individual's status.[3]

In the 1881/2 census, however, regulations for identity cards were substantially altered, due in part to the influence of foreign advisors. Identity documents would be crucial both in ensuring the population did not evade (conscription or taxation), but also actively sought, registration.

> Compliance with the census registration was insured by a rather compelling measure. Each registered individual was issued an official *nüfus tezkeresi* (population bulletin or identity card) which contained all the relevant information about the bearer in the register. This card came to be known later as *nüfus cüzdanı* (population book).
>
> Each individual had to show it to the authorities before buying, selling, or inheriting property, before being accepted in an occupation or profession, for obtaining travel documents, or for conducting other official business.
>
> Those without such cards, besides being unable to conduct official business, were punished by stiff fines and jail terms ranging from twenty-four hours to one month if they failed to present an acceptable excuse before the court.[4]

Historian Kamal Karpat estimates that because of these policies there was a low margin of error in the nineteenth century (1881/2) census of only 2 to 10 per cent, depending on the remoteness of the area. "The practical need", he explains, "for every individual to possess a *nüfus tezkeresi* used in all dealings with the government forced practically everyone to register".[5]

Karpat documents how this system was expanded, with some modifications, to cover the rest of the Ottoman Empire. Indeed, in a range of aspects some of its key features still survive in Turkey and other parts of the Middle East, including to an extent in Palestine.

In 1937 the British administration introduced an "order-in-council" that required the carrying of identity cards. This directive was reinforced in the emergency regulations of 1945, which, in turn, were revived by the Zionist movement (days after the regulations' May 1948 revocation by the British administration).

There are, however, some crucial differences. Identity cards in Palestine constituted very little in terms of "permissions" until 1948, when Zionist policy linked ID cards to mass sweeps and expulsions of Palestinians. Only from 1948 onward, therefore, did Palestinians as a group note the threat of identity documents, such that "dwelling in their homes without written permission [...] rendered them vulnerable to harassment, extortion, detention, and possible expulsion".[6]

## Clinging Like Sweat

The Israeli state refused to recognise the British and Ottoman identity documents, despite seeking to obtain by all possible means the population registries that contained Palestinians' identity details. The new state wanted intelligence, not to recognise Palestinian rights. While Israeli Jews were immediately given registration receipts on the day of the first census, and while these receipts were quickly replaced with identity cards, the same process was temporally extended for Palestinians; weeks and months passed between each stage of being counted, registered, given receipts, and exchanging receipts for IDs. In four small villages alone, for example, hundreds of Palestinians had yet to be given receipts by mid-January 1949 (Jish, Mghar, 'Ilabun, and Dayr Hanna, in the upper Galilee).[7]

In the interim, Palestinians were in danger. The receipts, when given, were the only indication of being counted in the registry.

> These rectangular stubs, if damaged or lost, became the equivalent of an ID, and the people clung to them the way sweat clings to the body, for it was their only hope not to be expelled during sweep

operations [`amaliyyat tamshit], which was a common thing in those days in our Arab villages.[8]

With no receipt Palestinians were afraid of any movement, such as getting to their land, working or even obtaining food. Moreover with only one option for food – rations – any Palestinian without a receipt was forced to risk expulsion by buying food at inflated prices on the black market.

Sweeps were a source of panic and terror:

> A typical operation entailed an early morning siege around a village, with the participation of [military government] soldiers, in addition to anywhere between one to two hundred soldiers including units of the "Minorities" or Druze Battalion, who often knew the area and had the requisite linguistic skills to issue orders. [...]
> An identification unit, comprised of soldiers as well as informants would then spend anywhere from seven to forty-eight hours verifying the identity of each person. At the end of the operation, those who were determined to be "legally" residing in the village were allowed to go home. Of the rest, most were immediately expelled, and a few were detained for further investigation.[9]

During these mass arrests, villagers were ordered to leave their homes unlocked and stand in fields, often for hours in the sun with no food, water or toilets. On returning home, they sometimes found their possessions had been stolen.[10]

Such sweeps continued intensely until 1956.[11] This period of extreme anxiety, and in particular the various documents distributed to Palestinians prior to the final ID cards, have rarely been documented. The following account draws upon the groundbreaking archival research and on-site investigation by historian Shira Robinson.

### The Red IDs

Yehoshua Palmon, who fought with the British as a commando, was one of three key figures in the compilation of the "Village Files" and blacklists (who "took a great personal interest in the implementation of the policy of selection, interrogation and sometimes execution");[12] he took on a new role after 1948. Officially called the "Prime Minister's Advisor on Arab Affairs", his mandate in effect included the reduction of the Palestinian population. The problem, in his eyes, was that he was limited somewhat by the world's gaze: trucks and mass expulsions could not easily continue. So in June of 1949, Palmon came up with an idea which by November took shape as "temporary residence permits" or TRPs.

Palestinians until this point had been not only persistent, but also inventive in their assertion of their rights as the indigenous landowners and nationals of Palestine.

> Returnees were hidden in attics and holy places; registration receipts were forged or passed on following the death of a relative or neighbor; and according to local lore, some men actually purchased weapons on the black market merely in order to turn them in and gain leniency during the sweeps in their villages.[13]

All of these strategies entailed great risk: a forged ID was grounds for immediate expulsion. The new documents would grant a small period of respite: a permit to remain for three months, or up to 12 months, but not more. Once in the system, these Palestinians were then easier to expel. Offering the hope of renewal, or exchange for an ID, the TRP thus encouraged obedience and undermined the assertion of Palestinian rights.

As the new TRP system was selective, it made certain Palestinians especially vulnerable. Robinson describes how anyone who had returned in the first half of 1949, and who had no papers from the Israeli military or police, was ineligible for a TRP. So too was any Palestinian who returned later, but had no cash to pay the "bail" required to assure freedom from expulsion or imprisonment. Finally, all steps toward gaining a TRP required a nod from the "local authorities" (*mukhtar*, communal leader, local notable, police, intelligence, military government representative, etc.), so anyone out of their favour, for whatever reason, was in trouble. A lack of property, by contrast, made one more eligible for a TRP. One category of eligibility, for instance, was "Residents of the Little Triangle who were employed but lacked property".[14]

As with all such procedures affecting Palestinians, the TRPs were long in coming. Meanwhile all Israeli officials, including the "Rations Inspector", had been instructed to recognise only TRPs and IDs. Thousands of people waiting for TRPs were denied food. Some of the thousands of men detained during mass arrests and in the Israeli labour camps were also left in limbo, without TRPs and IDs. Moreover, even a TRP or ID was no safeguard against expulsion – as shown by the experience of the 400 ID-carrying villagers of Saffuriya (expelled in January 1949), the 11,000 townsfolk of Majdal (a centre dating back to the 1500s), and the villagers of Ghabsiyya, Iqrit, and Kafr Bir'im.[15]

In late 1950, Palestinians in two Western Galilee villages (Bi'na and Dayr al-Asad) "waged a legal and grassroots political battle against the distribution of TRPs".[16] One simple strategy was to call TRPs "red IDs" (*al-hawiyyat al-hamra'*), since IDs were ordinarily blue. The villages boycotted the TRP registration procedures and instead obtained blue IDs through court proceedings. The campaign's success drew attention to the discriminatory and disempowering nature of TRPs. Yet TRPs continued to be distributed, and Palestinians continued to be expelled.

In 1954, as expulsions entered their eighth year, Palestinian returnees received an official designation via the "Law to Prevent Infiltration". Returnees remained eligible to apply for TRPs, rendering them of course visible for expulsion, and at least 300 Palestinians did so in the year of the new "law". Some went a step further, applying to the courts established in 1948. Their efforts, however, were stymied by repeated invocation of "emergency powers" to continue expulsions, thus reinforcing and prolonging the insecurity of the TRPs and their legacy for decades and generations.

There are no known, official figures for the numbers of Palestinian residents who received TRPs instead of civil IDs. Historian Elias Shoufani estimates that some 16,000 Palestinians carried these permits long after the dust of the citizenship law debates had settled [...]

Other TRP holders enjoyed no legal protection and did not have the right to vote. Without citizenship, they also could not obtain a passport, which barred them from leaving the country [...]

Other TRP holders did not receive civil IDs until the 1980s. Still other Palestinians, their precise numbers unknown, resided in Israel for several years without any paperwork at all. These individuals lived in constant hiding from the authorities and through court cases were able to obtain military IDs, if not TRPs. Their stateless status was passed on to their children, if they married someone with the same papers.[17]

### Systematic Discrimination

A new and unique feature of the TRPs and IDs, was to unite in one selectively issued document a series of "permissions" that had previously been rights enjoyed by all Palestinians. Thus Palestinians became extremely vulnerable when stopped and searched, and when dealing with any Israeli representative. Arabic-language newspapers at the time reported "the daily absurdities that people endured as a result of the authorities' obsessive checks for IDs". And it was not only the "authorities" that felt entitled to exploit the systematically engendered vulnerability of Palestinians; armed "civilians" felt at liberty to carry out "random beatings, ID confiscations, and evictions".[18]

The administrative segregation between Jew and Palestinian introduced to separate, exclude, and maintain political control over Palestinians in Israel deepened this vulnerability. In 1950, a memorandum was distributed to top Israeli officials to remind them that Palestinians were only permitted contact via the military. "Your offices", wrote Foreign Minister Moshe Sharett, should contact "the appropriate local military authorities", after which "it would be preferable if the answer would not be given to the applicants directly, but that the final decision should be transmitted via the local military governor or the regional officer for Arab Affairs".[19]

Final decisions on any given application, for "permission" to enjoy any given right, could take an indefinite amount of time, and also result in detention or expulsion. Meanwhile, Palestinians were left open to harassment and extortion. The administrative segregation of Palestinians (except Jewish Palestinians) from Israeli Jews underscored this systematic targeting and discrimination. Military tribunals were reserved solely for Palestinians, and could not be appealed in the civilian court system, reserved for Jews. Military "committees" covered the three geographic regions into which Palestinians were confined, and comprised military representatives, intelligence, police, and members of Palmon's office (the Prime Minister's Advisor on Arab Affairs) – the same office tasked with masterminding the administrative segregation and denationalisation of Palestinians.[20]

By the late 1950s, the results were obvious. The "State Controller" noted that while in theory the emergency regulations were to apply to all equally, in practice Jews are not "expected to carry such permits and in general are not prosecuted".[21] The reality of daily life was one of segregation.

Since 1948 the social and ecological segregation of Jewish and Arab citizens has been a characteristic feature of Israeli society ... it is nearly impossible to find mixed Arab–Jewish residential districts.

Indeed, social contacts of any kind between Arabs and Jews are very limited. Arab–Jewish intermarriage rates are negligible. In a study of Israeli high school students conducted in 1975 only 16 percent of the Jewish students interviewed said they had opportunities for contact with Arabs.[22]

This segregation meant that Palestinians' livelihoods were essentially criminalised as working without "permission". Thus cultivating one's own land, or being found anywhere other than where one's "permit" specified, were punishable activities forever resulting in Palestinians being blacklisted. Military "judges" justified the practice of blacklisting and its consequences (or "punishment") by invoking the argument of security, without defining its meaning or how a blacklisted individual had threatened it.[23]

Well into the 1960s, Israeli academics claimed that "only a few" Palestinians were affected, and that the restrictions "applied to Jews as well".[24] But it was only Palestinians who were subject to military commanders, military courts, military closed zones, and military force. Any semblance of equality evaporated when in 1958 the Israeli Prime Minister David Ben Gurion "refused the identity card issued to him because it was written in Arabic as well as Hebrew".[25] For Palestinians, meanwhile, simply not having an ID card, "vetted and approved by the Israeli Secret Service", was grounds for "a prison term for as long as a year and a half and immediate transfer to one of the pens to join other 'unauthorized' or 'suspicious' Arabs now found in Jewish-occupied areas".[26]

## 4.2   TRADING RIGHTS FOR NEEDS

### Extortion and Theft

ID cards were not distributed unless all former passports and identity documents were relinquished to Israeli authorities.[27] This was especially dangerous since Palestinians were forced to forfeit their rights – or at least the paper documents assuring those rights. The new cards would come to "represent" Palestinians in all their "institutional encounters".[28]

Under this system Palestinians were routinely at risk of beatings, extortion, theft, and "various acts of humiliation".[29] In one among many instances, a military "governor" imposed a curfew on an entire village, which prevented the villagers from reaching their places of work. Palestinian protests fell on deaf ears, so their Jewish employers intervened. The governor responded by proposing to lift the curfew in exchange for a fee from the employer.[30]

In return for "services rendered" Israeli officials might, for example, promise to remove "rumours" accumulating on files kept on certain *hamula* (extended family) members, or make farm machinery available for purchase at half the market price. They might also arrange for the speedy transport of a sick relative to a hospital in a city (as most Palestinians required special permission to enter cities), "approve" the return (entry only, not stay) of relatives who had been driven out in 1948, or "permit" the marriage of a Palestinian man and woman across the Armistice lines.[31]

When some Palestinian families could no longer afford the "weekly parties" they had been holding for Israeli officials (and their wives) in the Western Galilee, the officials informed them they "would have to leave the country", despite being eligible for TRPs.[32] Village leaders (*mukhtars*) collaborated in these "parties".

> In October 1950, for instance, the *mukhtar* in nearby Dayr al-Asad announced that the purpose of the "tax" he had collected from all registered villagers was to hold a "party" for the governor and the clerks when they come to distribute IDs. The scandal in Dayr al-Asad reached its height two months later, when it was reported that civil and temporary IDs had been distributed along the lines of local family politics, such that individuals belonging to families out of favor with the *mukhtar* who were supposed to receive blue IDs received red ones instead, and vice-versa.[33]

Village leaders also coerced villagers into "working for them without pay by threatening to tell the authorities to give them TRPs instead of civil IDs".[34]

> The small and impoverished village of Nahaf (Acre district) became particularly well known for the mafia-like rule of its *mukhtar*, who reportedly used the threat of the red IDs to coerce villagers into farming his land for no pay, abandoning commercial projects which competed with his own, ceasing all Communist Party activity, and offering him "reward" money when they obtained the papers which they were anyway scheduled to receive.[35]

Another known *mukhtar* "became quite rich by taking bribes or taking something if he fancied it; it was an extreme form of patronage".[36]

But the extortion and dispossession of Palestinian assets was more systematic and went far further than food, village parties, or petty cash; Israel "offered" many Palestinians the use of lands belonging to other Palestinians, in exchange for signing away their rights to their own property.

> While Israeli authorities also helped internally displaced Palestinians to rent empty homes in shelter villages or, in some cases, register the property in the name of IDPs, they also forced the internally displaced to give up their rights in their villages of origin.[37]

Palestinian refugees were afraid, quite rightly, "that by leasing other land they might lose their rights on their own land".[38] Even if they refused to lease other Palestinians' land, Palestinians could be intimidated in other ways. The threat of a building demolition or withholding of a building permit was another inducement to surrender claims to their lands or to "accept" compensation.[39]

These internal refugees were also granted the "privilege" of some rights before other Palestinians. They were generally the first to receive IDs, before Palestinians who had remained in their homes, and especially before returnees. Such divide-and-rule strategies were successful in crippling Palestinian efforts to develop a nation-wide campaign of resistance.[40]

### False Suffrage

A mask of legitimacy was given to military rule when Palestinians were allowed to vote. However, when elections took place, "only 32,000 of the 69,000 Palestinians counted in the census had received their IDs; although Palestinians comprised 14 percent of the counted population, they comprised only 5 percent of eligible voters".[41]

The symbolic act of giving suffrage has arguably been one of the strongest pillars in asserting authority over the population of Palestine. But even the vote was an act of coercion in many instances. Palestinian reliance on "permissions" meant that what little they had to give – their food, their property, their wealth, and now, their vote – was an object of barter. "Through the military government", said Teddy Kollek, who had been elected mayor of Jerusalem, "Arab votes were secured".[42]

The TRPs were powerful tools in denying suffrage, in addition to all other rights:

> The only right accorded to those Palestinians who managed to obtain a TRP was the right not to be deported so long as their permits remained in force. Other than this, TRP holders had no rights to *political representation* or private property, which meant that their land could be confiscated [emphasis added].[43]

But Israeli officials were able to coerce any Palestinian, irrespective of a TRP or ID. Building permits and revocations of demolition orders were "traded" for Palestinians' agreement to "deliver the votes of kinship groups to a particular Zionist political party".[44]

Finally, not only were Palestinians told *for whom* to vote; they were also told for whom *not* to vote.

> Military authorities threatened land confiscation or loss of work permits to Arabs who supported the Communist party. A complaint to the UN Human Rights Commission in 1961 by a group called the Third Force Movement recited that the military governors "see to it that a worker who has expressed sympathy with the anti-Zionist party should get no permit to go to look for work, and he and his family should remain unemployed and hungry".[45]

In exchange for a new permit or a renewal, Palestinians were expected to "show their loyalty", to vote "for the ruling party, Mapai", and crucially, to refrain from "any independent form of political activity".[46] The converse was also true, and Israeli officials used sticks as well as carrots: Palestinians who attempted to form political organisations were denied "permissions", put under house arrest, and expelled.[47]

### Transplanting the System

In 1966, the restrictions on Palestinians living in Israel were mostly lifted. Demand for cheap labour required mobile workers, and the Palestinians by this time were, for the most part, dispossessed of their land and property, making them ideal to replace the now upwardly mobile Jewish settlers.[48] Some of the British administration's "emergency regulations", however, had been adopted by Israel as "laws" rather than emergency regulations.[49] Thus, even when "military rule" was ended, these "laws" continued. The 1949

"Registration of Inhabitants Law" and the 1954 "Law to Prevent Infiltration" are two examples significant for their emphasis on population control. The State of Emergency was never lifted.

Israeli officials wanted to ensure that Palestinians understood the fragile status of their rights. Long after 1966, "Palestinians continued to be fearful of speaking out against state policies".[50] Moshe Dayan, at the top of the armed forces, argued succinctly:

> [L]et the individual know that he has something to lose. His home can be blown up, his bus license can be taken away, he can be deported from the region; or the contrary: he can exist with dignity, make money, exploit other Arabs, and travel in [his] bus.[51]

Following the Israeli occupation of the West Bank and Gaza Strip in 1967, Palestinians there were about to experience what their fellow Palestinians across the Armistice lines had been living for the previous 18 years. Extortion and acts of humiliation were once again tied to the withholding of rights via a Population Registry, identity cards, and a system of permits. As the occupation progressed, earning a living became increasingly difficult without "permissions". Extortion, as a result, became highly profitable. In the late 1980s, one Palestinian collaborator "earned" about $1000 a day selling permits, giving "permission" to depart for Jordan for a short period, and return via the Ben Gurion airport.

> I used to call [the secret services] and ask them to sign permits for me. They made their own inquiries and forwarded the names to the Ministry of the Interior. I would come to the Ministry of the Interior after office hours, and they would sign the forms for me.[52]

Extortion continued well into the 1990s, as the following incident illustrates:

> Z.'A., the *mukhtar* of a town in the West Bank and a known collaborator, used to help obtain different permits from the Civil Administration in return for a fee. In August, 1993, several Palestinian laborers who worked in the settlement of Ornit near Qalqiliyah had their work permits revoked on the grounds that they owed income tax.[53]

The *mukhtar* then asked the labourers if they wanted their permits back:

> I said that I did. The *mukhtar* said that it would cost me 500 Shekels. I told him that this was a lot. The *mukhtar* told me that not all the money was for him and that I shouldn't ask him where it was going. I took 500 shekels from my pocket and paid him. The *mukhtar* called his son and told him to go up to the house and to bring me the permit.[54]

The practice was not limited to the West Bank. Israeli officials and Palestinian collaborators extorted hundreds of thousands of dollars from Palestinians in Gaza seeking various permits: family reunification, approval of land purchases, and magnetic cards.[55]

### Using ID Cards to Control and Humiliate

When the system of military rule was transported wholesale to the West Bank and Gaza Strip, legitimate rights became mere "favours and expressions of goodwill", which could be "revoked at any time".[56]

> [A] Palestinian cannot plant a tomato without an unobtainable permit from the military government. He or she cannot plant an eggplant without such a permit. You cannot whitewash your house. You can't fix a pane of glass. You can't sink a well. You can't wear a shirt that has the colors of the Palestinian flag. You can't have a cassette in your house which has Palestinian national songs.[57]

The punishment of individuals was borne collectively as the confiscation of a breadwinner's permits or IDs affected their entire family.[58]

When military rule started, rights were consciously taken away from each and every Palestinian; then selective exceptions were made, conditional on compliance and collaboration. The first "operations coordinator" of military rule in the West Bank and Gaza Strip, Shlomo Gazit, described his policy as "directed toward creating a situation in which the population would have something to lose, a situation in which the most effective sanction is the revocation of benefits".[59]

Palestinian resistance from the 1920s to the 1990s survived such restrictions, and involved "civil disobedience, general strikes, nonpayment of taxes, refusal to carry identity cards, boycotts, and demonstrations".[60] In this context, the confiscation of identity cards was used to crush these forms of resistance, affecting both blacklisted persons and their families. Through ID confiscation (or the threat to do so), family members of blacklisted persons were forced to "surrender", or to pay the taxes that the blacklisted person had refused to pay as a form of civil disobedience.[61]

Confiscation was thus used by the military occupation to force Palestinians to police other Palestinians. Examples documented in the 1980s included: four elderly residents of the Gaza Strip who were compelled to cut down fruit trees allegedly used as cover for stone-throwers; a 19-year old in Tulkarem who was asked to guard a main street from stone throwers from 7 p.m. until 1 a.m. – he refused and lost his ID; soldiers frequently forcing Palestinians to remove barricades or flags, extinguish burning tyres, or paint over nationalist graffiti; one person was ordered to remove tin-cans hanging from high-tension electricity wires, and died as a result of electrocution.[62]

When asked about the use of IDs for coercion, one man recalled:

Yes, they told me to clean the street. Many times; three or four times. People don't talk about it because it's normal. They would tell someone to count his melons. He would have to take them all out of the truck, and then put them all back in again. They would tell people to insult their grandfathers, who were walking with them.

[In the early 1980s] They would tell people to dance – especially people with beards. My friend had a beard and I didn't. I was 13 or 14 years old. They asked him, "Do you like Khomeini?" And he said no. He wasn't lying. The soldier said, "If you don't dance, I won't give you the ID". He started dancing and he got the ID back.[63]

Palestinians arrested and then freed during the Israeli military invasions that began on March 29, 2002 faced further danger on their release, because most of the West Bank was under direct re-occupation, and the population under total curfew.

In many cases prisoners were released on to the streets in areas several hours' drive away from their homes. They were forced to seek shelter during the curfews, when anyone leaving their homes risked being shot by Israeli soldiers.

The military did not give discharged prisoners documents showing that they had been released, and failed to return many confiscated ID cards. Consequently these released detainees risked not only being shot, but also being re-arrested if Israeli soldiers stopped them.[64]

Thus the continuum of the indispensability of the ID – which since the 1940s was essential for Palestinian daily activities – continued under occupation, as Dayan had promised in 1967.

*Figure 4.1*  Pleading at checkpoint. IDs became indispensable from the 1940s to the present, and created the potential for coercion at every stop-and-search moment: at checkpoints, sweeps of villages, raids on homes, and confrontations of Israeli armed forces against Palestinians in their daily lives. (Tom Kay)

A Palestinian refugee from the Jaffa region, living in Gaza, explained in 2007:

If they get your ID – it's a problem – you can't even sign into a school. [Even when dealing with] Palestinian officials – if you don't have an ID then you are lost. For example, even at the University of Gaza, you can't enrol. No – you have to have your ID. If you get a job, you have to have an ID. Even Palestinians will not help really.

You're lost, you're lost – you can't have your children registered
on your ID. If you don't have an ID you can't get an Egyptian
travel document – you're stuck, you can't go anywhere.[65]

The risk posed by concentrating human rights in a single, seizable
document is limited only by the imagination of the Israeli military,
who routinely stop and search for IDs, threaten to confiscate, and
actually confiscate them.

### "Fuck the Donkey"

Samer [name changed] is a 27-year-old shepherd in a village near
the town of Tulkarem, in the northern West Bank. For ten years, he
took his flock out at 6 a.m. every day, and returned them home in the
afternoon. One Thursday, in June of 2003, he walked the flock to a
gate (that the Israeli army had erected to prohibit Palestinian farmers
from reaching their land), along with his brother and cousin, where
they were confronted by a Border Police jeep...[66]

Two male border police officers were in the jeep, and they let
the flock pass through the gate. They also let my brother pass,
and told him to continue walking. One of the border policemen
demanded my ID card and started to check it.
I had a donkey with me and was holding him by a rope.
The officer who was sitting next to the driver asked me if I
had ever been in jail. He spoke very good Arabic. I told him that
I had never been in jail.
After the policeman checked my ID, he took the rope from my
hand and tied it to the front of the jeep. Then he told my cousin
to unleash the donkey's saddle. He unleashed it. Then he told
him to put the saddle on the ground.
Then he told me to wear the saddle. I put it on my shoulders,
and my cousin tied it on me, like the policeman told him to do.
Then the policeman told me to walk to the greenhouses not far
away and to come back. I did that several times.
Then he ordered me to sit on the donkey. He bound my hands
with the rope that was tied to the donkey. After I sat on the
donkey, he told me to ride toward the greenhouses and to come
back.
He still had my ID card.
He had me do it three times. The first time, my hands were
tied. Then he untied my hands. The saddle remained tied on my
back. Then he told me to ride to the nearby grove.

I asked him about my ID card.

He told me that we hadn't finished, and that he would be behind me. He and the other policeman followed me in the jeep. When we reached the grove, he tied the donkey to a tree and told me to fuck it. He repeated his demand a couple of times.

He also told me to lift up the tail of the donkey and tie it around my head. I told him that the tail was too short, and that I wasn't able to do it.

Up until this point, Samer's emphasis is on the ID card. It is only after this that Samer mentions the threat of weapons.

He stood facing me and aimed his weapon at me. The other policeman was in the jeep, watching what was going on.

I stood behind the donkey, took out my penis, and told him "enough." He said, "I'll tell you when it is enough." I was frightened to death, and I couldn't get an erection, so I couldn't do anything. He made me continue, and I pretended that I was doing what he wanted me to do.

I tried to look over at them, but the policeman yelled at me and told me not to look, and that if I did, he would shoot me. This went on for about thirty minutes, before he told me to stop.

In the end though, it is the return of the ID card that marks the end of the day's coercion.

He tightened the saddle on my back and gave me back my ID card.

Then he told me, "Ride over to the flock, fuck them, and I'll chase you." I rode away, the saddle still on me, and he watched me go.

After I got some distance away from them, I untied the saddle and walked over to my brother ... and told him what happened.

My cousin and lots of other people saw what happened to me. I have not gone [back there] since then. I am afraid that I'll come across border policemen again.

In one such testimony, of a student used as a human shield, the first thing soldiers did was take everyone's IDs.[67]

## 4.3   INFORMANTS AND COLLABORATORS

### A "New Class" of Palestinian

The pressure to collaborate is one of the most difficult demands on Palestinians who either need IDs or need to retrieve them. This pressure permeates and is instrumental to the perpetuation of the system of control.

Cases of Palestinian collaboration with the Zionist movement date back to the early 1900s when, by 1941, Yaacov Shimoni (one of those involved in creating the Village Files) was appointed to supervise the "treasurer", a Palestinian who in turn supervised other collaborators. These collaborators were integral to Zionist military planning; Shimoni met David Ben Gurion every Sunday in Jerusalem with Syrian-born Eliyahu Sasson, who served as head of the Jewish Agency's Arab department between 1933 and 1948. Palestinians who had collaborated prior to and during 1948 were later given special treatment. Those who had left Palestine, and who applied to return, were selectively given temporary residence permits (TRPs) for "freedom of movement". Some were even given IDs.[68]

Israeli officials were careful not to give out too many permits, however, and adopted a quota system. From April 1950 onward, the secret services had to "request a specific number of permits for their agents in advance, to be valid only in a specific location and only for a few days at a time". In November, another rule was made. Permits would only be given when "necessary for or beneficial to one of the recognized institutions of the state, the market, or the public". All other requests, "including those certified to have assisted the security services in the past, will be generally rejected".[69]

As old collaborators were discarded, new ones were recruited, using the same incentives, but with stronger emphasis on status. In a context of mass expulsions and an ongoing hunt for returnees, no Palestinian could take for granted that s/he would get "status", that is, "permission" to escape expulsion. The introduction of the temporary residence permit (TRP) in the summer of 1949, argues Robinson, "produced a new class of Palestinians whose future legal status depended upon their willingness to satisfy the whims of Israeli military governors, police officers, and intelligence operatives".[70] TRPs were also used to obtain information (to enable expulsion) without giving rights, tempting Palestinians with temporary rights in the hope that they would ultimately receive a permanent one.

Just as votes were coerced, so was the surrender of rights and collaboration. A 1958 Israeli Arab Affairs Committee strategy document describes how "at the personal level, Palestinian individuals are to be directly connected to the state through personal interests".[71] Essential services and permits were to be made conditional on collaboration.[72] The reinstatement of rights, as "favours", should be "awarded in such a way as to commit them to the relationship with the State".[73]

In issuing TRPs, Israeli officials favoured Palestinians with a "clean past", a "quiet and straightforward" character, and a (family) history of fighting alongside Zionist forces prior to and during 1948.[74] TRPs could only be exchanged for IDs if Palestinians "could convince the local Governor of their 'good behavior' once their permits expired."[75] The situation was even more precarious for those who had been barred from obtaining an ID:

> Once you were barred from obtaining a civil ID, your local Military Governor could *choose* to issue you a TRP for anywhere from a month to a year, at the end of which you would be expelled, obtain a civil ID, or have your TRP renewed [emphasis in original].[76]

According to their inventor, Yehoshua Palmon, TRPs would test Palestinian behaviour, discipline, loyalty to the state, and trustworthiness.[77] Loyalty was "exhibited through willingness to transfer information to the authorities and helping to promote the policies of the military government".[78]

By the 1950s, the network of informants and collaborators had become "like a plague", because the "system of favours worked for absolutely everything one needed", indeed replacing the need for cash.[79] Former Israeli officials have described how they would approve or expedite applications (for work, "exit", or anything else), as a cheap means of coercing or "buying" Palestinian collaboration:[80] "[T]here were cheaper informants who didn't have much power, but for instance in return for a permit to go and work in Haifa or Tel Aviv they would inform."[81]

Such collaboration-for-permits continued after military rule ended in Israel (in 1966) and after 1967 spread to the military occupation of the West Bank and Gaza Strip.

> A resident of the territories who wants to bring his wife from Jordan has to choose between making an annual payment of 100 dinars for a summer visitor's permit, finding another

wife, or collaborating in order to obtain [approval for] family reunification.[82]

Controlling Palestinian "status" – through IDs, family reunification, and expulsion – was the principal form of coercion, garnering land, political compliance, and informants.[83]

### Informants, Returnees, and Blacklisting

In addition to those in desperate need of a "status", blacklisted individuals were also particularly vulnerable, and attempts were made to lure them using "forgiveness":[84]

> In exchange for cooperation and awarding "special services", suspicions could be removed, rumors confuted, indictments dropped, files closed, or even criminal proceedings stopped at a later stage.[85]

The problem, of course, was that blacklisting was a vicious circle. All that was needed to blacklist someone was an informant or collaborator: "If you needed a permit for something, you just went and gave the police a bit of information about someone."[86]

Once on a blacklist, permits became out of reach:

> It wasn't easy getting permits because of the collaborators. You would go and apply for permits but the collaborators would interfere.[87]

So a collaborator placed a person on a blacklist, who in turn was under pressure to collaborate. Collaborators would also, in letters to Israeli officials, identify returnees, and even the children of returnees – especially those who "illegally" married ID-holding Palestinians:[88]

> Given the nature of Arab communities where the village was their whole world, there would be feuds. A feuding family might go and inform on those trying to return to the Israelis. Then the Israelis would come searching for someone.
>
> The people of the village accepted that he would try to escape and that the Israelis would shoot. I remember more than one who was killed on the edge of the village trying to escape.[89]

Informants would take part in sweeps, accompanying Israeli armed forces and intelligence, who would "cordon off a locale, gather its residents in a holding pen (often without food or water), check each person for their ID, and expel or detain those without proper papers".[90]

> The police used to come and search in our village for smuggled goods or people who might have returned from outside. They would come and arrest people who were informed on.[91]

Informants also helped to point fingers at Palestinians who, "though living on their land, might be deemed absentees, so their land could be confiscated".[92]

In addition to building blacklists and identifying returnees, collaborators were recruited to work across the Armistice lines. Initially collaborators provided intelligence, but after 1967 they were employed as officials, police, and in the prisons:[93]

> Since 1977, prisoners have reported that torture is also administered by a small group of collaborators in each prison, some of whom are not actual prisoners but informers posing as such. Whether prisoners who collaborate or informers insinuated into the prison, the procedure has been institutionalized.
>
> In each prison and detention center, special rooms are set aside for the collaborators, who are known as "asafir" or "song birds". Common among the "asafir" are violent criminals selected for their fierceness. Others are selected from those held on political charges, even though they lack a political past. The latter are allowed privileges in accordance with the services they perform.[94]

There is ample documentation of the routine use of coercion and torture to pressure Palestinians to "turn informant".[95]

Keeping Them Tied

Much of the information sought by Israeli officials was on informants themselves, as well as blacklisted persons (according to interviews conducted with former officials).[96] Thus informants could be blackmailed, and their private details would be known to the officials who wished to recruit, retain, or discard them. Pressure was increased by denying permits for work, exit, and so on, to force collaboration. One villager, from Dura, described his experience in the early 1990s:

I was at the bridge, with an exit permit for studies in Egypt, but it was returned to me with no explanation [...]

In the room was a man named Q., who said, "I know a lot about you and I can send you to jail. It's important for me to know about your activity in the village." He also said: "There is no one who can approve your departure except myself, and your whole future is in my hands. You want my help now, and in return I want your help." He did not elaborate, and of course I did not agree.

He offered me money, saying: "As much as you want. You will have a new car, and I will give you an Israeli ID card with which you can travel freely in Israel."[97]

Israeli officials in the 1950s openly acknowledged this strategy and system. Palestinians "pass on information because they are dependent upon us; had this dependency not existed, there would have not been cooperation between us and them".[98] The system enabled rights to both be taken and then granted back selectively "in the name of security", and rewarded collaborators "with security clearance to facilitate access to certain jobs, building permits, travel, and the granting of business licenses".[99]

Palestinians were impoverished – via dispossession and military rule – and then brought back in as labourers, but never in numbers that could threaten Israeli economic interests. Palestinians were to be kept at the "periphery" of the economy, ensuring that economic enterprises were not only "highly profitable", but also useful to "turn Arabs who engage in them into an oppositional force to any Arab separatist movement".[100] Those Palestinian labourers in the West Bank and Gaza Strip who were denationalised and without passports, were viewed as more vulnerable and therefore more pliable.[101]

Since 1967, there is no one in the territories who has requested a service or permit of some kind from the Military Government who did not receive an offer from the GSS [secret services] to act as a collaborator in return for his request being fulfilled. That is the nature of the occupation. Whoever wants to get ahead a little in life, whoever has ambitions, encounters the dilemma at a certain stage.[102]

It was very hard to break or challenge this cycle of dependency, as described in the 1992 testimony of a Y'abad villager who, in late

1991, had given a can of olive oil to a collaborator in exchange for a movement permit. After two meetings with secret services, in which the villager declined to provide requested information on others, he decided to skip the third meeting and end relations. A few days after his missed meeting, Israeli forces drove into the village.

> The soldiers started collecting ID cards from the residents, and after checking them returned them to their owners. But they kept my ID card. P., who was there, came up to me and asked: "Why didn't you come on the appointed date?" Then he said, in a quiet tone, "I can get you at any time. If you see a sign on the olive press in Y'abad, you will know that we need you." My ID card was returned, and a month later I contacted P. and we arranged another meeting in the same apartment in Netanyah.
>
> He began asking and interrogating me about people from Y'abad and about my relations with them, where they worked, what their activity was in the Intifada, etc. I emphasized that I knew nothing about the activity of these people, and I always replied in the negative.[103]

Again, after about three meetings, the villager resisted collaboration; he had been asked to take part in a military operation.

> I decided not to cooperate anymore and not to show up at the meetings that were arranged.
>
> But five months after the last meeting, in early July 1992, I heard a crash outside, and I saw through the window that a military vehicle had collided with my car which was parked in the courtyard of the house, far from the road. The soldiers asked for my ID card, my driver's license, and my car insurance, claiming they wanted to compensate me for the damage, and asked me to go over to the jeep, which was some distance away.
>
> Then I understood that the accident was a trap. The soldiers took me to the jeep, in which was seated a GSS officer who asked me to come to a meeting with him.[104]

The villager continued to refuse collaboration, recognising that accepting "compensation" for the destruction of his vehicle would amount to acquiescence.

## Manufacturing Dissent

Due to the system of blanket bans and selective permissions, collaboration could be rewarding. Collaborators – especially those with historic ties to the Israeli army – could wield power via military rule; they could be "masters in their own society":

> There were many collaborators. This is maybe not so well known. First there were collaborators from before 1948 who collaborated with the Zionist movement like the Druze. In our village there were Druze, Christian and Muslim. The Druze went into the Israeli army – they were betrayers.
>
> Then there were people who collaborated because they had connections with the military and the security. Finally there were some very well known collaborators. The reward for collaboration was that these people could be masters in their own society. They could earn money.[105]

Collaborators could "dispense favours" to "whoever they wanted", in the words of a 34-year-old collaborator living in Jaffa:

> I was young. I was attracted by the idea of having power and status and earning fast, easy money. I liked walking around with a concealed weapon, getting through [military] roadblocks with no problems, dispensing favors, especially permits, to whoever I wanted.[106]

The network of collaboration made "everyone suspect everyone around them":[107]

> I was aware of informants from when I was very young. Everyone talked about it, and people were also scared to talk with each other about some things. There was a feeling that there were informants all over the place; you cannot know who is one or not. But always you are afraid that if you say something it will get to the Israelis and you will be punished for it – arrested.[108]

Israeli officials aimed to project a unified image as "the all seeing, all knowing body".[109] In addition, local collaborators could provide the appearance of internal Palestinian conflict, when in fact it was Israeli officials who were launching attacks on any political opposition.[110] In the 1950s, Palestinians "scheduled for expulsion in the next sweep" would be promised IDs if their relatives publicly slandered the Communist Party,[111] or even in one instance, "set fire to the local party headquarters on the night before the election".[112] Village "leaders" (*mukhtars*) were often collaborators who contributed to this image of internal conflict, by discouraging any support for opposition parties or activities. The following experience, of a teacher in search of work, illustrates this point:

> Usually permits were given on the recommendation of the *mukhtar*. They didn't give permits to communists. This *mukhtar* wasn't the real *mukhtar* but had been appointed by the military governor. He was a collaborator. He would recommend who should and shouldn't get permits.
>
> When I was about 17 in 1949, there was a public meeting in the village about the war in Korea. I clapped for the communist speaker who spoke against the war and the *mukhtar* saw this. When I applied I couldn't get a permit to go and work as a teacher. I wanted to go to talk to the Ministry of Education in Jerusalem. But in Nahariya they said to me "your file is closed – there is no way you can work as a teacher". And they were desperate then to recruit teachers as they had been ordered to open the Arabs schools.
>
> So without a permit I somehow managed to get to Nahariya and then to Jerusalem. I put on a Jewish hat and dark glasses and went to the Terra Sancta College, where the Ministry of Education was, and saw Mr Bloom the chief inspector of Arab education in Israel. I had taken a risk. I spoke to him and said, "why have you blocked my application? I am not a communist. I am just against the war in Korea." Bloom then rang someone in charge of Arab education in the North in Nazareth and told him to give me a permit. So I went to work in Nazareth and had to live there.[113]

The function of collaborators in discouraging opposition or fuelling the appearance of informal conflict persisted as *mukhtars* continued to submit weekly reports about Palestinian property, returnees, emergency regulations infractions, and opposition activities.[114] The role of informants was "instrumental in the breakdown" of resistance launched in 1967.[115]

## Conclusion

> They make everything difficult so if they give the slightest release
> – you think it's something great.[116]

A young Palestinian accountant summed up her experiences, as a woman, wife, mother, and professional, in the above statement. It reflects the roots of the power held in the identity card: the blanket bans on all things normal. Without special "permission", a Palestinian has few if any of the rights enjoyed by citizens elsewhere in the world (or by Zionist colonists in the same geographic space as indigenous Palestinians).

Coercion and collaboration are used to enlist the population's participation in their own oppression: gradualism, blanket bans, and "permissions" in exchange for cooperation. Such strategies treat Palestinians as right-less unless granted the temporary "privilege" of a restored right – in effect equivalent to a violation of rights, but rarely phrased that way. The initial clawing back of rights during the mass denationalisation of 1948 and subsequent years became so embedded, that now many view Israeli official permissions as genuine gifts to Palestinians, as signs of democracy, freedom, and tolerance. In reality, Palestinians' own rights are now used as both carrot and stick in a cycle that is illegal under the Fourth Geneva Convention. Article 51 prohibits using pressure, taking advantage of an individual's distress, or making vital services – especially those to which every person is entitled, like freedom of movement and the right to reside together with one's spouse – conditional on collaboration.[117]

# 5
# Movement Restriction and Induced Transfer

After registering and effectively denationalising the majority of Palestinians, while distributing identity documents to a small minority, the Zionist movement – by 1948 having declared itself to be the state of Israel – added a third layer of bureaucracy and force: movement restrictions. And while population registries and identity documents had precedents in the past, nothing like these movement restrictions had ever existed before in Palestine. The first section of this chapter describes how, over a few decades, Israel crowded Palestinians into what were in effect open-air prisons first in 1948, and again in the late 1990s and subsequent years. Although the bureaucratic mechanism for these restrictions originated in British colonies like India, it was only applied intensively in Palestine by the Zionist movement in the mid-twentieth century.

Restrictions continued for 18 years, and in 1967 similar restrictions went into force in the West Bank and Gaza Strip. A vast military bureaucracy evolved to deal with enforcing the complex pass system with the aim of controlling Palestinian movement. The second section describes how discrimination via identity documents – combined with movement restrictions – made life so difficult for Palestinians that it amounted to a policy of "induced transfer".

The third section maps the changes in Palestinian population distribution over time, through expulsions, forced removals, movement restrictions, and induced transfer. While the Oslo interim agreements are best known for creating a patchwork of Areas A, B, and C out of the West Bank and Gaza Strip, perhaps their more indelible mark is the dual system of roads: blocked passages for Palestinians, and clear highways for colonists. Then in 1994 the Israeli military erected a wall around the Gaza Strip. And finally in 2002 building started on the 810-kilometre wall around the West Bank which sliced off 90 per cent of Jerusalem, isolated over 200,000 Jerusalemites from the West Bank, and left a further quarter of a million Palestinians in the West Bank without fundamental services, cut off from their own lands, families, and physical and social infrastructure.

## 5.1   ENTRENCHING MOVEMENT RESTRICTIONS

### Shutting Palestinians Off from their Land

In the 1830s, the Ottoman government gave a travel certificate (*mürür tezkeresi*) to individuals to help them monitor substantial increases in the population.[1] In the late 1800s, travel certificates were issued in much the same way as certificates of birth, death, or marriage. Thus, these were in no way restrictions on movement of the kind that would be imposed a century later.

In 1937, the Palestine Order-in-Council listed a number of ways to restrict movement, which were later incorporated in the 1945 Emergency Regulations. Repealed in May 1948 by the departing British administration, and reinstated by Zionist forces in the same month, these regulations gave free rein to military commanders to take Palestinians captive indefinitely, forbid anyone to make use of his or her own property, and restrict any person to his or her home or locality.[2] Identity documents, containing identity numbers to match the Population Registry, were key to monitoring compliance with movement restrictions.

In addition to limiting each individual, a military regime fell like a net over Palestinian space and lives. It trucked, transported, and drove Palestinians on foot into three areas – the Galilee, Naqab, and Triangle (an area northwest of the West Bank, as shown in Figure 5.1 later in this chapter) – and then subdivided those areas further. The Galilee, for example, was broken into 58 pieces, effectively confining every Palestinian to her or his neighbourhood, village or town.[3]

> The restrictions were very strict unless you could get a permit and not everyone could ... I recall the atmosphere that people were afraid to go anywhere unless they really had to.[4]

Main arteries were "out of bounds", such as the road between Haifa and Nazareth, where permits were "hardest to get".[5] The Bedouin in the south, who had lived in the Naqab for 1,500 years, were forced into a reserve; they were "removed to an area north-east of Beersheba [Bir al-Sabi'] and forbidden to stray outside it".[6]

Article 125, considered the most vital of all the Regulations, allowed for the exclusion of Palestinians from a given area to make way for Zionist colonisation.[7] It was immediately supplemented in May 1948 with an ordinance for "law and administration", and again enabled Israeli commanders to arbitrarily declare areas of exclusion. Such declarations accompanied most of the expulsions in the subsequent period, including in the Naqab and Galilee (for example, Iqrit, Kafr Bir'im, Majdal, and Umm al-Faraj). All destroyed villages were out-of-bounds to their Palestinian landowners and inhabitants.[8]

### Labelling Palestinians As Outsiders

A month later another ordinance, which called Palestinian properties "abandoned", again excluded Palestinians from their privately owned land, but fell short of outright land theft.[9] Instead, it held Palestinians responsible for costs of "improvements" and entitled them to the "net income" of their land – to be decided by Israeli officials, and to exclude all crops and access. But such colonial generosity was short-lived, and in March of 1950 a "property law" designated most of the Palestinian population as "absentees". This move marked a shift in terminology from land ("abandoned") to people ("absentee"), as well as an explicit expropriation of Palestinian lands, homes, and belongings.

Even before declaring themselves a state, Zionist military leaders had established a committee to control Palestinian lands, whose "powers" were concentrated in a "custodian", who later under the 1950 property law received the "right" to transfer Palestinian land to the "development authority" that then passed it on to the Jewish National Fund.[10] By 1949, Israel claimed to have taken a quarter of a million acres of Palestinian land and given it to "other owners who will cultivate it for the public benefit".[11]

From 1949 to 1951, the Israeli leadership debated the pros and cons of whether the "custodian", or a "judge" in civil courts should designate a Palestinian as "absentee". The former accused the latter of being "subjective" as "there can be no proof that an individual left his home out of fear". The courts responded that, "evidence presented by the Custodian to certify [a Palestinian] as absentee were frequently groundless". They felt the labelling of absentees was "arbitrary", and relied on the Custodian's "own judgement, which may be prompted by heartlessness or obstinacy", in addition to the Custodian's ability to make exceptions regarding absentee status for those who feared and did not assist "Israel's enemies".[12] Whatever the rationale, all parties knew that the label of absentee provided a convenient cover for denationalisation and mass dispossession. The debate was over who would get the spoils.

A slew of civilian laws in the 1950s exceeded even the military regulations in enabling land and property expropriation. As

Palestinian property slipped from hand to hand, Palestinians themselves were confined in reserves. Even within cities, special quarters were designated for Palestinians, and all those living outside those areas were crammed into them. In Haifa, for example, the Israeli army ordered Palestinian residents from the upper and western parts of the city to move into the old Wadi al-Nisnas neighbourhood. Similar cloistering took place in Jaffa, Acre, and al-Majdal (until its complete expulsion). In Lydda, Palestinians "were unable to walk outside their own quarter alongside the railway which was soon to be known as the 'Arab ghetto'".[13]

Given the inconsistency evident in holding about 160,000 Palestinians in open-air prisons while claiming that 91,000 of them were "absent", the paradoxical term of "present-absentee" was invented and applied to those returnees who were given "permission" to reside in the new reserves. In addition to these present-absentees, and the 69,000 counted in the census, were the tens of thousands of returnees (estimated by the military government in 1953 to number 50,000), most of whom never received identity documents and were again expelled – sometimes repeatedly – from their homeland.[14] All returnees, whether labelled "present-absentee" or "infiltrator", as well as all refugee landowners (labelled "absentees") were stripped of their land and livelihood, thereby erasing the category of Palestinian landowner and national in this new lexicon.

If non-absentee Palestinians married absentees, they could not pass on their lands to their children – since they were given the lesser status of absentee.[15] Israeli officials then seized these lands and tried to encourage Palestinians to take part in their own dispossession and labelling as outsiders. Palestinians resisted, but this was limited.

In 1951 when they began to register the land of the refugees, the villagers wanted to set up a village council to organise against this land registration. This was taking place through the military governor's custodian and they wanted to force the refugees to exchange their land in return for compensation. Again the *mukhtar* went running to the military governor saying a meeting was being arranged ... So they stopped the meeting.[16]

In the end, if Palestinians agreed to be called absentees, they would be given either another Palestinian's land to lease or money in exchange, as "compensation" for their lands at less than one-tenth of their value.[17] If they did not agree, their lands would simply be taken and they would still be labelled absentees.

## Forced Removals

Forcible removal or induced transfer were at the extremes of movement restrictions and from 1949 onwards in order to pack Palestinians into reserves within the Armistice lines, Palestinians were rounded up from across the country. Israeli soldiers expelled Palestinians from their home villages and watched as they found shelter in other Palestinian villages. The villagers of Iqrit, for instance, went to the village of Rama; those of al-Jalme were forced into Jat; and the villagers of Saffuriya were pushed into nearby villages and eventually into the city of Nazareth.[18]

As Palestinians were forced into smaller spaces, their former homes and lands were taken by Jewish immigrants. The lands of al-Jalme were given to the kibbutz of Lehavot Haviva, and Israeli forces blew up the homes of the Iqrit villagers on Christmas Day, 1951. In total, Israeli forces grabbed 93 per cent of the land within the Armistice lines, squeezing Palestinians into tiny cantons comprising the remainder. By 1953, 350 of the 370 newly established Jewish settlements had been built on Palestinian private property, according to an Israeli government press release. Palestinians witnessed Jews-only settlements spring up in place of their destroyed villages, "orchards withering away before their very eyes because there was nobody to tend them",[19] and colonists moving into their urban homes and estates.[20]

The military forces also took over communal Palestinian land, such as land in trust under the Islamic *awqaf* (endowment of money or property or land for communal benefit) – all of which was taken and given to Israeli Jewish settlers. Graveyards were dug up, and the dead exhumed and dumped into collective graves. The trusts' administration was dismantled and replaced by a Jewish official. Israel openly justified these measures of enclosure and forcible expulsion citing "the need to make room" for colonists.[21]

Moreover "security" had no credence as a reason for land expropriation, as settlers would be given land in the midst of an inhabited Palestinian village. In addition, lands would be taken from a Palestinian only to be leased back to the same Palestinian. This practice was attractive for two reasons, neither related to security. First, income was generated from the rent paid by the dispossessed owner-turned-tenant. Second, Palestinians' own land could act as bait to manipulate Palestinian behaviour – especially, as noted in Chapter 4, voting behaviour. The punishment for activism, by extension, was to deny Palestinians access to their land. Additionally, forced removals undermined Palestinian cohesion, as returnees struggled home only to find another Palestinian "leasing" their home from the "Custodian".[22]

Family or neighbours would take risks in giving food or shelter to returnees:

> In the early 1950s many people would sneak across the borders. We would hear knocks on the door at night and my older brother and my mother would recognise the people as from our village. They would come at night, tired and hungry and they would want food and something to drink.[23]

The relatives of returnees, sometimes living in the same courtyard as the lessees, tried to protect their relatives' properties awaiting their safe return.

Returnees' relatives in shelter villages "often ostracized the refugees [from other villages who were "leasing" homes], denying them work and preventing their registration for public facilities like drawing water, supplies of wood for fuel, or picking the 'Sabr' fruit". The lessees faced a double dilemma: their own homes, lands, and villages were taken and given to others, while they were used by Israeli officials to keep other Palestinians from their own properties. In some cases, entire villages were emptied and repopulated by other Palestinians.[24]

The untenable situation for many displaced Palestinians meant they had to move again in a few years. From the late 1950s and into the 1960s, Palestinians across the country were forced from their shelter villages into urban areas. Historically, prior to Zionist colonisation, Palestinian villagers were reluctant to concentrate in urban centres and give up their culturally and environmentally integrated way of life. The departure of villagers for an uncertain future in the newly segregated cities, therefore, showed how desperate economic conditions had become. Over a third of the Palestinians flowing into the city of Shafa 'Amr, for example, were pushed there for survival.[25]

### The Forced Removal of Kafr Bir'im

Nihad Boqai has provided a detailed study of the forced removals, from the village of Kafr Bir'im, illustrating this incremental, painful, and ultimately permanent process.[26] Over the course of five years the village was gradually wrenched from its owners with long-lasting effects. In October 1948, despite a violent raid on their homes, all 1,050 villagers were home for the census visit by Emmanuel

Friedman, intelligence officer of the Seventh Brigade (villagers today have since learned their file number, 15/13, in the "Office of Minorities" for the Safad region). Based on the intelligence "village files" compiled in 1942, the village was understood to be friendly to Zionist forces; the village had also assisted the Zionist movement in 1945, working personally with Yehoshua Palmon, later to become the architect of the "red" temporary IDs, and an advocate of Palestinian expulsion.

Six days after the census, Friedman returned with a gently worded expulsion order:

> Our intelligence sources say that Kafr Bir'im is in serious danger, but you are fortunate because my men can protect it. Your lives, however, may be in danger. Therefore you have to close your houses, give us the keys and head to the surrounding hills for a few days. I promise you that none of your belongings will be touched.[27]

The soft words were accompanied by soldiers to ensure compliance with the marching orders to Lebanon "five kilometres north" (that is, one kilometre past the border). Fearful from the massacres by Zionist forces two weeks earlier in surrounding villages (Safsaf, Jish, Aylabun, Majd Al-Kurum, Saliha, Sa'sa, and Khirbat Arab al-Samina), but still in defiance of the expulsion order, the villagers escaped to the nearby caves and woods. One of the caves had been used as a tomb, and Palestinians were horrified to find themselves hiding beside human bones. Seven children died of hunger and illness in this period of exile.

While the villagers were still in hiding, the village leader and priest went together to the village of Jish (where a massacre had taken place a week earlier, and the villagers had been expelled) when they heard of a planned visit by the "Minister of Minority Affairs" Bechor Shitrit and the "military governor" Elisha Soltz. The leader and priest were told to move Kafr Bir'im villagers into the homes of the expelled Jish villagers, for a period of only "two weeks". They did so but the villagers still overflowed into the streets, so Friedman told the remaining 250 villagers to go to Rmaish, in Lebanon, promising this would not affect their right to return.

The two weeks passed, and the villagers continued to move back and forth to Kafr Bir'im over the next months, to pick crops, feed the poultry, and renovate their homes. Six months later, in a meeting in Ben Gurion's offices, village leaders received reassurances from

Yehoshua Palmon that they would be allowed to return to the village. That same day, Jewish colonists entered and surveyed the village, and took over the homes of the Kafr Bir'im villagers. The villagers wrote directly to Ben Gurion, and received the following reply:

> The [expulsion] ... does not derive from a wish or a tendency to punish the people of Bir'im or to cause damage to them, and you should certainly not consider it an injustice or a negative response to your loyalty to the government. At this stage, the government is not intending to uproot the residents of Bir'im from their lands and means of sustenance, and it will make arrangements for you to live a regular life in Jish.[28]

But the plans to destroy the village of Kafr Bir'im had been made in June 1948, as part of "retroactive transfer", a policy which contained six measures, including home destruction, that continued into the 1960s. (The policy, contained in a three-page memorandum entitled "Retroactive Transfer, A Scheme for the Solution of the Arab Question in the State of Israel", was approved by David Ben Gurion and proposed on June 5, 1948 by Jewish Agency officials Yosef Weitz and Eliyahu Sasson, and Hagana intelligence member Ezra Danin.)[29]

Sami Zahra, one of those who had taken refuge five years earlier in the tomb with human remains, remembers the day of the bombing in mid-September, 1953:

> When the planes appeared about the village, and the houses were bombed, we all went up a hill located in the high area of Jish overlooking Kafr Bir'im. Every time a bomb fell on a house, the people would mention the name of the house owner and cry, and wait for the next bomb which would destroy the next house. They were unable to intervene against the destruction ... Ever since that time, the hill has been called the "Bir'imites wailing place".[30]

The villagers wrote again to the Zionist leaders they had once supported, saying they "would have preferred to be slaughtered by the racist oppressor" rather than having their "houses demolished before their eyes in a situation of calm and without justification". The "bombing of the houses", they continued, "will not make the owners cede their rights".[31]

But Palestinians were replaced in Kafr Bir'im. A 70-year-old villager recalls in 2006:

Ten-thousand dunums for grazing only 50 cows of Kibbutz Bar'am! We told them that we were ready to live with the 50 cows and to feed them if necessary. We even suggested that we would buy the fodder for the cows, but they refused. They prefer the cows over us.[32]

Even the mention of their village in applications for various "permits" would bring about punishment in future years. Sami Zahra was forbidden to work,

[B]ecause I mentioned in the application that I was from Kafr Bir'im and lived in Jish [...] The officials told me that I had to say that I was from Jish in order to get a permit, but I refused.[33]

Kafr Bir'im remains a reminder of the many forced removals within Palestine, and expulsions outside the Armistice lines.

### The Pass System

Initially a relatively large apparatus was needed to maintain the very harsh movement restrictions. By the end of 1949, military rule over Palestinians employed over 1,000 individuals, engaged in the cycle of population registration, identity documentation (including enlisting and using collaborators), and expulsions. Ben Gurion described this cycle as follows:

The governor takes care of the registration of the population, the supervision of its movements ... and fights against infiltration by combing the area and checking identities ... The village heads have been ordered to report infiltrators [...] to seize weapons [and] evacuate semi-abandoned villages.[34]

A Ministry of Minority Affairs was established in May 1948, but was quickly replaced in July 1949, when total control over Palestinians was handed to the military.[35] Even this short-lived Ministry, however, was headed by the same person as the Ministry of Police, thus clearly denoting Palestinians as separate from Israeli Jews and as civilians under military occupation.

If the military found Palestinians without a pass, or with an expired pass, or on a different route from that prescribed in the pass, they fined or imprisoned them. Each day, the military issued hundreds of travel permits, some for a single trip, and others for longer periods. Any Palestinian wishing, for example, to travel from a Galilee village to nearby Haifa to look for work had to apply several days in advance, and could only access institutions and offices through the military, given the administrative segregation between Jewish colonists and Palestinians.[36]

Various ministries objected to the concentration of administrative power being in the hands of the Military Governor for all matters concerning the Palestinians in Israel. So in March 1949 Ben Gurion appointed a committee to look into how to deal with the Palestinian population and whether to retain military rule. Its composition – two senior military officers, chaired by the head of the military administration – assured its conclusions: namely the need to retain a forceful military administration for "security, demographic and land settlement reasons and for dealing with the issue of refugees".[37]

> One military person issued all the permits for each area, such as the Galilee.
> Three military commanders were appointed to serve as governors. Each district was divided into smaller sub-districts, each one of which included a branch of the military government and an appointed officer. The movements of Arabs between the three districts were restricted and permits were required [and] ... closed areas were restricted to permit holders only.[38]

Thus a single individual virtually ruled over broad swathes of territory and their indigenous, civilian population. The lack of resources combined with such concentration of power was not only open to abuse, but condemned Palestinians to endless queues in order to obtain any permit for movement.

> Getting a permit was torture because you needed to go to the military governor's office in Shefa 'Amr, the only place for permits for the whole of the Galilee. Everyone had to go there. And only one individual dealt with it. People used to wait maybe a whole day and not get seen and have to return the next day.[39]

The travel permit was limited to a particular purpose, with a pre-set route and timings. The permit specified: "the dates for which it was valid, the purpose for which it was issued, the destination, the route, and the date of return".[40]

Palestinians needed a permit not only for short-term travel but also for a change of residence; any Palestinian who resided in a locality without permission might be evicted, and his or her property confiscated. The permit system proved particularly profitable in Bedouin areas where a special military "green patrol" drove them off their lands and reduced their flocks through the pretext of permit enforcement.[41]

## The Self-propagating Regime

With time the size of the required apparatus dwindled, as the regime of movement restrictions became more entrenched and self-sustaining. Presenting the simplicity of enforcement in an interview years later, the former military governor of the central and northern districts explained that a weekly visit of an army or military police patrol sufficed to control the different areas.[42] Palestinians also noted how a limited number of checkpoints served to restrict large numbers of Palestinians.

> I first became aware of movement restrictions when I started high school in Nazareth in early 1949, I was 13. There weren't checkpoints like now. The only place where they inspected people would be in one spot on the bus journey at the entrance to 'Akka and another going into Nazareth on the road east to Tiberias.[43]

The strict enforcement of restrictions was conducted by the military and police over ordinary citizens of all ages.

> The military government had a centre in the police station. Everyone who wanted to travel needed a permit to go anywhere outside the village. If you left without a permit they would send you back. The Israeli soldiers and police used to check all the buses. Everyone needed a permit whatever their age.[44]

Enforcing the military regime effectively criminalised Palestinians. Between 1948 and 1967, Israeli police records show a dramatic disparity between Jews and Palestinians in the numbers accused and punished. Dozens, sometimes hundreds, of Palestinians were taken prisoner every month for transgressing the movement restrictions. About 40 per cent of the charges (and "convictions") levelled against Palestinians were for breaking the movement restrictions and military regulations.[45]

> Many people were arrested for entering the city without a permit. I remember one of my school classmates was arrested several times for taking eggs to Haifa (about 35km away). Jewish people

wanted Arab village eggs, but the Israeli authorities considered this smuggling. He would have been 13 or 14 and was arrested several times.[46]

Military courts "sentenced" thousands of Palestinians every year to punishments for ordinary accepted behaviour, such as accessing their land, going to work, or marketing agricultural produce.[47]

> There were very few cars at that time. Although there were no roadblocks, the police could appear on the road and stop a bus at any time. Because you needed permits to go anywhere, they would stop the buses and ask everyone to produce their permits. If someone didn't have a permit they would be taken off the bus.[48]

Military and police stopped public and private vehicles alike, to search Palestinians on a daily basis.[49]

The use of a quota system for military and police funding gave an added incentive to harass Palestinians. Sociologist Alina Korn uncovered this mechanism through a series of interviews:

> Dr Levi Eden, the director of the Youth Probation Service, told me in a conversation that took place in January 1990, about something that he was accustomed to doing in the fifties when he was the commanding officer of the police station in Afula. A police station that opened more than a thousand files in a month on an average, was considered a large station, and as a result was entitled to certain benefits.
>
> Each year in December, when he estimated that he needed some more files in order to reach the required number of 1,000, he ordered his policemen to go to the central bus station in the city in order to arrest Arabs who did not have travel permits in their possession, and to open files on them. In that way he was able to fulfill the desired quota.[50]

## 5.2   INDUCED TRANSFER

### The Destruction of Livelihoods

Already in 1947, Ben Gurion had supported suggestions to induce Palestinians to leave by various means, including "starving them to death". By 1949, food production was virtually destroyed. The average amount of arable land for each village – some of which had been entirely self-sufficient – was reduced from 2,280 to 500 acres; villages within the Armistice lines faced severe shortages.[51]

A military governor was appointed in 1948: Moshe Reiss. He operated from Ma'alia near here. We had no rations, no wheat, no sugar. I remember my father went to the military governor and wanted a permit to get to Haifa to buy food. He was given a two-day permit.[52]

Nor could Palestinians work directly on the land to grow food. Even nearly 30 years later in 1974, the Israeli official responsible for all agriculture in the area declared Palestinians to be "a cancer in our body", and campaigned in 1975 together with the Jewish Agency to "eradicate the plague" of Palestinians cultivating lands and orchards in the Galilee.[53]

Under strict military rule, Palestinians had few opportunities to socialise or engage in social, cultural, and educational activities. After 1948, only one secondary school was left standing, with no institutes for higher education. Seeking an education required a permit, and nearly all permits were reserved for labourers to work for Jewish employers.[54]

We didn't really have any external life. It was all in the village. It wasn't a stable situation then.[55]

The few remaining permits were mainly issued to further facilitate the system of permits – seeing lawyers, going to court, and communicating with the military government.[56]

Such confinement in one place made normal life extremely difficult. The movement restrictions strangled villages' economies, already debilitated by the ongoing military assaults that left men in prison, crops rotting in fields, and a range of health problems from malnutrition (rickets and scurvy) and malaria to infectious diseases such as typhoid and diphtheria.[57]

Despite the serious health situation, medical practitioners faced heavy travel restrictions for over a decade. Even at the end of December 1957, "doctors from Nazareth were still being given a permit valid for six months with a specific list of the places where they were allowed to visit".[58] Equally, patients were banned from reaching medical facilities – Palestinians today remember that "If you needed to do some business or go to the doctor, you needed a special permit".[59] Family members were left unsupported as "breadwinners stayed in one area while their dependents stayed in another, usually only a short distance away".[60] Enforced separations were prolonged through permit postponements, "even for urgent cases like illness, births or death".[61]

Although Palestinians desperately needed income to survive, they could not sell their goods because of movement restrictions. Without access to markets, they were forced to sell to Israeli Jewish merchants – who could travel without a pass – at only a fraction of the produce's value. This strategy had early origins: Ezra Danin (who worked on the Village Files) had suggested in 1947 "destroying the traffic (buses, lorries that carry agricultural products and private cars) ... sinking their fishing boats in Jaffa, closing their shops and preventing raw materials from reaching their factories".[62] His plans materialised, resulting in mass Palestinian unemployment as rural and urban economic lifelines were destroyed.

As in all caste-like systems, Palestinians were "restricted to unpleasant jobs that Jewish workers would not accept, like in sewage".[63] Even such "regular" employment led only to a short-term permit, which needed to be renewed repeatedly to continue working:

> Sometimes the permit was for a day and sometimes for a week. It depended on the reason. If people were working somewhere regularly they used to put a cross by the name to make it easier to renew the next time.[64]

Wages were unequal, even for identical work. But Palestinians had little choice – changing jobs required a permit. Moreover, work was extremely limited; employers advertised jobs for "army leavers only" as a covert way of saying "Palestinians need not apply". Once hired, dismissal was easy, so Palestinian employment was always precarious.[65]

> In practice many jobs were closed to Arab workers and employees. The Arab worker who found a temporary job in a remote Jewish colony could be dismissed on the grounds that he was "not organized".[66]

This mechanism became systematic, relegating Palestinians to a "reserve army of labour" – a tap to be turned on to suit the requirements of the emerging Israeli economy. The permit system enabled Israeli authorities to close the bottleneck of Palestinian labour when Jewish labourers wanted work:

During the summer months and other periods when there was a reduced demand for labor, the military government was required to block the departure of the Arab workers to the Jewish sector. The military government introduced a type of "queue" system and supplied work permits for two or three weeks in a month.[67]

Such restrictions placed Palestinian livelihoods at the mercy of a systematically discriminatory regime.

### Curfews

In the first decade after 1948, "curfews became the most common method of controlling Palestinians".[68] Perhaps the best-known incident in this period took place in 1956, in the village of Kafr Qassem. The Israeli army gave only a half hour's notice to the village leader that a curfew would take effect at sunset. With no way of telling the villagers returning home at dusk, the villagers were surprised to be confronted by armed forces asking if they were from the village. When they said "yes", 47 men, women, and children were shot dead, one by one, at close range, in the first hour of the curfew alone.[69]

Defending the premeditated massacre, Brigadier Shadmi had told his forces, "A dead man is better than the complications of detention". Shadmi and his men eventually served short prison sentences, were formally pardoned, and then promoted to leading roles in Palestinian municipalities and the Dimona nuclear facilities.[70]

Curfews thus limited the movement of even those Palestinians with temporary permission to move between home and work. After a decade of military rule, still only one in three Palestinians were given a permit, and only half were for "extended periods". In 1959, Palestinians were allowed for the first time to remain in local centres and cities during daylight hours – although those in the Naqab were only given this "privilege" two days a week. Palestinians, however, could only use main roads and travel to their own "district capital", not to other villages or the cities of other areas. Particular individuals (like the Palestinian candidates banned from running in the 1965 elections), meanwhile, continued to be blacklisted, banished to remote Jews-only areas (to prevent contact with other Palestinians), and made to report twice daily to specified Israeli army offices. And at any given time, a curfew could annul a travel permit making every Palestinian vulnerable and his or her movement a "crime".[71]

## Cantonisation

Over time a geography of forced segregation emerged.[72] The exclusively-Jewish town of Karm'iel, for example, was built on Palestinian villagers' land, by dispossessed and impoverished Palestinian labourers.

[Y]et no Arab can either live or open a business there [...] when one man agreed to rent his villa to [a Palestinian] from a nearby village, most of the residents signed a petition demanding rescission of the agreement as "a matter of principle".[73]

A Palestinian who applied to open a marble quarry in Karm'iel was denied "on grounds that the area was closed to non-Jews".[74]

By 1964, plans were underway to truck out another 300,000 Palestinians, but were aborted before the actual expulsion (Ariel Sharon asked his staff to research how many buses and trucks would be required to "transport" Palestinian citizens of Israel outside the 1949 Armistice lines if a war broke out – as it did three years later; his subordinates, however, were reluctant to cooperate in case the plan surfaced to embarrass Israel).[75] Instead of outright expulsion, therefore, the policy of crowding Palestinians into reserves continued. Public housing was built for Israeli Jews only, and housing blocks explicitly excluded Palestinians:

When a few Arab families disregarded the law in 1975 and either bought or rented several flats, pandemonium broke out among the Jewish population. According to the Israeli newspaper, Ma'ariv, "The residents complain that the situation is intolerable [and] ... threaten to abandon the town en masse and move to neighbouring cities – if nothing is done to prevent the penetration of Arab families into that section of the city [i.e. Upper Nazareth], and in particular into the housing blocks where they live".[76]

In 1968, a plan was developed by Shmuel Toledano to reduce Palestinian numbers by other means: assistance to emigrate, financial incentives to have fewer children, and a further economic squeeze to force Palestinians to seek their livelihoods elsewhere. The plan was implemented in 1974 as the Koenig Report and, according to Toledano, remained in force until 1991. If the effects of this plan were ever measured, they were not made public, so little is known as to its impact on the Palestinian population. What is known, however, is that it was merely one among many: a number of other proposals were simply not implemented for various reasons (such as Toledano's offer of 1,000 passports, bought from a South American country, as a mechanism for encouraging Palestinians to leave).[77]

Despite movement restrictions officially ending in 1966, Palestinians remained under "strict social control", armed forces patrolled the reserves, and the state of emergency was never lifted. Previous emergency regulations on population registration and movement restriction remained as "law". Markings enabling discrimination persisted in the Population Registry (and on ID cards until 2002, when the entry for "nationality" was blanked out due to debate on how to define "Jew", as described in Chapter 3). Heavy surveillance continued through wiretaps, through the 2007 "Big Brother Law" on communications data (giving Israeli police and other authorities unlimited access to private telephone information), and through the biometric databases made official in 2008 (details in Chapter 3).[78]

The model of mobile workers – who worked in Jewish areas during the day and returned to the reserves (the Palestinian-only city quarters, towns, and villages in Israel) at night – remained, even if not overtly regulated through movement restrictions encircling the reserves. By the mid-1980s, this model accounted for more than two-thirds of all employed Palestinians within Israel. But even after the end of military rule, the mainly Palestinian areas suffered discrimination. They remained without communication networks, health centres, public services (as but one example, there was not a single library in any Palestinian area in 1980), sewage lines, or paved road networks. Water and electricity also took a long time to arrive.[79]

### Transferring the System to the West Bank and Gaza Strip

The restrictions of 1948–66 were reincarnated on the other side of the Armistice lines, in the West Bank and Gaza Strip, in 1967. The population registry and identity cards provided information to the Israeli army about where Palestinians "belonged" and where they would be punished. Vehicle license plates were instant giveaways: yellow for Jewish colonists, black for the Israeli army, and white, green, blue, or red for Palestinians (depending on the level of permits granted).[80] Thus the Jewish colonists in the West Bank and Gaza Strip (constituting a population shift into occupied territory in violation of the Fourth Geneva Convention) were exempt not only from the movement restrictions, but also from all the military orders applying to Palestinians from 1967 to the present.

The first step taken by the Israeli army in 1967 was a blanket ban on leaving the West Bank and Gaza Strip. After four years of confinement, Palestinians were told in 1971 that they might request permission to pass outside the Armistice lines – during the daytime only; overnight stays were still prohibited without special passes. From 1971 to the present, to travel anywhere outside the borders of historic Palestine entailed obtaining a "certificate of exoneration" and then a permit from the Israeli army.[81]

A number of departments in the Israeli military authority (misleadingly entitled the "civil administration") responsible for the West Bank and Gaza Strip, had to clear the certificate. These departments included the income tax department, the customs and excise department, the police, the municipality, the village leader, and the Village Leagues (bodies staffed by Palestinian collaborators appointed by Israel). There was no formal appeal procedure for decisions on movement restrictions; if a lawyer sought a review, the case was simply re-submitted to the secret services.[82]

Contrary to international law, in March 1993 Israel prohibited Palestinian movement between the West Bank and Gaza Strip; some exceptions were "granted" prior to 2000, and none after.[83] The result was that "thousands of Gazans currently living in the West Bank are considered illegal residents and, if caught at a roadblock, could be deported back to Gaza".[84] (While exact numbers are not known of people deported from the West Bank to Gaza, estimates are high, and include people born in the West Bank.)[85] Curfews, meanwhile, not only prevented entry and exit from villages, but also prevented people from leaving their homes. Such curfews extended at times for weeks.[86]

## Pass Laws and Punishments

Between 1967 and 1992, over 1,300 numbered military orders were issued in the West Bank (with corresponding orders in the Gaza Strip), many of which were illegal under international law. Perhaps the military orders best known for being illegal under international law were those annexing East Jerusalem and the Golan Heights. The military orders and subsequent activities were declared "null and void" by the UN Security Council resolutions 478 (1980) and 497 (1981). But Israel persisted in issuing and enforcing numbered military orders. Over 20 per cent of the West Bank was closed off from Palestinians through military orders issued in the 1960s alone.[87]

Together with other, unnumbered military orders, regulations, notifications, and instructions, the numbered military orders served to "legislate" every detail of life, from mechanic shops (No. 395) to gas canisters (No. 480) to cow marking (No. 263). Most significantly, they layered the West Bank and Gaza Strip with a web of restrictions on movement so stringent that Palestinians could scarcely pass from one village to the next without risking retribution. In a five-year period, 1991–6, over 112,000 workers spent more than 224,000 days in prison. And this was one of the better periods. In the same period, workers paid over US$16.8 million in fines. The penalty for not carrying an ID was a year's imprisonment; the Israeli army administered additional punishment at their discretion:[88]

If you are caught they might beat you up (if you don't have the right papers), maybe imprison you. Maybe they arrest you for two hours and then they would release you. There was a young man, a friend from Masha, they broke his hand.

Many people were caught that would sell vegetables in Kufr Qassem. They were forced to eat hot chilli, maybe half a kilo, or a full kilo of hot chillies. Forced to eat onion, no bread nothing, just plain onion. One, two, three – it didn't matter. They would even feed potatoes to the people. They would [forcibly] take off all their clothes and tell them to leave.[89]

Military orders were also supplemented with Israeli laws that had historically been used only against Palestinians, such as the labelling of "absentees". Although Israel maintained that military rule (not Israeli law) applied to Palestinians in the West Bank and Gaza Strip, Israel (and its courts) nevertheless made an exception for the Absentee Property Law.[90]

Albeit on a lesser scale than previous decades, expulsions still continued, especially of blacklisted persons, prompting protests from the UN Security Council, European Economic Community, and United States.[91] A 1994 UN report warned that:

[Any] form of forced population transfer from a chosen place of residence, whether by displacement, settlement, internal banishment, or evacuation, directly affects the enjoyment or exercise of the right of free movement and choice of residence within States and constitutes a restriction upon this right.[92]

Descriptions of movement restrictions and expulsions cannot convey the psychological effects. For Palestinians prohibited from returning home, or forced to choose between the village of their birth or the town of their work, or between the home in which they grew up or the home in which they raised their children, the expulsions and bans on movement were dispiriting. In the words of Fawaz Turki, a Palestinian's home and lands provided the "essential repertoire of consciousness, the props of daily life as a peasant, a professional, a tradesman, or an artist", from which were drawn personal "myths, metaphor, laughter, and ethos", and with which each person identified as a "spiritual being".[93]

Breaking Palestinian resistance to colonisation was not only a matter of destroying all sources of revenue; it was also about making daily life seem so futile and unfulfilling that emigration would appear preferable.

## 5.3   ENHANCED MOVEMENT FOR COLONISTS, RESTRICTED MOVEMENT FOR INDIGENOUS PALESTINIANS

### Maps of Movement Restrictions

It is through maps that we can chart over time the evolution of movement restrictions: where Palestinians were once free to live and enjoy fundamental human rights, and where they are now confined and deprived of these rights. In Chapter 2, Figure 2.1 mapped Palestinian villages, towns, and cities that covered the country – some of these dated from as early as 5000 BC, and most in their modern form from the 1500s[94] – until 1922. Figure 5.1 shows where Palestinians now live, with varying degrees of confinement, while Figure 2.2 and Figure 5.2 tell part of the story of how a shift of this magnitude came about.

Figure 2.2 denoted the destroyed villages and the lines drawn around the West Bank and Gaza Strip in 1949 by the self-proclaimed state of Israel during armistices with Egypt, Lebanon, Jordan, and Syria. Palestinians were excluded from these armistices over Palestine, and the agreements themselves forbid the lines from being "construed as political or territorial boundaries" or from prejudicing the "ultimate settlement of the Palestine Question".[95] What the lines illustrate, however, is the degree to which movement restrictions were imposed on Palestinians from a very early point in Zionist history. The Armistice line around the West Bank partitioned villages and communities across its 320 km length.[96]

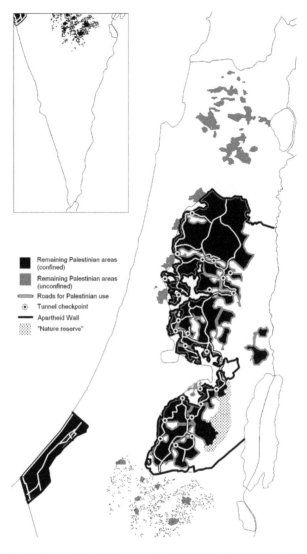

*Figure 5.1* Constraints on Palestinian movement. Grey areas show the rural spaces reserved for remaining (10 per cent) Palestinians in the 1940s, and to which they were confined for 18 years (urban ghettoes not shown). Black areas show the spaces reserved for Pal-estinians in the West Bank and Gaza Strip, and to which they remain confined by a system of Israeli-issued bans and permits, as well as physical obstacles including concrete blocks, trenches, barbed wire, a concrete wall, and an iron wall in Gaza. (Reproduced with permission from *The Arab World Geographer* [AWG] http://arabworldgeographer. metapress.com)

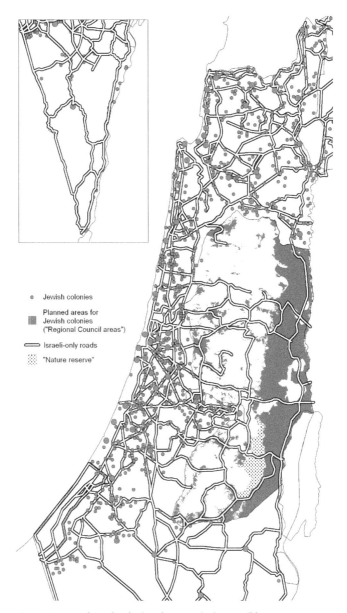

- Jewish colonies

Planned areas for
Jewish colonies
("Regional Council areas")

Israeli-only roads

"Nature reserve"

*Figure 5.2*   Roads and colonies that remain inaccessible to 90 per cent of Palestinians. Over 1,660 kilometres of such roads crisscross the West Bank alone, forcing Palestinians into ever-smaller spaces, with Palestinian movement bound downward into a series of tunnel-checkpoints. (Reproduced with permission from *The Arab World Geographer* [AWG] http://arabworldgeographer.metapress.com)

Figure 5.2 shows the network of roads and colonies that remain inaccessible to 90 per cent of Palestinians today. The 1.4 million (less than 13 per cent of today's eleven million)[97] Palestinians who are "permitted" to travel on these roads (that is, those living in Israel), for the most part still live clustered in the same spaces reserved for them in 1948 – and to which they were forcibly confined for 18 years. These spaces (excluding the urban ghettoes into which they were forced in the 1940s)[98] are shown in grey on Figure 5.1. This 13 per cent of Palestinians, moreover, are deprived of one of life's most basic rights: to marry and live with whom they choose.[99] As they are forbidden from entering the West Bank, and the Palestinians in the West Bank are forbidden from crossing the Armistice line, villages and even homes are literally cut into two pieces. Palestinians who live in these homes mockingly speak of having a head in the West Bank and feet outside it.[100]

Figure 5.1, therefore, is the current situation, resulting from a number of key events. The most significant in terms of physical barriers to movement was the construction from the 1980s onward of a road network which Palestinians were forbidden to use, and from 1994 onward of the walls in the West Bank and Gaza Strip.

## Apartheid Roads

In the early 1980s, Israel developed a master plan for taking over the West Bank, bearing a strong similarity to a road-and-colony plan proposed in 1978 by the colonist group, Gush Emmunim. The 1983 master plan outlined special roads for colonists to "bypass" as well as restrict the growth of Palestinian villages and cities. By 1993, 400 kilometres of these colonist-only roads had been laid down.[101]

The 1993 and 1995 Oslo interim agreements between Israel and the Palestinian Liberation Organisation did not change the status of Palestinian land or people, but they did shape the movement restrictions shown in Figure 5.1. Perversely, while they were meant to indicate colonist evacuation – in stages toward a future, as yet undetermined final agreement – they were instead used by the Israeli army to justify expansion of the colonist-only road network. The argument was that colonists needed roads without Palestinians for their safety, to compensate for a reduced army. Over US$600 million was spent on these roads in 1995 alone.[102]

The Oslo interim agreements sliced the West Bank and Gaza Strip into minute pieces, with Area A categorised for Palestinian occupancy, Area C categorised for full continued military occupation by the Israeli army, and Area B categorised as something in-between

– generally areas where Palestinians were living, but where the Israeli army wished to retain (and eventually gain full) control. The Oslo categories graphically showed how little space remained for the millions of indigenous Palestinians in their own country: all of Area A was only 5 per cent of historic Palestine. This tiny fraction was in turn fragmented into non-contiguous areas, with 13 in the West Bank alone (comprising 17.2 per cent of the West Bank).[103]

In the decades that followed, these categorisations became more apparent, as colonists intensified in Areas B and C, while the Israeli army laid siege to Area A. A map published in January 1996 by an Israeli newspaper labelled Area C as "state lands", revealing Israel's expansionist intentions, and openly contradicting international law.[104] The same 1996 map indicated routes "recommended" and "non-recommended" for Israelis, and "restricted to operational forces". Later that year, Israeli soldiers erected hundreds of checkpoints and blockages to Palestinian movement inside the West Bank and Gaza Strip.[105]

While physical restrictions created a reality "on the ground", political manoeuvres gave a misleading impression of flexibility and change. On closer analysis, however, a series of Israeli proposals offered little freedom and kept Palestinians enclosed: the Sharon proposal of 2001 entailed keeping 121 colonies and 99.6 per cent of colonists, and the "disengagement" plan of 2004 and the "convergence" plan of 2006 kept 86.7 per cent of colonists (367,646 people) despite claiming to evacuate as many as 47 per cent of them.[106]

By 2004, an unwritten but highly enforced policy demarcated roads forbidden to Palestinians. Over 124 kilometres of roads were prohibited to Palestinians, restrictions that sometimes even prevented them from crossing; another 244 kilometres were confined to Palestinians with special passes (while permitted for all Jewish colonists); and an additional 364 kilometres of roads were blocked by military forces. Between 2002 and 2010, over US$557 million was sunk into the network of roads and tunnels.[107]

In 2005, a military order banned Palestinians from crossing the Armistice line (or into Jerusalem) except at eleven prescribed locations. All other routes were open for "Israelis" only, defined – using reference to an Israeli regulation welcoming all Jews of the world to settle in all of historic Palestine – to exclude all West Bank and Gaza Strip Palestinians (thus also excluding Palestinians in Jerusalem) but to include all Jewish colonists. This left only a handful of routes open to Palestinians (shown in white on Figure

5.1), all blocked by checkpoints running below the rapid-transport thoroughfares of colonists (represented by circles in Figure 5.1). The numbers of physical restrictions on movement in the West Bank climbed to a peak of 752 in 2008 (including 122 around the Old City of Hebron alone, and excluding the roads reserved for Jewish colonists in the West Bank), and remained well above 600 in subsequent years.[108]

By 2010, over 1,660 kilometres of roads layered the West Bank, hemming Palestinians into smaller non-contiguous areas, and accelerating colonist movement across the Armistice line. As colonists drove overhead, Palestinians' only form of permitted movement was to pass through 44 tunnels, which gradually replaced over 600 checkpoints and other military obstructions (including trenches, roadblocks, and metal gates) in the West Bank.[109] These tunnels were marked by fortified checkpoints. In total, three main terminals, nine commercial terminals, and 22 terminals for cars and workers controlled all Palestinian movement.

By the end of 2010, 149 colonies and 100 "outposts" were in place across the West Bank (including East Jerusalem), with half a million colonists. Over four million Palestinians, including 1.5 million refugees from across the Armistice lines, were encircled in dozens of cantons, with a total area equivalent to 12 per cent of historic Palestine. Yet despite the expanses of confining infrastructure, the built-up areas within colonies remained relatively small.[110]

> They are just one per cent of the whole West Bank population, but they are claiming 60 per cent of the land. The settlements are actually just built-up pockets, but the settlers include huge tracts of land around them by laying down barbed wire. So in effect it's more like estates, containing just a few houses.[111]

It was the desire to live without seeing Palestinians (except as shipped-in workers) that forced Palestinians into small spaces, not a physical requirement for space.

### The Wall

In 2002, Israeli armed forces (and private-sector firms) began building a wall of concrete and steel, to eventually run for 810 kilometres (and 30–100 metres wide throughout), which they called a "security fence". The International Court of Justice in 2004 recommended it be named for what it was, a wall, and judged it illegal based on its regime of movement restrictions and its route –

well over twice the length of the Armistice line, claiming swathes of the West Bank.

By the summer of 2010, and at a cost of US$2 million per kilometre, 520 kilometres of barbed razor-wire, patrol routes, sniper towers, electrified wires, ditches, surveillance cameras, and eight-metre high concrete slabs (over 60 kilometres alone) sliced through villages, agricultural lands, homes, families, and livelihoods.[112] The thick black line in Figure 5.1 traces the wall's route and its divergence from the Armistice line, reaching instead up to 22 kilometres into the West Bank. In Jerusalem alone, only four of the 142 kilometres of wall are located on the Armistice line. The consequence of this divergence is the dispossession and forced displacement of thousands of Palestinians.

Of a population of 2.3 million in 2003, 22.6 per cent of Palestinians in the West Bank were separated from their lands by the wall, and another 16.9 per cent were left isolated outside walled areas (the proportion of these Palestinians given permits to work in their own land decreased each subsequent year, for example from 10,037 in 2006 to 1,640 in 2009). Fourteen villages were under immediate threat of expulsion. The village of Nu'man, for example, was gradually deprived of all contact and services: in 1992, villagers were informed that without Jerusalem IDs they would be deported and their homes demolished. In 1994, the children were forbidden from attending Jerusalem schools, construction of a school was forbidden, and in 1998 vehicles transporting the children to West Bank schools were forbidden. Waste disposal vehicles were forbidden, burning the accumulating waste was forbidden, fuel and vegetables from the West Bank were forbidden, and in 2003 much of the village's land was taken for the wall, a colony (Har Homa), terminal, and army post. Ambulances, fire fighters, physicians, and veterinarians were forbidden, as was anyone without an ID specifying residence in the village. Women who had married Nu'man villagers were therefore also forbidden from going home to their husbands and children. This type of situation affected over 6,300 people.[113]

Another 8,550 were trapped between the Wall and the Armistice line, with their only movement confined to a rarely opened gate (with similar circumstances threatening another 16,500 Palestinians). These people were required to apply for permits to live in their own homes and, alongside over 200,000 Palestinians in Jerusalem, were cut off from the rest of the West Bank. Taken together, 6,300 people were under immediate threat of expulsion, 8,550 were between the

Wall and Armistice line, and a similar scenario of entrapment was the reality for another 16,500, plus 200,000 in Jerusalem isolated from the West Bank – 231,350 in total. A final 257,265 people were hemmed into enclaves, walled on three sides and severely restricted on the fourth, bringing the number of severely affected Palestinians to 488,615 (a conservative estimate and less than that given by Israeli researchers).[114]

The wall, and the impediments to movement depicted in Figure 5.1, were thus a means to induce nearly half a million Palestinians to seek refuge in the areas shaded black, or outside historic Palestine. The alternative to induced transfer was a life without health services, land, education, housing, and the freedom to begin and raise a family. In the words of Nu'man villager Jamal Der'awi, the aim was to "create a situation where we ourselves reach the conclusion that our lives are unlivable".[115]

The situation in the Gaza Strip was worse. In addition to a complete ban on entry and exit, with temporary exceptions given to less than 5 per cent of the population, a tight embargo was placed on essential goods for food, housing, education, and health services – leaving 83 per cent of the population in a situation of food insecurity. The most visible demonstration of all came in 1994, when an iron wall ringed in Palestinians in Gaza (taking with it 25 per cent of the most fertile lands), drones effected a ceiling over the Strip, and warships closed in on Palestinians' small fishing boats.[116]

### Keeping Up Appearances

While Palestinians were confined, Israeli colonists were free to expand further onto Palestinian land. Figure 5.2 is the mirror image of Figure 5.1, and demonstrates the extent to which the wall, checkpoints, road network, colonies, and even the Oslo categories of A, B, and C, facilitated rather than hampered colonist movement. All these obstructions were coded to block Palestinians but not colonists, through the filter of IDs and racist stereotypes. Israeli human-rights group B'tselem describes restrictions on movement as "based on the assumption that every Palestinian is a security threat". This "racist assumption", they explain, illegally violates the rights of "an entire population based on national origin".[117] In the village of Nu'man, children over the age of six were required to carry their birth certificates wherever they went.[118] Reflecting on the absurdity of their reality, Der'awi wondered, "It makes you laugh and cry at the same time".

Internationally, restrictions on movement and their long history were played down, in favour of an appearance of "strict separation between nations". A series of "cross-border industrial zones" – historically known for exploiting the captive labour force – received a benevolent veneer of "development" funding from Germany, the US, Japan, and France. A "humanising image" was projected of the hundreds of checkpoints: progressive, scientific, and positive, using scanners, sensors, biometrics, computers, private security guards, and turnstiles.[119]

The system of permits, according to a study of checkpoints conducted by Physicians for Human Rights, was not only a violation of human rights, it was a cover-up of that violation: "there in order to preserve appearances".[120] Over 65 gates in the Wall maintained an illusion of permeability and movement; in reality, they remained closed except for a few minutes a day, a few days a year, for a few "permitted" Palestinians. The Wall cut off Palestinians from their lands, and then Israeli army officials denied these landowners permission to their lands for failing to prove their "connection" to it. Over 90 per cent of the applications for permits rejected between 2006 and 2009 were due to a failure to prove "connection to the land".[121]

Israeli officials took it for granted that Palestinians should submit to such discrimination on an ethnic and national basis, which violated – without due process – freedom of movement, and the rights to work, property, and livelihood. A spokesman in 2002 defended the regime (as it was later called by the International Court of Justice in 2004) saying, "We haven't figured out the logistics of daily life for the Palestinians yet. We'll just have to wing it".[122]

Armed colonists and the Israeli army were not only free to travel roads and lands, but even to violate Palestinian homes. Researcher Nir Gazit noted "a kind of mental erosion among the soldiers that makes some of them trigger-happy", and in 2004–5 collected a number of testimonies from all ranks that he concluded reflected wider trends:

You are always curious about what happens behind that closed door and, hey, you can just cross the street and find out ... When you enter the house you really feel you are in charge. Leaving aside your platoon, leaving aside the entire army outside ... now it's you and him.

You are inside his home, and you are the one in charge not him! You can tell him to raise his hands up; you can enter his bedroom, his toilet ... Hey, you can do everything! In there you have the maximum direct control you can gain.[123]

Soldiers had even given a name to their intrusions, which were "routinized and exercised around the clock" – "ineffective fire":

> We shoot buildings, not people ... we were shooting at buildings, windows and sunheated water tanks, but not humans. Sometimes we were shooting just for the fun of it ... You know a kind of targeting-fire competition. Look, from our perspective every window is a potential firing [crack] and every building is a legitimate target.
>
> We don't look for people in these windows, although we may have killed someone during these shootings ... I can't really tell because it was very far. Still, we know some people got killed in such fire incidents.[124]

### Colonists as Enforcers of Movement Restrictions

In the first ten months of 2011 alone, the United Nations Office for the Coordination of Humanitarian Affairs documented 377 colonist attacks, injuring 167 Palestinians and damaging nearly 10,000 Palestinian-owned olive trees and other trees. Colonists killed three Palestinians in hit-and-run incidents. Such killings were not new: from 1987 to 2011, they killed 165 Palestinians. Despite claims by Israeli police to have followed up 642 cases of colonist attacks on Palestinians, between 2005 and 2010, only 9 per cent resulted in identification and indictment. A study of attacks in the West Bank between 2007 and 2011 found that Palestinian violence had decreased by 95 per cent, while colonist violence increased by 315 per cent, in a steady annual rise that has yet to plateau or drop.[125]

Over 90 per cent of attacks took place within Area C; the attacks were one more means to restrict Palestinian movement into enclosed cantons. This was illustrated by the example of the village of Qusra, home to about 6,000 Palestinians and located near the central West Bank city of Nablus. Human rights organisations documented 17 attacks by colonists on Qusra villagers between January and October of 2011. In all of these, colonists acted not only with impunity, but also with the aid of Israeli armed forces when present. On March 7, 2011, colonists assaulted Qusra villagers with guns, baseball bats, and metal bars.[126] They shot a Palestinian in his left wrist; when soldiers arrived, the soldiers shot another Palestinian in the leg, then moving closer, shot his second leg at close range. As he lay on the ground with bullets in both legs, a colonist then kicked him in the face. Israeli police arrested none of the colonists, and suggested the Palestinians "file a complaint" at one of the colonies.

One of the villagers, Fathallah Abu Rida, who was attacked on September 16, 2011, and shot in the left leg by a colonist, had twelve dunums of grapes, figs, and olive trees, and recalled:

> We used to go to our land all the time, not only for farming but simply to be there, to enjoy it. Each of my children has planted their own trees and flowers. Now my youngest daughter, Rahani, who's eight, tells me, "Dad, don't go to the land. I don't want you to die".[127]

Qusra villagers lost hundreds of trees to colonist attacks, and hundreds of acres to colonisation. Such attacks, especially from the 1990s onward, served as a final informal layer in the restrictions on Palestinian movement.

## Conclusion

> We will not allow other people to make us strangers in our country.[128]

The ongoing invasions into Palestinian space, privacy, and security are one more way of making life unbearable, which – in combination with the infringements of the population registry, IDs, constant surveillance and movement restrictions – act to induce Palestinians to leave.[129] Despite this and numerous violations of international law, it is the dignity of living in one's own ancestral home, lands, and pluralistic community that is perhaps most instrumental in preventing Palestinians from succumbing to induced transfer.

# 6
# The Health System

The "green" [1949 Armistice] line separated Palestinians from their homes, from their cities, and from their villages. [It separated] everything from everything in exactly the same way. It interned Palestinian society in 1949.

But the Palestinian people got used to it, and built their lives in a way that it became normal again. I am afraid that the Israeli government has learned from that.

It says to the Palestinians, it says to itself, and it says to the world, "Maybe it will be difficult with the separation wall, to go to school, but you will build schools on the other side of the wall. Maybe it will be difficult to go to the hospital, but you will build hospitals on the other side of the wall. And you will find work on the other side of the wall. Because it happened once, and it will happen again.[1]

This chapter and the next focus on the recent decades in the West Bank, and examine the cumulative impact that population registration, identity documentation, and movement restriction have had on the public health and education systems. In doing so, these two chapters highlight daily reality: what do people face, how do people cope, and what are their thoughts for the future?

The first section of this chapter considers the impact of movement restrictions in reducing public access to health care services, and in undermining the actual health care system. This takes place within the context of growing health care needs resulting from increasing poverty and Israeli army attacks. The second section describes the transformation of a functional health system into a context fraught with danger. Examples include ambulances being attacked or denied access, births and deaths at checkpoints, patients with chronic conditions requiring regular treatment being prevented from reaching medical help, and young Israeli soldiers at checkpoints taking on the role of medical diagnosticians.

## 6.1 COLLAPSING PUBLIC HEALTH STRUCTURES

### Blocking Basic Care

Half of the Palestinian population has been unable to consult with their usual health services due to closures and curfews.

Detours and long waiting hours at checkpoints have often forced Palestinians to divert to different health facilities.[2]

In 2004, the United Nations Office for the Coordination of Humanitarian Affairs reported that, as a result of movement restrictions, 39 per cent of the people surveyed stated they had to find alternative health facilities to the ones they normally used. Since 2000, impediments to health access were particularly dangerous in a context of ongoing military attacks and induced food insecurity. During the attacks on Palestinians in the West Bank and Gaza Strip in 2002 and 2003, for instance, demand for blood transfusions rose by 178 per cent; the need for hospital emergency wards rose by 52 per cent; and admissions to hospital and surgery increased by 20 per cent and 31 per cent, respectively. Disability, both physical and mental, became a major concern as a result of ongoing attacks from the 1980s onward.[3]

In a situation of a besieged economy, large numbers of homeless, and increasing food insecurity, health access was even more vital. Attacks on Gaza in 2006 and 2009, as well as ongoing Israeli military activities against Gazan civilians, killed and injured thousands, and rendered thousands more homeless (over 3,400 in 2006 and 20,000 in 2009). Home demolitions between September 2000 and May 2005 numbered 41,783 (partial demolition) and 2,855 (complete demolition) in the West Bank, and 23,561 (partial) and 4,778 (complete) in the Gaza Strip. Poverty rates in 2008 – excluding food aid and remittances, and before the 2009 attacks – were 79.4 per cent in the Gaza Strip and 45.7 per cent in the West Bank.[4]

> The ordinary person from a village who needs medical treatment faces major problems. First of all there is poverty, which is a huge problem if someone wants to get to hospital but has no money. Then the Israelis will either delay or obstruct or deny access to a certain clinic. Then there is the waste of time even if you have the money and get there.[5]

The right to health is part of the 1946 World Health Constitution, 1948 Universal Declaration of Human Rights (UDHR), 1966 International Covenant on Economic, Social and Cultural Rights (Article 12), 1989 UN Convention on the Rights of the Child (Article 24), and 1997 Maastricht Guidelines.[6] Article 25(1) of the UDHR states:

Everyone has the right to a standard of living adequate for the health and well-being of himself and of his family, including food, clothing, housing and medical care and necessary social services and the right to security in the event of unemployment, sickness, disability, widowhood, old age or other lack of livelihood in circumstances beyond his control.

Yet in the West Bank and Gaza Strip, Israeli movement restrictions eroded health conditions and constrained health access:

If you live in a village near Nablus and need to get to Nablus – [such as in] one of the villages in the northern West Bank near the Wall – instead of a 20-minute drive it can take you two hours. That delay increases the chances of complications if, for instance, you suffered heart failure or chest pains, or are in labour.

That is why the Ministry of Health estimates that in 126 cases people have died because of obstructed access at checkpoints and there have been nearly 70 births actually at checkpoints.[7]

Patients were forced to stay longer as in-patients, or near the services they needed, as travel to and from home became more difficult. But even that stop-gap and resource-draining solution was insufficient for the 266,442 Palestinians trapped into one of 27 enclaves in the West Bank, surrounded by barbed wire, walls and sniper towers, and restricted to entry and exit through gates or similar mechanisms.[8]

For instance, one gate in Jenin affects the three villages of Um al-Rihan, Barta'a al-Sharqiya, and Dhahr al-'Abd. The people from these three villages can't leave them without permission, and someone who isn't from those villages can't enter them.

In this small cluster, five to six thousand people are affected, and they only have one nurse and a doctor who works privately, and people can't afford to pay him because of the bad economic situation.[9]

Leaving these areas to seek care elsewhere was not merely difficult, but rather impossible, unless the locked gates were opened by the Israeli military. Restrictions on movement hampered the referral system at every stage, between villages, to a town, another district, and beyond.

It is even difficult to get referrals from villages within the same district to clinics. Before the wall, someone from a village with a level 1 clinic who needed more sophisticated services would be referred to another village nearby with those services, or to a hospital in the same district, or a hospital in a different district with specialised services, like from Qalqilya to Nablus or Ramallah or Jerusalem. This type of referral has been completely disrupted, because of access problems, as people can't move easily with the wall, the checkpoints, and the curfews.[10]

### Blocking Specialist Care

Every health system functions on the assumption that there is free passage of patients, doctors and relief teams. [...] Modern health management aims to specialise specific units in specific services. If it were not so each medical centre would be obliged to provide all medical services available in that country.[11]

A public health system for a population of several million should have a large number of primary care centres within communities, complemented by secondary and tertiary care centres in areas accessible to the general population. Intensifying movement restrictions over a period of decades in the West Bank and Gaza Strip made this "difficult, if not impossible".[12] Instead, over 70 per cent of the population faced restrictions to reach secondary and tertiary care.

We are talking about a new geography of health. According to the World Health Organisation system we don't need clinics everywhere; this depends on a number of factors such as population size and distance to facilities.

But, for instance, people in Dhahr al-'Abd used to go to the clinic nearby, which is five minutes away. Now with the Wall, people outside the Wall can't go to clinics inside.

So there is a big dilemma facing the health sector: does each isolated place need their own clinic? For instance in Qalqilya and Salfit, they want their own hospital. But Nablus is only 20 minutes away. So in the future, if the Wall goes up, what will happen to the health system, to all these structures?[13]

The system in the West Bank and Gaza Strip was designed to function according to public health principles, with a hierarchy of primary, secondary, and tertiary services. With freedom of movement, this would function well. Without it, however, the system could not meet health needs. For instance, the greatest need for disability services was in the north of the West Bank, but the services were strongest in the south.[14]

Historically, urban centres, and particularly Jerusalem, served as service points for specialised and emergency care:

> Jerusalem had the largest number of specialised hospitals serving Palestinians, but from 1994 access to these hospitals in East Jerusalem became difficult. If you wanted to get to Jerusalem you needed a permit. This means you have to apply for a permit; you can't just get into your car or a *servis* [shared taxi] and get to Jerusalem. You need to supply reasons for the permit, and even when you provide these you can be refused. Or you get a permit, but it's for the wrong date or time when it's too late.
>
> So from this period on we saw a sharp drop in the occupancy rates of these specialist hospitals, which people used to access from all over the West Bank and Gaza.[15]

Given the high rates of heart disease – the number one cause of death, accounting for 21 per cent of all recorded Palestinian deaths in the West Bank and Gaza Strip – the obstruction of access to Jerusalem facilities was a serious concern. Jerusalem's Saint John's Hospital was the only Palestinian centre for specialised heart care, and al-Maqassed Hospital was a key facility for cardiac emergencies. Beyond heart services, Jerusalem also housed vital provisions for disability, and offered life-saving dialysis.[16]

Without access to Jerusalem or any area within Israel, Palestinian medical personnel were forced to refer their patients to Jordan, Egypt, or further afield. Given the economic situation, this kind of referral was an impossibility for many. More importantly, movement restrictions were increasingly imposed on exiting either area, with a blanket ban on Palestinians leaving either the West Bank or the Gaza Strip, and a starkly reduced number of exceptions.

In 2007, Israeli officials blocked entry to Egypt for all Palestinian patients referred from the Gaza Strip. That year, 282 patients had hoped to find care in Egypt; 32 patients died between October 2007 and March 2008 – all had been denied access to specialist care outside the Gaza Strip.[17]

Similar Israeli denials to outside care were seen in the West Bank. The thousands affected included Rahma Hamed, who was referred to neural specialists to save her baby daughter's sight, but was turned back in July 2011. Intervention by the International Committee of the Red Cross failed to gain Palestinians access. Amal Gomaa required urgent treatment, while facing a number of health complications from her battle with uterine cancer:

> She suffers severe stomach bleeding and chronic pneumonitis, which exceeds the pulmonary crisis. The findings of the radiograms indicate that her condition might develop into a lung fibrosis. This is in addition to [damage to] the cartilage in her left foot.[18]

Amal had already had a panhysterectomy and doctors in the West Bank felt they could not help further; she needed urgent care from specialists outside the West Bank. In 2011, Israeli officials turned back more than 4,000 Palestinians from the border between the West Bank and Jordan.[19]

### Displacing Clinics

> Health services in the occupied Palestinian territory are on the verge of collapse.[20]

This assessment, from the World Health Organisation in 2006, describes the long-term systemic impact of movement restrictions. Without freedom of movement for patients who frequent local clinics, these clinics cannot survive. The case of Dr A., who faced obstacles trying to open and maintain a practice first in a nearby town, and then in his village, shows this process in detail.[21] Dr A. left Palestine for Venezuela with his family in 1968 and returned in 1996 after studying medicine. In the late 1990s he opened his own orthopaedic clinic in Nablus, as he could not get an Israeli-issued ID, and thus could not work for the Palestinian Ministry of Health:

> Before this Intifada there weren't so many problems in moving around. I started my private orthopaedic clinic in Nablus in 1998. I had a car with yellow plates and at that time it took about 20–25 minutes to get there from Marda. I chose Nablus rather than Salfit or Marda, since then they weren't large enough to support the type of specialist equipment I use. You need a big city for that.

Movement restrictions in 2000 forced Dr A. to close his clinic:

> We couldn't use private cars any more and had to travel by *servis* [shared taxi]. Sometimes I had to change *servis* 3 or 4 times, at

Jama'een, Bur'in and then walk and then take another *servis* to Till and then walk again and get another one into Nablus. This was all because the soldiers closed the Huwarra road into Nablus and we had to take a roundabout route through mountains and it was difficult in the winter. You never knew how long it would take to reach Nablus.

And if there were soldiers at the checkpoints, they often shot at people. Sometimes they would close the checkpoint for 3–4 hours or turn us back. These [Jama'een, Bur'in, Till and others] were flying [randomly set up] checkpoints.

My patients dried up as they couldn't reach me and I couldn't reach them. That's why I closed the clinic.

Dr A. describes the lengths he had to go in order to reach patients, after he had returned to his village and had tried to keep a practice open:

After I closed the clinic I came back to try to work in [the village of] Marda. It was hard, as the Israeli soldiers closed both entrances to the village. I stayed without working really, apart from seeing a few patients from neighbouring villages, for about two years.

The little hospital in Salfit, which had an emergency suite, used to ask me sometimes to come and treat people injured in clashes with the Israeli army. Once they sent an ambulance to take me, but the soldiers prevented me from leaving the village. So to get to Salfit, I had to walk for around 45 minutes over very hilly rough ground, and go past settlers from Ariel and Taffuh. It was dangerous.

Salfit is only about seven minutes' drive away – 1 ½ km. But when the road was closed to Palestinians you wouldn't know how long the journey might take. So for those two years I sat at home really, and ate the money relatives sent from Venezuela.

After 2004, when it became easier to travel to Salfit, Dr A. opened a clinic there. But he could not use his own car for what should have been a ten-minute journey. Given movement restrictions that banned the use of private vehicles, he had to use a *servis,* and the journey never took less than 45 minutes, as there were always flying checkpoints. Finally, he moved his work to Ramallah in 2005, since the Za'tara checkpoint was easier and more people could access Ramallah. Dr A.'s situation was typical; by 2004, only 44 per cent of nurses and health workers and 24 per cent of doctors lived locally to their work.[22]

## Cutting Off Supplies

Since 1967, Palestinians in the West Bank and Gaza Strip were forbidden to import medical supplies, and forced instead to purchase all supplies from Israel. Even supplies given by international donors to Palestinians were subject to confiscation and delays. Médecins du Monde reported in November 2003 that Israeli officials had been holding birth delivery kits at the airport for seven months (sent by the United Nations Population Fund, UNFPA). The Ministry of Health in Nablus had been waiting for these kits since February 2003. In 2002, when Palestinian needs were greatest after Israeli attacks, Israeli officials at the airport kept medicines for eight months – until one third of them had expired – that had been sent from Germany, the US, and Italy to the Union of Palestinian Medical Relief Committees.[23]

Over time, Palestinians in the West Bank and Gaza Strip developed a domestic pharmaceutical industry, supplying 45 per cent of needed medications. But this also relied on imported raw materials. Furthermore, much of the production was centralised in key towns like Ramallah, meaning that movement restrictions threatened shortages throughout the West Bank and Gaza. Some essential drugs for life-threatening illnesses were still underproduced: insulin, hormones, and hospital infusions (such as the anesthetic lidocaine, the anti-epileptic phenobarbital, and pentazocine for pain control). Power outages, and especially the cutting of power and fuel to the Gaza Strip for extended periods, threatened the refrigeration of vaccines and hospital infusions.[24]

Palestinian families developed coping mechanisms for supply shortages, stockpiling in anticipation of curfews and incursions. But such options were only open to those who could afford them; others reduced or interrupted their dosages, risking their own health to accommodate the restrictive circumstances.[25] In 2002, when Palestinians in the West Bank were placed under curfew for 23 consecutive days, essential supplies dropped below critical reserve levels – not only in dispensing clinics and pharmacies, but also in the central storage facilities. Heart disease medications were substituted with locally produced generic brands, but these were not necessarily bioequivalents and could lead to increased side effects. Infant formula was also insufficient to meet public needs. Shortages were faced in medications for asthma, epilepsy, hypothyroidism, hypertension, and diabetes, as well as crucial hospital infusions.[26]

Effective health networks in the 1980s brought immunisation levels up to 90 per cent for children aged 18 to 30 months.[27] The intensification of movement restrictions in recent decades, however, caused a significant decline. Vaccines spoiled when Israeli soldiers exposed them to light at checkpoints – a particular issue for BCG (tuberculosis) and measles vaccines.[28] A doctor working in a village near Bethlehem confirmed the attendant risks to the vaccination programme:

> Recently we had to vaccinate all the children against measles. Last year there had already been a vaccination campaign organised by the Ministry of Health. But the boxes were opened so many times by soldiers at checkpoints.
>
> Measles vaccines are very sensitive to heat and sun. So we had to do all the vaccines again in June and July this year. The Wall will have a direct impact on vaccines, because there will be a gate which only opens certain hours.[29]

Other vaccines were damaged in "back to back" delivery, when soldiers force Palestinians to unload goods from one truck into another, on the other side of the checkpoint. A pharmacist in the Salfit area near Nablus described how he transported vaccines in 2004 and the problems caused by checkpoint delays.

> I use an icebox to transport medications such as insulin and other vaccinations. I usually fill it with blocks of ice to keep the medication at the correct temperature. Usually I keep them between 2 and 8 degrees, because over 8 degrees they get spoiled. But the medication is kept cold in the icebox for maximum 3 hours. The delay can affect the temperature of the medication and spoil them.
>
> I spend hours at checkpoints. Sometimes the soldiers send me back, so I have to go over the earth mound with the boxes of medications. Sometimes I reach the clinics with broken vials.
>
> This puts me under great pressure, especially when I have to take all the medication out of the car until they [soldiers] check them one by one, and then I have to put them all back in again. This creates a delay in delivery to the clinics.[30]

By 2003, more than a third of surveyed infants (and in some areas up to 50 per cent) lacked effective antibody protection against measles, a major cause of child deaths.[31]

## 6.2 HEALTH SYSTEM SHUTDOWN

### Taxis into Ambulances

Within the body of international humanitarian law, the 1907 Hague Conventions (Fourth Convention, Article 43) and Fourth Geneva Convention mandate specific provisions for the protection and safe transport of pregnant women, the wounded, sick, and infirm (Fourth Geneva Convention Articles 16 and 20), access to emergency care (Article 17), protection for civilian hospitals (Article 18), safe transport of medical supplies and essential food and clothing (Article 23), and appropriate health services and conditions (including resources necessary for public health and hygiene) (Article 56).

> The provision of medical treatment to the wounded and the immunity of medical teams and hospitals are fundamental principles [...] Since the beginning of the current Intifada [September 2000], [the Israeli human rights organisation] B'Tselem has documented many cases in which the IDF [Israel Defence Forces] violated these principles.[32]

In defiance of international human rights and humanitarian protocols, from September 2000 to March 2006 there were 383 attacks on ambulances, in addition to nearly 1,800 reported cases of ambulances carrying ill and injured people being denied access. The situation was particularly severe from September 2000 to October 2003. During this period the Palestinian Red Crescent Society (PRCS) and Union of Palestinian Medical Relief Committees (UPMRC) reported 991 instances when soldiers stopped their ambulances. Especially since 2000, there is extensive documentation of how Israeli soldiers delayed at checkpoints, obstructed or attacked emergency medical teams and their vehicles.[33]

Cases cited by Médecins du Monde confirm the difficulties and danger Palestinian medical staff routinely experienced when trying to reach patients.

On September 20th 2004 in the morning, I was coming to work to Battir (near Bethlehem) together with another nurse. At the checkpoint the soldiers did not let us pass. We showed them our medical cards but they did not care. They told us we had to go home. We climbed on the hill nearby and they shot tear gas at us. We ran, and after a while we eventually managed to take a car to Battir. As Palestinians, we are used to it. It is our daily life.[34]

Roadblocks and barriers and flying (randomly set up) checkpoints prolonged journeys undertaken on roundabout routes precisely to avoid the fixed checkpoints:

At the start of the Intifada ambulances couldn't enter [Marda] village because the roads were blocked off. They would come to [the edge of the village to] take patients to the Huwarra checkpoint where they would be checked and maybe had to wait a while for another ambulance to meet them at the other side and take [the patients] to Nablus.[35]

Especially at night or during curfews it was impossible to do such journeys.

Testimonies in numerous reports illustrate the arbitrary application of existing protocols regarding medical access, and the ability of soldiers to ignore permits and Israeli-issued documentation:

We are often delayed at Tayassir checkpoint (in the Northern Jordan Valley). Even if the medical teams in the ambulance show the soldiers their cards, they don't care. Our medical cards mean nothing to them. I find that I have less time to do my work, because sometimes we are delayed reaching the clinic. Yet the number of patients has increased; this delay affects the quality of service provided for the patients.[36]

When ambulances were blocked, emergency patients were forced to rely on drivers of ordinary vehicles or taxis:

Social solidarity and resilience have nurtured the Palestinian health response to occupation from pre-hospital care to rehabilitation. When ambulances are unable to reach their targets, the injured and the ill are transported by neighbours, friends and families.[37]

*Figure 6.1*    Amputee through Surda checkpoint, 2003. Surda is one of the "flying" check-points established erratically, but with physical obstacles to movement such as concrete blocks, earth mounds, and trenches dug deep in the middle of the road. Palestinians are forced to walk up to two kilometres, exposed, and can face random live ammunition, tear gas, and sound bombs when Israeli soldiers choose to "close" the checkpoint. Surda is the most crucial passage between the north of the West Bank and the hospitals and care facilities of Ramallah, and further south, Jerusalem. (Tom Kay)

But these ad hoc solutions are insufficient to deal with critically ill patients, births, or transporting dead bodies:

> Once [in December 2004] our ambulances were transporting a pregnant woman in labour. She was expecting twins and this was her first pregnancy after a long time of IVF treatment. She was agitated and it was a complicated pregnancy.
>
> She was stopped at the Dahhiye checkpoint on her way to Jerusalem and the Israelis forbade her entry to Jerusalem by ambulance. They wanted to see a permit but our ambulances at that time were not requesting medical permits on principle. In the end the Israelis decided to call an Israeli ambulance to pick her up from the checkpoint and take her to al-Maqassed hospital.
>
> Although the Israeli ambulance came quickly she had already been delayed 40 minutes at the checkpoint. They refused to take her to al-Maqassed hospital, which was Palestinian. Eventually

the soldiers decided to let her pass the checkpoint and to reach the hospital only by private taxi and not with our ambulance.

So she took the taxi but gave birth in the taxi alone only with the driver. Then she arrived at the hospital with her babies. Imagine this picture. This is one of hundreds of such stories.[38]

### Pregnancy and Childbirth

Prior to 2000, antenatal health care coverage was high, with 95 per cent of births in the West Bank taking place with qualified birth attendants and 92 per cent in hospital. In the period 2001 to 2002, however, home births increased from 8 to 14 per cent, and by mid-2002 only 67 per cent of births were with professional attendants. From the end of 2002 to the end of 2003, the provision of essential reproductive health services decreased from 82.4 per cent to 71 per cent. Women were less able to reach clinics for antenatal care, and without this essential monitoring and care, hospitals had to deal with more obstetric emergencies. Women also faced difficulties in reaching post-natal care, an element so crucial in overcoming the after-effects of trauma or complications.[39]

Movement restrictions and curfews thus led to a significant increase in high-risk, complicated pregnancies, stillbirths, and home deliveries:[40]

In the past five months [of 2004], Health Work Committee [HWC] clinics, in partnership with Médecins du Monde [MDM], have identified 263 pregnant women who have at least one high risk factor for a poor delivery outcome for the mother and baby. These women represent 10% of all antenatal visits who are seen in the HWC/MDM clinics.

There is a looming crisis if the Wall prevents these women from reaching hospital in time to deliver their babies. Premature birth, low birth weight and congenital malformations cause more than half of all infant deaths in the occupied Palestinian territories.[41]

Médecins du Monde reported that, in October 2003, 28.7 per cent of women attending their clinics could not reach hospital for delivery because of closures and curfew. By 2005, more than 30 per cent of births occurred at home, increasing the potentially fatal risk of complications to mothers and babies. More women began asking for caesarean sections, as they were worried they would not be able to access medical help. From 1999 to 2009, caesarean births increased by nearly 10 per cent. With anxiety over blocked access to professional care and facilities, birth had become something fearful rather than something to be celebrated, and this fear also compounded the potential for complications.[42]

From 2000 the statistics on the numbers of births, and the number of deaths associated with births, that occurred at checkpoints gave rise to great concern. The Israeli military issued checkpoint soldiers with very basic birthing kits. Palestinian health agencies developed guides for women on birthing alone, especially at checkpoints. They also trained health care workers for home births, and developed networks of birth attendants who could give telephone advice to family members to guide them through the birth.

In 2005, the United Nations Population Fund (UNFPA), United Nations Relief and Works Agency, and the World Health Organisation submitted data to the UN General Assembly on the issue of birth and death at checkpoints.[43] In this report the UNFPA stated that between 2001 and mid-2005 they had recorded more than 70 cases of "women in labour who were delayed at checkpoints, resulting in unattended and risky roadside births, causing maternal as well as newborn deaths". And in 2007 the Palestinian Ministry of Health reported to the UN that between 2000 and 2006, in addition to 69 births at checkpoints, 10 per cent of pregnant women in labour were delayed for two to four hours on the road to the maternity facility, whereas the average time without roadblocks to reach health facilities was 15 to 30 minutes.[44]

In a case reported by Amnesty International, on August 26, 2003, Rula Ashtiya was forced to give birth on the ground, on a dirt road by the Beit Furik checkpoint, after Israeli soldiers denied her passage:

> We took a taxi and got off before the checkpoint because cars are not allowed near the checkpoint and we walked the rest of the way; I was in pain. At the checkpoint there were several soldiers; they were drinking coffee or tea and ignored us. Daoud (her husband) approached to speak to the soldiers and one of them threatened him with his weapon. Daoud spoke to them in Hebrew; I was in pain and felt I was going to give birth there and then; I told Daoud who translated what I said to the soldiers but they did not let us pass.
>
> I was lying on the ground in the dust and I crawled behind a concrete block by the checkpoint to have some privacy and gave birth there, in the dust, like an animal. I held the baby in

my arms and she moved a little but after a few minutes she died in my arms.[45]

Her husband had pleaded with the soldiers:

> I spoke to them in Hebrew; I know Hebrew because I used to work in Israel; they understood what I was saying but did not let us pass. After the baby was born Rula screamed, then after a while she screamed that the baby died. She was crying. I burst into tears and ran toward the cars on the other side of the checkpoint, ignoring the soldiers.
>   I brought a taxi and went back to Rula; I felt so bad to see her in such condition; she was holding the baby in her arms, covered in blood and the umbilical cord was on the ground, in the dust and still attached and I had to cut it with a stone; I didn't have anything else to cut it with. Then I picked up Rula in my arms and she was holding the baby and I carried her to the car and we went to the hospital. Rula and I are still suffering a lot.

## Soldiers into Diagnosticians

From 2000 to 2003, 94 people died at checkpoints waiting to get to hospital, and more than 83 people died because they could not access emergency health care or because of lack of treatment for chronic disease, including 27 children, and 19 newborns. A study by the World Health Organisation found that nearly 64 per cent of people needing kidney dialysis treatment had no access to care in the summer of 2002, and 43 per cent in the subsequent six months. For the same time periods, access to chemotherapy was blocked for more than 65 per cent, and 29 per cent of patients, respectively. And for those with diabetes, 43 per cent in the first period and 15.6 per cent in the second could not reach help.[46]

The case of 34-year-old J.A.M., diagnosed with renal failure in 1997, illustrates the hurdles to evade the constant danger of a missed treatment. After a failed kidney transplant, he needed dialysis treatment three times a week:

> When there were dirt barricades blocking the roads out of Marda in 2003, my brother would call the ambulance and they would wait on the other side of the barrier. My brother would carry me across the barrier for about five metres to the ambulance. The checkpoints often made us very late for the appointments. There were problems at Huwarra and also with flying checkpoints.

Sometimes they kept me waiting at the checkpoint for 4–5 hours. They would check my ID and the ambulance driver's.

Probably around 2–3 times they wouldn't let me pass the checkpoint and get to Nablus. Everyone in Marda has a Tulkarem ID and they said that people with this ID weren't allowed to go to Nablus. This was even though I always carry papers with me – hospital appointment and reports. But they are always changing the soldiers, and it depends on their mood whether they will let you through. Those times I still managed to get to Nablus but [once I was there] I had to come back to Marda and call a private ambulance to get me [home] there.

I have never had to miss a treatment. But if I did miss a treatment it would be serious and could lead to blood poisoning and death.[47]

J.A.M is typical of many such patients who function with regular treatment but who could die of self-toxification within weeks without it. This happened to Sabri 'Abd al-Qader, who died from kidney failure at 40 in October 2001. He had been delayed at a checkpoint, and was attempting to walk his way to hospital in Tulkarem. His friend Abu Ali explained:

Sabri needed dialysis at the hospital, so he used to travel to the city all the time. When they closed all of the roads (in 2003) he couldn't reach the city or the hospital. Sabri tried on a number of occasions to cross the checkpoint but soldiers refused "because he didn't look sick". As Sabri said: Of course he didn't look sick. As long as he had dialysis he was healthy. That was the point.[48]

Soldiers and commanders had assumed the role of medical diagnostician, with fatal consequences. Dr Scaafi cites another case from May 2002, of a young woman of 21 from the village of Qibya (northwest of Ramallah) who needed dialysis three times a week and suffered renal failure. "She experienced renal failure on May 22nd but the soldiers completely denied her access to the hospital in Ramallah. She died the same day."[49]

Given prolonged periods of movement restriction, people with chronic conditions – that could be controlled with regular access to medical support – increasingly transferred to hospital, with implications for both the individuals and the scarce hospital resources:

One of the major objectives of our mobile clinics is to try to control chronic conditions as much as possible, like diabetes, neo cardiac infractions and cancer, to prevent complications. It really is a vital service. We provide medications, and do blood and urine tests. But given the movement restrictions, we increasingly try to refer the more serious cases to hospitals.[50]

A study of the effects of movement restrictions, conducted in three hospital emergency departments in Bethlehem and Nablus over a one-week period in January 2005, found that 18 per cent of the 2,228 people seeking emergency assistance, or 394 people, were delayed en route. Only 13 per cent of those not delayed were hospitalised, and most of the rest could return home following treatment. In contrast, 32 per cent of those delayed were hospitalised.[51]

The higher hospital admission rate in this group suggests that restrictions in access to hospital services influence the severity of the medical conditions presented [...]

One possible explanation for this is that people who have to pass checkpoints live at a greater distance from the hospital. The need to pass a checkpoint might discourage sick people from seeking medical care for fear of being denied access or held back. When they eventually do seek help, their condition has deteriorated and admission is needed.[52]

By 2007, 36 per cent of health care providers said that many patients could not access services. More than half of the providers reported mobile team delays and problems in getting medicine for people with chronic conditions.[53]

### Doctors into Human Shields

Problems facing medical personnel were not limited to obstruction of movement; the Israeli army detained, arrested, used as human shields, beat, and killed some emergency staff. During 2002 and 2003, under the most extreme conditions of curfew, delivering medications to patients was highly dangerous and complex. Whenever possible, and often under fire, teams of medical staff, volunteers, and ambulances delivered medicine for patients with chronic diseases, as well as formula milk and food. Dr Scaafi, Director of Emergency Services at the Union of Palestinian Medical Relief Committees, described these efforts:

At that time we provided a range of services to people, like transporting people to hospital, giving out medicine, checking people in their houses and giving medication, supporting families with food and [infant] milk. We did this by walking and with ambulances. It was very dangerous.

I divided my team into five teams. Each team contained a doctor, a health provider, volunteers and 2–3 internationals. They moved around together as a group, either by car or on foot. They used to be stopped by the Israelis and some were beaten. Some of the internationals were arrested, and I remember two of them were forcibly deported: taken to the airport and put on planes. We worked from the early morning till late at night every day.[54]

Dr Scaafi related his 2002 experience, when Israeli soldiers took him as a human shield:

They took me as a human shield on the third or fourth day of the invasion. I was here at the emergency centre. We had a lot of volunteers and internationals and emergency teams – about 40 people. The soldiers came and asked to speak to me. When I came down, they told me that they wanted to check the building and the building next door, as they were searching for wanted people. I said, "You can check any time."

They said everyone had to leave the building, including the four families who live in the building. They gave us 15 minutes. Then they decided to take me as a human shield to check the buildings. We went through our building, and they put explosives on all the closed doors and detonated them. They took me next door and did the same. I had to stand in front of them, and enter each room first with the dog, and when I saw there was no one in the office or the apartment, the soldiers came in. It took about four hours. And they didn't find anything or arrest anyone.

I had very bad feelings. First of all it was very dangerous for me – suppose that someone was in one of the offices or houses and started to shoot. It was violence against a doctor – not just anyone, violence against the doctor who was leading the emergency team. In addition, during those four hours, the emergency services couldn't do anything. They were all waiting outside the building until the Israeli soldiers finished checking them. I had the medications with me in storage.[55]

For all medical personnel, movement restrictions and the dangers of Israeli military intervention made it impossible to plan, were stressful, and ultimately affected the amount and quality of medical care. As a means of coping, health providers developed mobile clinics in the 1980s, like those described above by Dr Scaafi, to reach patients. When mobile clinics were blocked, their staff often carried heavy equipment by hand through checkpoints.

> We wanted to develop the capacity of villages to meet their own health needs, especially through providing high quality nursing training for village women, based on the Latin American experience of training rural health workers. So far [in 2005], we have trained 274 women from 102 villages, out of a potential 600 localities.
>
> It's a diploma course, which is accredited by the Ministries of Higher Education and of Health. Last year, all the 22 women we trained are from villages around the Wall and from Bedouin communities.[56]

But even the mobile clinics in which these rural health workers operated faced challenges reaching patients. For instance, from January 2004 to April 2005, mobile clinics attempted to reach isolated villages through gates in the Wall 18 times; they were denied access on 15 occasions and delayed several hours on three occasions.[57] It was practically impossible for Palestinian mobile clinics to access some isolated clusters of villages in Jenin and south of Qalqilya; only Israeli or international organisations could get through. Even this was impossible, however, for villages (like Nu'man, described in the previous chapter) where access was forbidden except to those with identity documents linking them to the village.

Conclusion

> The right to health of residents of the Occupied Territories is bound up with the right to freedom of movement, since this determines their access to healthcare.[58]

The structure of a health system relies on mobility to retain an effective range of primary, secondary, and tertiary care services. But in Palestine, the Israeli military denies access to patients, personnel, ambulances, and medical supplies – with immediate and long-term impact on women, children, and vulnerable people, despite demonstrated resilience and coping mechanisms.

Statistics, reports, and cases all point to a catalogue of human casualties that can be traced directly to restricted movement. The right to movement becomes increasingly medicalised, as the reason to pass of last resort. In the attempt to work around the barriers, roles become subverted: taxis into ambulances, soldiers into medical diagnosticians, and doctors into human shields.

The snapshot this chapter provides – of the implications of movement restrictions on Palestinian access to health services – demonstrates that the basic human right to health has, in very broad terms, been degraded. The various international legal provisions to respect and protect civilians seeking health services, as well as health care staff seeking to provide services, appear to have little meaning in the context of identity documentation and a layered system of movement restrictions.

The evidence highlights how an under-resourced health system has struggled to maintain provision. But as with education, discussed next, aspirations to improve are being constantly undermined.

# 7
# Education

The first part of this chapter looks at obstacles to student and teacher movement, and how each developed innovative but ever-stretched coping mechanisms. For instance, in 2002 over a quarter of a million Palestinian children could not reach their schools. And in 2004, one third of Palestinian children faced physical obstacles on their way to school.

Then we look at the impact of direct attacks on schools, schoolchildren, and teachers by the Israeli military and colonists, during the first years of the new millennium. These assaults took a toll on what had once been the region's leader in education, and on the emotional and psychological wellbeing of students and teachers.

## 7.1   COLLAPSING EDUCATION STRUCTURES

### Blocking Students

> Children adapt and are resilient. But do we want them to adapt, to think it's normal to have to go through checkpoints to get to school?[1]

For schoolchildren, mobility restrictions were especially frightening, as school journeys and arriving safely were unpredictable. UNICEF reported in 2004 that, "On any given day, one third of all school-aged children are struggling to the classroom through checkpoints, earth mounts, bars and trenches".[2] On their journeys to school, children and teachers were routinely tear-gassed and harassed. Children were present when soldiers fired guns, and children regularly experienced humiliation or saw soldiers humiliating and insulting adults. In 2005, the Palestine Monitoring Group observed that:

> Israeli restrictions on Palestinian freedom of movement such as checkpoints, curfew and closures of roads, Wall gates, schools and Palestinian locales, have directly and drastically obstructed access to education.[3]

By 2003, around 17 per cent of Palestinian households in the West Bank had moved for education reasons. In the period 2003 to 2004 school dropout rates rose, as students had to transfer to other schools given movement restrictions.[4]

> [Resistance] is all the kinds of coping strategies women have to do. They have to find a way to get the school closer for the kids when the school year starts. They have to find a way to extend a small bit of money to cover a large – a whole week of eating. They have to borrow. They have to look for all sorts of social welfare.[5]

Although schools, education administrators, and nongovernmental organisations struggled to keep schools functioning, it proved increasingly difficult to maintain academic standards given such ongoing disruptions. Teachers could not know from day to day whether a school would open. The Palestinian Ministry of Education tried to encourage schools to stay open even during curfew, but in such situations head teachers were faced with very difficult decisions, since they could not guarantee the safety of teachers or students.

In October 2002, UNICEF, whilst acknowledging that most Palestinian children had returned to school, noted that nearly a quarter of a million children and 9,300 teachers could still not reach their regular classrooms. At least 560 schools were closed because of Israeli military curfews, closures, and home confinements. Between September 2000 and May 2004, such measures closed 1,289 schools. The Israeli army also used military orders to close down schools and universities. In Hebron for instance, in 2003, military orders closed Hebron University and the Palestine Polytechnic for eight months, affecting 6,000 students; in the same year, ten Hebron schools were closed.[6]

In 2002, the Wall began separating 22 areas from their schools. By 2004, in three districts of the northern West Bank alone, 2,898 children were affected, trying to reach twelve different schools.[7] Where schools were still within reach, journey times were greatly prolonged, permits were required, and students were subject to daily searches at the Wall gates. The United Nations repeated its warnings regarding the effects of movement restrictions on the education system and on Palestinian children: "Access to education is directly correlated with Israeli closure and curfew policies and military operations. Teachers and pupils cannot reach their schools."[8]

Between September 2003 and June 2005, the Israeli army closed districts, roads, Wall gates, and schools on 93 different occasions, mainly affecting the northern West Bank and also Hebron. Qalqilya, for instance, which had three closures between 2003 and 2004, experienced 26 in the first half of 2005, since a large number of Palestinian communities were in "closed zone" areas, and because of extensive searches and delays at the gates to the Wall.[9]

Accessing universities was equally difficult. For instance, for two and a half years (between June 2001 and December 2003), the Surda roadblock on the road between Ramallah and Birzeit University severely hampered access to the university. The Wall also affected student intake at all the West Bank universities, and particularly at al-Quds University Jerusalem, where the Wall divorced the main campus from the city of Jerusalem, containing 36 per cent of its students.

### Blocking Teachers

> The numbers of schooldays lost can only be roughly estimated, but it is important to point out, that teachers are facing the same or even worse problems in reaching school as their pupils do, and frequent losses of classes are due to the inability of teachers to reach school.[10]

During the 2002 to 2003 school year, the United Nations Relief and Works Agency for Palestine Refugees (UNRWA), which runs 95 schools in the West Bank, serving more than 60,000 children, reported that on average every day 9 per cent of their teachers (145 teachers) were unable to reach school, and that children lost 1,475 days of teaching. During 2003 to 2004, curfew affected students in 26 per cent of government schools losing 1,152 school days in the West Bank and Gaza Strip.[11]

In Qalqilya, a town in the north of the West Bank completely encircled by the Wall, some teachers who previously took five to ten minutes to reach their schools now had to travel 25 kilometres to get through a checkpoint which was often closed or blocked for hours.

N., a teacher living in Bethlehem's Aida refugee camp, described the routine difficulties teachers encountered during 2002 and 2003 when trying to get to school. It was not only the extended journeys, but also having to cope with the arbitrary behaviour of the soldiers controlling the checkpoints.[12] Her account also illustrates the extraordinary lengths to which teachers went, in order to reach schools:

In September 2001 I started teaching in a primary school in al-Ram, just beyond the Qalandiya checkpoint. My sister also taught there and we would travel together from Ramallah. This was a really difficult checkpoint as the soldiers would check everyone and stop people passing, so we used to go round the checkpoint through the quarry below. It was a difficult rocky path and often the soldiers would spot us and run after us. To get to school for 8am we had to leave home at 6:30am; normally the journey should take around 15 minutes.

Once some soldiers stopped me and my sister in the quarry and said, "Give us your IDs." I said, "I don't have my ID." So a soldier grabbed my bag and took out my ID. They sent us through the checkpoint and made us wait for two hours. Then they said, "Today you're not getting your ID, come back tomorrow morning at 7:00."

So of course we had to go home. Usually when they caught us like that we couldn't reach the school. This would happen a lot – one day we would get through and for two days we couldn't.

At one stage the soldiers were only letting schoolchildren through the checkpoint. I asked a woman soldier, "How can you let the students through but not the teachers; I have a teachers' ID?" She replied, "That's the law – shut up."

I thought about what I could do. Because I look young, I decided to dress in a school uniform, leave my teachers' ID at home and carry my 14-year-old niece's birth certificate. When I got to the checkpoint I would wave at the other teachers and sail through. I would arrive at the school and everyone would say, "Miss Nisreen is wearing a school uniform."

This worked for two weeks but then the soldiers started stopping all the students who looked a bit tall. So I had to choose between either going through the quarry, or taking a longer more expensive roundabout route through Birzeit village. We often couldn't get back to Ramallah, as the quarry or the Birzeit roads would be closed, so I had to stay over with a teacher who lived near the school.[13]

Understandably, such daily experience wears people down and many decide to move nearer their place of work in the hope that journeys will be easier. N. describes what happened when she tried to work nearer her home in Bethlehem in Autumn 2002:

After 18 months in Ramallah, I decided to get a teaching job in Bethlehem because often when I tried to return to Bethlehem on Thursdays for the weekend they would close the roads. I could only get to see my family every two weeks. The longest time I stayed in Ramallah without returning to Bethlehem was during the long siege in 2002 – I was stuck in Ramallah for 50 days. Of course during that period it was really hard, as my family was in Bethlehem and we were very worried about each other.

The closest place where I could find a job was in al-Sawahira al-Sharqiya and I moved back home in October 2002. I thought it would be easier, but every single day they would stop me and three other teachers from Bethlehem at the "container" [highly militarised civilian] checkpoint. Sometimes they would stop everyone passing. Sometimes they would let one older teacher through, but not us younger ones. So in the school they would ask, "Why could so-and-so arrive and not the others?" At the school no one could really understand the situation unless they actually really lived the checkpoint experience.

So we decided that we had to find other ways of reaching the school. Of course the mountains of Wadi al-Nar [the "valley of fire", so named because of the high number of vehicles falling off the road and down its semi-arid cliffs] are very high and have countless paths, and we tried many of them! We had to leave at 6:15 to get to school for 8:00. At that stage the soldiers weren't accepting the teachers' IDs that were issued from the Palestinian Ministry of Education. But sometimes even if I left very early, I wouldn't get to school on time, as the soldiers had a flying checkpoint at Beit Sahour. If I didn't make it to school on time, the school would ask me to make up the hours as I had to finish the syllabus.

In 2002, I couldn't reach the school at all for a total of six weeks.

Sometimes the soldiers would ask really stupid questions, or they would say, "Abu Dis is closed today; no one is allowed to go, just return to Bethlehem." But even when we were leaving to go back, they would stop the cars returning to Bethlehem from going through Wadi al-Nar. Then people had to walk the whole length of Wadi al-Nar until you got to Abu Dis – this would take around two hours. And the army was sometimes moving across the mountains, taking people's IDs, and maybe keeping you there for the whole day, or they would fire tear gas.

I have a colleague with a Jerusalem ID, so she is forbidden to go through Wadi al-Nar or Bethlehem. About a month ago, soldiers picked her up at Wadi al-Nar and beat her, [then] gave her a big fine. They told her that if she tried to pass again, she would be put in prison. So she has decided to live with her family in Jerusalem and find a job there. But her husband lives in Bethlehem.[14]

## Localising Teacher Recruitment and Training

Unlike government schools, the schools run by the United Nations Relief and Works Agency for Palestine Refugees (UNRWA) had the advantage of already being relatively decentralised into refugee camps and villages. This enabled localisation of recruitment, as an adaptation strategy in response to increased movement restrictions. But the new strategy came at great cost to the quality of education.

Beginning in 2000, UNRWA began attempts to replace teachers who could not reach schools due to movement restrictions. In doing so, however, they reduced the pool of applicants for each school by narrowing the geographic area: UNRWA had previously divided the management of their educational activities in the West Bank into three areas – North, South, and Jerusalem; after 2000, these areas were divided into seven, five, and six sub-areas, respectively. Teacher recruitment then proceeded in these isolated 18 sub-areas.[15] The head of the UNRWA's education program described how, before 2000, "if a teacher was the best in a certain subject and lived in Nablus, and there was a vacant post in Tulkarem, that teacher would commute to Tulkarem".[16] Although movement restrictions in the 1980s and 1990s had made that difficult, it had still been possible. After 2000, however:

We suffered severely from movement restrictions on teachers, who were used to travelling freely within each of the three areas. From 2000, we couldn't use the pool [of applicants for teaching positions], as so many teachers couldn't reach their schools. In 2000/2001 when internal closure was imposed – we lost 60–70,000 teachers days – i.e. out of 2000 teachers, around 500 (25%) couldn't reach schools.[17]

In selecting teachers, the UNRWA had to prioritise teachers' ability to reach the school, over their relevant teaching experience or academic specialisation:

So if I get someone in area x who is really an excellent teacher but the vacancy is in area y, I can't put them in area y. And if someone is satisfactory and lives in area y, then that person gets the job.

As we had to recruit a lot of teachers we couldn't use our normal procedures, the first priority was to find teachers willing to work under the emergency. As it was an emergency it wasn't a secure job. But because of movement restrictions people couldn't find other jobs, so we were able to find people, including trainee teachers.[18]

Trainee teachers were the stop-gap solution in a number of areas. Because of movement restrictions the UNRWA was forced to re-allocate teachers closer to their homes, and then search for substitutes.

We couldn't do this all at once; we had to do this wherever we could, and wait for teachers to come up, and [we would try to] match locations with specialisations, and so on.

But in some remote areas we couldn't find teachers with the required specialisations, like areas deep in the south of the West Bank, or the four most western West Bank villages near the Green Line.

So we have to do everything possible, like finding new graduates to get them into those schools, and then transfer the [original] teachers to their own localities. But that also affects the quality of the education.[19]

Compromising teacher quality was not the only problem. Students and teachers did not know one another, having been flung together for short periods at a time. Furthermore, the new arrangements were not immune from movement restrictions; sometimes even the new, more closely located teachers could not reach schools due to movement restrictions. Finally, the entire restructuring of the educational system to match movement restrictions was a considerable financial drain, drawing heavily on the UNRWA's much-needed Emergency and General Funds.

R.H., head teacher of the UNRWA secondary girls school in the Al Amari refugee Camp in Ramallah, illustrates what happens on the ground:

There are now only two teachers who come from outside Ramallah, and they meet difficulties daily. They come from villages near Ramallah (Arura and Deir Dibwan) [...] but if there are flying checkpoints [at Atara, Surda, and Ein Yabrud], then it's difficult and they will be late.[20]

*Figure 7.1*   The long walk through the checkpoint to reach schools and university, 2003. Israeli soldiers blocked the Surda intersection with heavy earth mounds and trenches bulldozed into the road, forcing Palestinians out of their vehicles and into the dust and mud. The intersecting road still serves as a thoroughfare for colonists and the Israeli army, while Palestinians are forbidden on it. When the checkpoint is closed, Palestinians are forbidden even to cross the colonist-only road. (Tom Kay)

Therefore, by 2005, of the 30 teachers working at the Al Amari school only two came from outside the Ramallah area.

For the few UNRWA teachers who continued to commute, and the many others in government or private schools, settling down to teach after gruelling journeys affected teachers' performance. N. from Aida camp describes how checkpoints forced her to disembark with her belongings and walk at several points in her commute:

The journey to school is very stressful. There would be pressure at the checkpoints, being stopped, and seeing others prevented from passing ... and you would also arrive at school very tired indeed. Also there was the weather to contend with – rain and sun. As a teacher you want to give your all to the students. But if I don't feel good, I can't do that.[21]

The UNRWA was also forced to decentralise teacher-training where possible, or work without it when necessary.[22] Foregoing teacher-training was a problem common to all educational sectors: public, private, and refugee.

> Because of movement restrictions, people who need to visit schools like school supervisors waste a lot of time waiting at checkpoints. Out of an eight-hour working day, they could wait four hours at the checkpoint.[23]

Whereas previously regional supervisors might have been able to visit a number of schools in one day, after 2000 each journey was unpredictable and often vastly inflated due to long waits at checkpoints. It was difficult for teachers and school counsellors to undertake professional development activities – such as training, meetings, and discussions with other teachers – as it was impossible to access venues or, during periods of intense pressure, teachers needed to return home.[24]

### Localising Educational Activities

> Military occupations are another appreciable curb on the human right to education, the most egregious example being the Israeli–Palestinian conflict.[25]

Children have a right to education, and to have their interests as the "primary consideration" in all actions concerning them.[26] Before intensifying movement restrictions in the West Bank in the 1990s, the Israeli military targeted education in other ways: censoring books and teachers (for example, replacing all reference to "Palestine" with "Israel", back to the Crusades), prohibiting teachers' unions, detaining teachers and students, and closing schools and universities for up to four years at a time.[27] Under these closures and later movement restrictions, Palestinians established home schools, as joint efforts between neighbourhood committees, government, private schools, and schools run by the UNRWA. When the events of the 1980s repeated themselves in the 1990s and subsequent decades – mass arrests, curfews, closing of schools and universities – Palestinians again responded with similar coping strategies and resilience.

Two villages, spaced a mere three kilometres apart, illustrate the compounding of movement restrictions over time, its effects on education, and how Palestinians adapted the educational system to keep going. Kafr al-Deek and Deir Ballout lie near the 1949 Armistice line, northwest of the town of Ramallah. Families were spread across both villages, and accustomed to visiting one another daily. In 1989, the Israeli army erected a checkpoint at Deir Ballout's entrance. Until 2000, children in both villages went to the Kafr al-Deek high school, or to Qarawa and Biddya, for *tawjihi* (matriculation) exams. Public transport was scarce, so students shared whatever private transport they could find.[28] The short-distance journey took on average two hours, from 5:30 a.m. to 7:30 a.m. Prior to 2000, villagers also accessed health services and acquired supplies in Nablus. In 2000, however, the army gated Deir Ballout, eventually trapping it between the Wall and the 1949 Armistice line. Cut off from Kafr al-Deek and thus at a loss for secondary education, Deir Ballout tried to start its own high school, with teachers coming from Kafr al-Deek:

> But because of the checkpoint and the roads, [the teachers] couldn't always get [to Deir Ballout] and were often absent. So now all the teachers come from Deir Ballout and al-Zawiya [another encircled village in the enclave].[29]

Similar situations were repeated across the West Bank:

> Right now the Israeli military is preventing thousands of Palestinian children and teachers from attending school. [...] A generation of Palestinian children is being denied their right to education.[30]

During curfews it was impossible for students to reach their schools. For instance, in 2002, for over five weeks between April 2 and May 10, Bethlehem was under 24-hour curfew with only a few hours' relief every few days. In response to this, the Bethlehem Directorate of Education drew up an emergency plan so that twelfth grade students due to take their *tawjihi* exams could study in certain centres. The location of these centres was not publicised, in order to prevent the Israeli army disrupting them. They managed to ensure that 900 students – out of 2,150 *tawjihi* students living in areas under curfew – got lessons in these centres. But this was not easy, as both students and teachers risked breaking the curfew, and had to study and teach in unfamiliar centres.[31]

The Tamer Institute, a nongovernmental organisation that promotes children's literacy, felt a particular responsibility to respond to the needs of children during the extended periods of curfew in 2001 to 2003. The organisation had received funding to publish eight books translated from English and to run workshops with children in different parts of the West Bank and Gaza. Because of closure during that period it was impossible to run these workshops, so Tamer decided to publish 14 books (50,000 copies each) using local children's writers and editors for the additional six books. They distributed most of the books to government and UNRWA schools. They also included these books in the 3,000 educational kits they distributed to children in the areas most affected by closure, such as Hebron, Jenin, and the western Ramallah villages. These were children who either could not get to school, or if they did were particularly traumatised given the number of checkpoints they had to negotiate.

Some Tamer staff also tried to run some local informal schools during this period, and at the height of the curfew period, in March and April 2002, ran education activities with children in apartment blocks and libraries. "During this period it was amazing, whenever curfew was lifted children used to come to libraries in different areas – up to 50 used to come."[32]

As Palestinians had done when movement restrictions and curfews peaked in the 1980s, they again began to turn their homes into schools, as a means of coping with the restrictions of the 1990s, 2000s, and the subsequent period.

## 7.2   EDUCATION SYSTEM SHUTDOWN

### Attacks by Freely-moving Israeli Soldiers and Colonists

I was in Hebron recently and saw the checkpoint in the city that so many have to get through. You know, if they live in H2, they have to go across the roofs.[33]

The situation of Palestinians in the Old City of Hebron (in an area designated by the Israeli army as "H2") has become notorious, as not only do they have to contend with frequent closure or curfew, but they are increasingly surrounded by Jewish settlers illegally living in and continuously colonising more of their city. It became routine for schoolchildren in the Old City of al-Khalil (Hebron) to have to take circuitous routes across rooftops in order to reach school:

> A woman who lives at this house would have an old rickety ladder that she would put out – and that was before the staircase came along – and she would place it on the side of this metal shed. The children would climb down and come out of her house.
>
> What made it so unique was that sometimes the kids had to climb over certain rooftops in the Old City just to get to her house, to be able to come through her house, and then walk down, climb down that ladder and come out, to come onto the streets. [International observers] would stand here to make sure that the children were protected, that they weren't being threatened by the settlers or the army in regards to where they could and couldn't go, to try to get to the school.[34]

This homeowner became known as the "ladder-lady".

During the academic years 2003 to 2005 the Israeli army or settlers were responsible for 180 assaults on or near schools including firing tear-gas canisters, assaulting students or teachers, physically damaging schools, or opening fire. Most of these incidents took place in Nablus, Hebron, Jenin, and northern Gaza.[35]

From September 2000 to June 2004, the Israeli army broke into or shelled 298 schools, destroying 282. In addition, eight universities were broken into or shelled by the Israeli military, a further 97 schools were vandalised or bulldozed, and yet another 48 schools were turned into military bases.[36]

I.B., who teaches at the Palestinian Open University, describes the period when one of her daughters sat her matriculation exams in 2002:

> When my younger daughter was studying for her *tawjihi* here in Ramallah, it was one of the worst years of my life. Imagine in the same city, where I was living in Balloua – it was under occupation for seven months – while the rest of the city was free. The northern part of Ramallah was occupied by the Israelis, while the rest of Ramallah wasn't. So we had soldiers all the time in the neighbourhood.
>
> At one point, at the checkpoint near the City Inn Hotel (near the city centre), every day youngsters used to come and throw stones at the soldiers, and there was shooting. So we couldn't sleep at night. To go to school every day in Ramallah [my daughter]

had to go through the checkpoint. Sometimes she couldn't find any transport to our house and we couldn't use our car.

Sometimes for days our house was under curfew. Sometimes she had to go and sleep with a friend, who lived in a safe part of Ramallah. I thought many times of renting somewhere else in Ramallah, but I couldn't afford that.

That was a very decisive year for her. She couldn't afford to be absent from schools; she was in the science stream, and if she missed a class, it was serious.[37]

In some cases children were forced to sit exams whilst their village or town was under curfew or there was gunfire near the school. I.B. recalls how, on the final day of her daughter's *tawjihi* exams in 2003, Israeli soldiers did their best to disrupt proceedings:

On the Monday of the final *tawjihi* exams in 2003 the Israelis had patrols outside the classrooms at the school fence. The classroom was right near the fence. The soldiers were just outside the windows. Imagine sitting for your physics exam and having soldiers shooting randomly just under the window. They were doing it on purpose.[38]

Between October 2000 and February 2003, 132 students were killed and 2,500 were injured on their way to and from school. For the academic years 2003 to 2004 and 2004 to 2005, the Israeli army killed 174 students and seven schoolteachers, and injured 426 students and 28 teachers in government schools. Some were injured or killed whilst inside schools.[39]

### Undermining the Ability to Focus and Study

Education shall be directed to the full development of the human personality and to the strengthening of respect for human rights and fundamental freedoms.

Article 26(2), Universal Declaration of Human Rights 1948

While movement restrictions seriously impeded children and youths' learning environments, nevertheless the West Bank and Gaza Strip continued to lead the region in terms of equality in enrolment (by gender, rural/urban community, income, and refugee status). In 2006, the World Bank noted considerable Palestinian accomplishments in education in the West Bank and Gaza Strip. The literacy rate among 15 to 24-year-olds was over 98 per cent; and nearly 59 per cent of young Palestinians aged 10 to 24 said (in 2003) that their first concern was education.[40]

The West Bank and Gaza Strip offered eleven universities, eleven technical colleges (with four-year diplomas), and 19 community colleges (with two-year diplomas).[41] By 2006, over 40 per cent of 18 to 24-year-olds were registered in these institutions. Meanwhile primary and secondary schools in 2005 enrolled over a million students: 70 per cent attended government schools, 6 per cent private schools, and 24 per cent UNRWA schools.[42] Yet, the World Bank added:

> [T]hese achievements are all the more remarkable if it is taken into consideration that since 2001, the restriction of movement of people and goods imposed by the Israeli closures, curfews and incursions have severely disrupted the daily life for all segments of the population in the West Bank and Gaza, and in particular for school children and young people.[43]

To find the effects of these restrictions, educational managers looked past the raw enrolment figures and more closely at the quality of education and the learning environment. They found that students were often absent-minded and panicked by the sound of ambulances or army jeeps. The United Nations reported concerns that children were "unable to concentrate on their studies".[44] Local studies revealed that:

> Children find it increasingly difficult to focus and learn in the current environment when schools are at risk of continuous disruptions. This is particularly severe during periods of military invasion or closure.[45]

Children often became worried by a sudden quiet outside, thinking curfew had been imposed, and they requested frequent breaks. A 2003 Save the Children survey noted an increase in violence and bullying in the classroom.[46] Teachers felt that students had become more violent toward one another, and boys interviewed felt that teachers smacked them more. Other information, obtained through group discussions with students in five West Bank and Gaza schools in 2005, highlighted two key concerns for students: the immediate effects of incidents arising from movement restrictions – like curfews, incursions, soldier violence, harassment at checkpoints or the Wall – and the resulting psychological impact.[47]

> According to students, Israeli military and settler activity in the occupied Palestinian territories has generated a systematic lack of concentration, a lack of comfort and desire to participate in the class, and an inability to study with colleagues at home because of curfew and closures.
>
> Perhaps more importantly, students conveyed that they have been experiencing involuntary bed-wetting, insomnia, stuttering and refusing to sleep alone in their rooms.[48]

The direct impact of this was seen in exam results – one of the most tangible indicators of education standards. UNRWA statistics for 2003 to 2004 showed a 35 per cent decline in overall pass rates for sixth-grade maths, a 33.5 per cent decline for fourth-grade science, and a 12.4 per cent decline in eighth-grade Arabic, compared to 2000 to 2001.[49] And despite the impressive milestones noted by the World Bank, the United Nations began warning in 2004 that, "A decade of efforts to improve the education of children is under serious threat as registration levels have declined and children are postponing higher education".[50]

Shift teaching and overcrowded classrooms became routine, due to school closures and teachers' inability to reach schools. As a result, the United Nations observed, "The quality of education is compromised and continues to deteriorate as teachers fail to meet curricula requirements".[51] Teachers under pressure to complete the syllabus within a certain amount of time reverted to traditional teaching methods such as rote learning. Also, because of time pressures, core syllabus subjects took priority over non-compulsory subjects such as art and physical education – precisely the subjects that could encourage self-expression and help relieve stress and anxiety. Finally, time pressure reduced teachers' ability to give extra attention to students with special needs.[52]

Another by-product of movement restrictions was that schools did far less extramural activities than previously. Parents were loathe to let their children stay late, and the teachers themselves were tired and keen to get home, in anticipation of possible problems on the journey. This was especially so during curfew. Moreover, the knock-on effects of movement restrictions on the whole economy affected teachers and their sense of being under pressure:

All of the teachers have different problems. For example, their husbands may have stopped working, as they can no longer work in Israel, or their business which relied on transfer of goods has folded. My husband, for instance, is a dentist, and now he earns a third less than he did before 2000, as the patients can no longer travel into Ramallah from the nearby villages.

The school counsellor's husband has a clothing store, but his situation has deteriorated, as he depended on people travelling to Ramallah from Jerusalem. These types of domestic problems concern the teachers, and obviously affect their ability to totally focus on the job or give more, as they used to do before [2000].[53]

### Limiting Experiences and Futures

In Palestine the annual high-school matriculation examinations, the *tawjihi*, are a significant event in the education system, a major rite of passage for thousands of Palestinian girls and boys. The results are published in newspapers, determine a student's admittance into higher education, and are of wide public and social interest. In June 2004, ten UN bodies issued a press release expressing concern that high-school students would be prevented from sitting their final matriculation exams because of movement restrictions:

> Ten United Nations institutions call on the Israeli Authorities to ease restrictions on movement in the occupied territory to enable 60,000 Palestinian students to sit for their *tawjihi* matriculation final exams beginning today 7th of June. [...]
> "If these children are denied safe access to their examination sites, their whole future is undermined," said Anders Dange, Director of UNRWA Operations in the West Bank.[54]

Against this context, teachers reported a decline in children's concentration in class as affecting not only their performance, but also their sense of self-esteem:

> People have low expectations of what they can do, and little tasks become big. Time means nothing. People are depressed because there is no hope for the near future; they become inward and want to protect themselves and their immediate family. Definitely it fragments. You become very limited; you are tired at the end of the day, you have to help the children with their homework. When you can't interact with others, your circle is very limited. It is not only killing people, it is killing a society.[55]

The narrowing of horizons was a constant theme. For children, the ultimate impact of movement restrictions was to limit their opportunities. This emerged time and again in interviews with teachers and educators:

> All the time children say, "We want to go on a trip, we need to go on a trip outside the school, we are stuck inside these walls."
> But we can't take them on journeys outside the school because even UNRWA says we are not allowed to go outside Ramallah, as there is a checkpoint and they are worried it might be dangerous. Within Ramallah we try to take the children to the public gardens or a book fair. But that's it.[56]

A school counsellor at the same school said her timetable was absolutely filled with students queuing up to talk to her:

> One of our students said that she likes nature and she wants to draw it. But when she started to draw all she sees are houses and windows.
> Another told me the best thing in her life was going on a school trip. The children really are confined to the camp now.[57]

Researchers and policy workers in the Palestinian Authority National Plan for Children were very concerned that movement restrictions amounted to a process of de-development, in which children's life experiences became very limited and localised:

> I worry about the societal effect of isolation, the lack of exposure even to people living in cities near you. For society as a whole, and children in particular, your world gets very small, your ability to interact with people, institutions. I wonder what the isolation of communities means for a child's development, when they are only exposed to a limited set of people, and their world doesn't go beyond that.
> I remember that when I was a child, I used to travel everywhere, the school used to take us. Now my son of [age] eight, he doesn't know anything about the north. He has never been to Gaza. But it probably doesn't mean as much to him as it does to me that he can't move around, as he doesn't know anything else.
> The movement restrictions affect everything in our lives. The feeling that I am afraid to move or I am not afraid to move, affects children. The question in the end is: do children really understand

how this affects them, or do they realize this isn't normal? Maybe they think that all children in the world live like this.[58]

The system of education, like health, and like many other infrastructural and basic systems required for human development, is being eroded through movement restrictions imposed on a blanket basis against the Palestinian population. Without the necessary prerequisites for building a future for the next generation, more Palestinian families may be forced to move, completing the induced transfer they resisted for more than six decades.

# 8
# Conclusion

In the spring of 2002, yellow and purple blossoms covered the fields and trees around Jenin, a Palestinian town named for the fertility of its earth, and known for the largest forested area in the West Bank. But that spring, the forest had a different use. Israeli army forces were sweeping through the West Bank, taking more than 8,500 Palestinians from their homes and workplaces and holding them captive in makeshift camps. Around Jenin, the army separated the men aged between about 18 to 50 from the children, women, and older men; then they took the men to the forest: handcuffed, blindfolded, in their underwear; they were forced to kneel or squat in the cold mud, and denied blankets, food, and water.[1]

Soldiers had written the ID numbers on Palestinians' wrists with blue ink.[2] Then each man was photographed, interrogated with the use of a digital file containing details about his life, and had his ID number written on the back of the photo. Using plastic shackles – described by Amnesty International as a form of torture because they stop blood circulation and cut into the skin – to bind captives' hands, they blindfolded them, and kept them, "squatting, sitting or kneeling, not allowed to go to the toilet, and deprived of food or blankets during at least the first 24 hours".[3]

Majdi Shehadeh was one of over 600 Palestinians taken from Tulkarem refugee camp:

> We weren't given any food, and when we asked for water they poured it over us. The handcuffs were tight and when the blindfolds were taken off on our arrival I saw some people with hands black and swollen.[4]

By 3:30 a.m. they began to shake with cold. Elsewhere, in the Ramallah area, so many Palestinians were taken that the army forced them into a dried-up septic tank for lack of space in the prisons.[5] After a day and a half, they were given their first food:

[F]or 10 people we got a tomato and an apple and we shared this. Every six people had a loaf of bread, but a very small one and 200 grams of yoghurt.[6]

From 1967 to 2006, Israel incarcerated almost 700,000 Palestinians, that is, nearly one-fifth of the Palestinian population of the West Bank and Gaza.[7] However, the Israeli State Comptroller still indicated that the restriction of Palestinian movement is ineffective in preventing attacks on Israeli citizens.[8]

The intrusion into the Palestinian private sphere began as early as the population registries in 1948 and 1967, and continued for as long as the registries have been in use. Understanding the degree of intrusion also allows us to re-interpret, for instance, the claim that Palestinians now "control" their own health and education systems, or that Israel "disengaged" from the Gaza Strip (and the West Bank, as claimed around 2005[9]).

Harvard professor Sara Roy, whose father carried an identification number imprinted on his arm in the Second World War, was one of those who noticed the connections between these so-called bureaucratic elements during the 2002 mass arrests:

[W]hat does it mean when Israeli soldiers paint identification numbers on Palestinian arms; when young Palestinian men and boys of a certain age are told through Israeli loudspeakers to gather in the town square; when Israeli soldiers openly admit to shooting Palestinian children for sport; when some of the Palestinian dead must be buried in mass graves while the bodies of others are left in city streets and camp alleyways because the army will not allow proper burial; when certain Israeli officials and Jewish intellectuals publicly call for the destruction of Palestinian villages in retaliation for suicide bombings or for the transfer of the Palestinian population out of the West Bank and Gaza; when 46 per cent of the Israeli public favors such transfers and when transfer or expulsion becomes a legitimate part of popular discourse; when government officials speak of the "cleansing of the refugee camps"; and when a leading Israeli intellectual calls for hermetic separation between Israelis and Palestinians in the form of a Berlin Wall, caring not whether the Palestinians on the other side of the wall may starve to death as a result.[10]

Roy's question draws a line from the population registry and its concomitant identification numbers, through to movement restriction, and eventually to the inducement to leave or "transfer" of Palestinians. It is this line, so rarely drawn, that provides a new way of looking at the history of Palestine and the Palestinians.

## 8.1   REVIEW OF THE BOOK

### Denationalisation and Blacklists

When Palestinians volunteered information about themselves and others to the 1948 and 1949 census takers, hoping that this cooperation would lead to acknowledgement and recognition of their rights, they did not know that it would be instrumental in expulsion. The years 1948 to 1952 were crucial for the new Israeli state in establishing a regulatory framework to justify the expulsion *ex post facto*, and in denationalising Palestinians *in situ*. A critical aspect of these years was the temporary residence permit – for Palestinians only – whilst at the same time introducing a mechanism to provide automatic citizenship to Jews.

Palestinians saw through the euphemisms that emerged between 1950 and 1952: the Law of Return blocked Palestinian return, the Law of Entry blocked Palestinian entry, and the Law of Nationality blocked Palestinian nationality. These "laws" deleted Palestinian rights. While Jews from anywhere in the world could enter and gain citizenship as a right under the Law of Return, today close to ten million Palestinians are denied that right and need a permit to enter, a permit to reside, a permit to work, a permit to move, a permit to exit, and so on.

The system of registration ran parallel to the development of blacklists, such that as early as 1948 the population of Palestine was falsely reassured that only "hostiles" would be "targeted":

> Special units of the Hagana would enter villages looking for "infiltrators" (read "Arab volunteers") and distribute leaflets warning the local people against cooperating with the Arab Liberation Army. Any resistance to such an incursion usually ended with the Jewish groups firing at random and killing several villagers.[11]

In the autumn of 1948, 10,000 leaflets were dropped from airplanes, encouraging surrender or cooperation with Israeli forces. The blacklists enabled executions in village after village, and countless Palestinians felt personally hunted. Some recounted how they hid in caves previously used as tombs, alongside the remains of human corpses.[12]

As a system for marking individuals emerged, religion and race substituted for citizenship on identity cards, marked as "Jew", "Druze", "Arab", and another 130-odd categories. Religion-specific regulations governed who could and could not easily marry outside the 1949 Armistice lines. Special numbering further identified who and what a person was, indicating how s/he obtained her "status" as an ID-holder. Later, in the 1990s in the West Bank and Gaza Strip, technological advances facilitated further rights violations: wiretaps, digital distribution of personal information from the population registry, magnetic cards, and a digital reward and punishment system that earned the nickname "the ultimate police state" (from former Deputy Mayor and Chief Planning Officer of Jerusalem).[13] In this high-tech world, hanging a map was a punishable offence, and walking in a group of ten or more could elicit ten years of imprisonment.

Special signs marked onto ID cards, and later the colour-coding of IDs, "modernised" into digital form, ensured that blacklisted individuals could be taken captive anywhere – in their homes, going to work or school, or in the street. Or they could be liquidated: summary assassinations by remote control became the successors of the undercover assassins (*misti'rivim*) of the 1980s and 1990s, and the shooting line-ups of the 1940s.

## Coercion and Collaboration

In Palestine now, identity documentation not only signifies what a person is, but more importantly what a person is *not*, that is, a member of a privileged minority with state-protected human rights. The right to residency, for instance, was denied to all Palestinians (numbering 1.4 million in 1948), and then granted back to a select few, gradually. The 69,000 Palestinians counted in the census waited for at least four years to obtain Israeli citizenship. Thousands of Palestinians waited for more than 30 years.[14] Today millions are still waiting for some kind of citizenship to acknowledge their indigenous rights.

Israel developed special rules from 1948 onward that meant a Palestinian could not so much as eat, work, live, or move without his or her identity card, which accessed rations, employment, residence, and movement. The least-known but most personally destabilising "red IDs" were temporary residence permits that could last as little as a few days, holding out hope of a more stable status, while providing information that the Israeli army used for their later expulsion. Although Palestinians who "behaved", serving as informants and collaborators, were looked upon more favourably, nothing was guaranteed. And that was precisely the point: no guarantees meant living in limbo, thus rendering Palestinians easier to control. In this way, the rules continued, and a dual system of "separate development"[15] assured impoverishment and large-scale expulsion for Palestinians, in parallel to enrichment and large-scale colonisation for Jews living in the new state of Israel.

Palestinians waiting for the return and reinstatement of their rights – or at least some of their rights – from the late 1940s onward were asked to provide something in exchange from what little they had: funds, food, votes, labour, information, and above all, acquiescence in their own dispossession. The "confiscation procedure" of IDs was so effective a coercive measure that by the 1980s it enabled Israeli forces to carry out "random beatings" and force Palestinians in the West Bank and Gaza Strip to "perform": to dance, to play the violin, to kiss a donkey's backside, or to die of electrocution when ordered to remove tin-cans hanging from high-tension electricity wires. Such "performances", and the coercive power facilitating them, were later accompanied by the "neighbour procedure": the taking of Palestinian human shields.[16]

Denationalised Palestinians and their descendants today number eleven million, with less than 1.4 million allowed a vote in Israel – the political apparatus that governs in most of their former homeland.[17] The system of identity documentation in place in occupied Palestine is one over which Palestinians have minimal control, but which holds powerful control over them.

## Movement Restriction and Induced Transfer

In the late 1940s, each Palestinian was assigned a locality and forbidden to leave it without permission. The movement of the 69,000 Palestinians counted in the census was highly circumscribed, and that of the 91,000 Palestinians excluded from the census and labelled "present-absent" (5,000 boys and men in prisoner-of-war camps, 31,000 in the Little Triangle, 40,000 in the Galilee, and 13–15,000 in the Naqab)[18] was even more so. After 1948 the remaining 1.25 million Palestinians – including half a million in the West Bank and Gaza Strip – were banned from entering what had been their country. For the tens of thousands who managed to return after being expelled in the late 1940s, life was a constant battle against repeat expulsion.

As the movement of Palestinians was restricted, their forced removal from place to place continued. Villages were emptied and urban neighbourhoods were evicted to "make room" for incoming Jews. Even graveyards were exhumed and compressed to make space. The evicted Palestinians were crushed into increasingly crowded areas, causing intra-Palestinian friction between refugees and host communities.

Palestinians, but not Israeli Jews, had to apply for passes for movement, which were valid for as short as a few hours, and rarely more than a specified number of hours per day for a few months. Although thousands of military personnel were engaged in registering and controlling the movement of Palestinians, only a few personnel dealt with movement passes, resulting in excruciating backlogs. The military instead were heavily deployed to seek out and punish Palestinians found outside their localities without passes. Children caught selling their village's eggs in the city of Haifa, for instance, would be imprisoned for "smuggling".[19]

The term "induced transfer" refers to the destruction of a way of life such that staying in place becomes physically impossible. Contemplated by David Ben Gurion as early as 1947,[20] induced transfer was implemented from a very early point through damaging food production, confiscating land, and preventing Palestinians from having access to their crops.

Induced transfer forced breadwinners apart from their families, prevented medical professionals from reaching patients, and stopped Palestinians from marketing their goods. Discrimination via identity documents ensured that Palestinians were given lower wages and unhealthy work, and frequently denied work altogether. Curfews on Palestinian villages reinforced a sense of constant vulnerability; in 1956, Israeli armed forces shot – in the space of a single hour – 47 men, women, and children at close range for "violating" a curfew they did not know had been called.[21]

A further stage, in the 1960s, was to enforce Jews-only areas. In 1962 the newly built town of Karm'iel excluded "non-Jews" from either dwelling or owning a business there, despite being built on Palestinian land by dispossessed Palestinian workers. Renewed efforts to induce Palestinians to leave their homes and lands were formalised in a 1968 proposal (including tactics such as providing financial incentives for Palestinian emigration and a reduction of children), which became policy in 1974 and remained in place until 1991.[22]

After militarily occupying the West Bank and Gaza Strip in 1967, the Israeli military forbade Palestinians from leaving either area for four years, after which individual Palestinians could only apply for permission to leave. The model of mobile workers that had been in place since 1948 – labouring in Jewish areas during the day and returning to the reserves at night – was then reproduced in the occupied West Bank and Gaza Strip. Colour-coded identity cards and license plates reinforced the discriminatory framework; Jewish colonists, meanwhile, rapidly entered the newly occupied areas, exempt from mobility restrictions and the regime of military orders and punishments.

By 1993, over 1,300 military orders had been issued in the West Bank (with corresponding orders in the Gaza Strip), while Palestinians in Gaza and the West Bank were cut off from one another. Hundreds of thousands of Palestinians were punished – through imprisonment, fines, beatings, and acts of humiliation – for violating the pass "laws". Some Palestinians in the West Bank and Gaza Strip were also labelled "absent" (in 2005 an estimated 17.2 per cent, or 640,000 people, had a parent, child, sibling, or spouse who was unregistered)[23] as a means of denationalising them.

The 1949 Armistice lines split villages and communities down the middle; remnants of the movement restrictions that clustered Palestinians into reserves from 1948 to 1966 are still visible in the segregated urban areas of today; and the roads and colonies in the West Bank are forbidden to Palestinians, while linking colonists with high-speed thoroughfares and metropolises west of the Armistice line.

Over half a billion dollars was spent in less than a decade (and mainly in 1995) to create a road network of more than 1,500 kilometres – all off limits to pass-holding Palestinians. Over 600 checkpoints gradually turned into complete blockages, with passage being redirected to 44 tunnel-checkpoints, passing beneath the colonists' freely moving highways; and 25 "terminals" further restricted Palestinians. As armed Jewish colonists staked out vast "estates", covering 88 per cent of historic Palestine, Palestinians were further isolated into non-contiguous, unviable living spaces.

In 1994, the Israeli army erected a wall around the Gaza Strip, taking with it 25 per cent of the most fertile land, and giving themselves *carte blanche* to shoot at Palestinians in their own lands.[24] Eight years later, work commenced on an 810-kilometre wall that penetrated up to 22 kilometres into the West Bank, often markedly departing from the 320-kilometre Armistice line. Slicing off 90 per cent of Jerusalem, and isolating 200,000 Jerusalemites from the rest of the West Bank, the concrete wall towered up to eleven metres high and made life in hundreds of communities impossible. In addition, more than a quarter of a million Palestinians in the West Bank were deprived of access to fundamental services, separated from their own lands, families, and physical and social infrastructure.

The persistence of movement restrictions – and their accompanying regime of population registration and identity documentation – over a period of decades, violates international law. The right to movement is affirmed in the Universal Declaration of Human Rights (UDHR) and the International Covenant on Civil and Political Rights (Articles 13 and 12, respectively), and the rights to work, family, livelihood, health, and education are upheld in the International Covenant on Economic, Social and Cultural Rights (Articles 6, 10, 11, 12 and 13). Movement restrictions also violate the right to dignity (Articles 1, 22 and 23 of the UDHR).

Movement restrictions have created severe and harsh living conditions. Yet Palestinians remember well their lives before these restrictions, when many were prosperous landowners, agriculturalists, manufacturers, traders, intellectuals, and professionals. Health and education, for instance, remain two sectors in which Palestinians have fought to preserve not only functional but quality systems.

## The Health System

In the late 2000s, the health sector faced a 50 per cent decrease in public access to vital services, a steady rise in health needs due to restrictions and Israeli army attacks, and an unprecedented number of Palestinians living on the poverty line in what was previously a self-sustaining economy. Movement restrictions increased the cost of travel, resulted in over 120 deaths and 70 births at checkpoints, and forced patients to stay away from home in order to be near caregivers in case they could not return to health facilities. Over a quarter of a million Palestinians were placed in a dilemma: pass through the fleetingly open passage out of their enclaves to seek care, or stay at home where no care provider can enter without an ID certifying residence in the enclave.

The system of referrals – using a worldwide-recommended model of public health provision involving primary, secondary, and tertiary care – broke down under movement restrictions. Patients could not reach essential specialist care – a primary health care clinic five minutes away, or a hospital 20 minutes away. Patients with physical disabilities, heart conditions (the number one killer disease in the

West Bank and Gaza Strip), or kidney disease all suffered under movement restrictions. In a half-year span between 2007 and 2008, 32 Gazans died waiting for the Israeli army to let them access care in Egypt. Over 4,000 Palestinians were denied passage – by Israeli officials – from the West Bank to Jordan, including cancer patients and children.

Much-needed clinics in villages and small urban areas became unsustainable because of recent impoverishment and, in the words of one doctor, "my patients couldn't reach me and I couldn't reach them".[25] In search of patients, doctors were forced to service major population centres only. By 2004, the workplaces of less than half the West Bank's nurses and less than a quarter of doctors were near their place of residence – the rest commuted or were unemployed. But work was sporadic: soldiers barred vital routes, and the possibility of attack by Jewish colonists made detours dangerous.

In response to longstanding Israeli practices of withholding imported pharmaceuticals from their Palestinian importers, Palestinians developed an indigenous pharmaceutical industry to supply 45 per cent of the medication required. Even this, however, was insufficient for crucial hospital infusions and life-saving medications, including insulin. When movement restrictions intensified from 2000 onward, and Israeli attacks killed and injured thousands in the West Bank and Gaza, Palestinians were forced to cope without these urgently needed supplies. Furthermore, power outages and deliberate withholding of fuel for generators meant that the limited supplies of immunisations and hospital infusions were ruined. Patients reduced and interrupted their dosages amid shortages of medications for diabetes, heart disease, epilepsy, asthma, and hypothyroidism. Birth delivery kits, infant formula, vaccinations, and anaesthetics were all blocked by restrictions on the movement of persons and goods.

Denial of access and attacks on ambulances – numbering over 380 in a six-year period – violated the Hague Conventions, and seven articles of the Fourth Geneva Convention. Soldiers arbitrarily chose when to allow passage, irrespective of Israeli-issued documentation. Impromptu solutions – like taking taxis instead of ambulances – were insufficient for the transport of critically ill patients, dead bodies, or births. Due to movement restrictions, women were less able to seek antenatal and postnatal care, and by mid-2002 a third of all births lacked professional attendants (as compared to 5 per cent before 2000). Stillbirths and complicated pregnancies increased significantly.

With the decision of whether to allow free passage lying with Israeli soldiers, the military, and not the doctor, became the diagnostician. Patients were obliged to "prove" their illness; those whose medical documentation and Israeli-issued documents were rejected at the checkpoint suffered the consequences: from 2000 to 2003 94 people died at checkpoints waiting to get to hospital, and more than 83 people died for lack of treatment, including 27 children and 19 newborns. Kidney dialysis, chemotherapy, and other treatments were accessible or inaccessible at the command of checkpoint soldiers. Checkpoints not only blocked care to those attempting to pass, but even discouraged the attempts themselves – patients often stayed home in the hope of recovery rather than risking an exacerbation of the illness through the arduous journey. Were movement restrictions not in place, clinics could have been reached, on average, in as little as one-tenth of the time.

Doctors and emergency personnel were detained, arrested, used as human shields, beaten, and killed. Despite the dangers, they established mobile clinics to reach blocked communities, as well as training local health workers to respond *in situ*. To the best of their abilities, they attempted to reach patients to deliver medications, infant formula and food during emergencies, and to assist patients to access the care they needed. In the end, however, a diminishing pool of people, such as internationals and Israelis working with human rights organisations, were able to move in smaller and smaller areas (with villagers being the only ones allowed to be in their village and everyone else prohibited from entering).

As with education, the basis for building a present and future in Palestine is gradually but systematically being eroded for its indigenous people.

### Education

By 2003, over a sixth of households had moved house in order to access education, given increased movement restrictions: checkpoints, earth mounds dug up by army bulldozers, or trenches gouged into the roads. Movement thereafter only became more difficult. The Israeli army closed over 1,200 schools, the Wall blocked access throughout the West Bank, and universities were cut off from their student base. During the 2002 to 2003 school year, every day an average of nearly 10 per cent of UN-employed teachers could not reach their classrooms.

Faced with such obstacles and conditions of prolonged curfew, the Palestinian Authority and UN education systems regrouped and adapted. But this was at a cost to the quality of education. Five-minute journeys were transformed into 25-kilometre journeys, taking several hours each way. Roundabout routes were dangerous and subject to the arbitrary and violent behaviour of Israeli checkpoint soldiers. Teachers who managed to keep up the commute arrived exhausted and emotionally drained from the ordeal (some having walked two hours in the semi-arid "valley of fire" between towns). The United Nations was forced to recruit locally to replace teachers who were blocked by movement restrictions. This often entailed a compromise in quality: trainee teachers, teachers in unrelated subject specialisations, and rotating or temporary teachers who frequently had to re-establish connections with students. Teacher-training also suffered, as regional supervisors could not make it to schools, and teachers had difficulty meeting to collectively discuss professional development issues.

In addition to localising teacher recruitment and training, Palestinians had to decentralise schooling even further, setting up schools in small villages simply because the village children faced difficulties escaping the enclosures set up by the Israeli military (checkpoints, walls, gates, fences, and so on) to go to the existing school in the neighbouring village. Palestinians also established alternative educational activities when movement restrictions made formal schooling impossible or insufficient, and drew up emergency plans for ad hoc study centres for students preparing for their matriculation exams. They developed educational packages for students to teach themselves literature, environmental health, and other subjects, and they ran local informal schools in homes, apartment blocks, and libraries.

From September 2000 to June 2004, the Israeli army and colonists assaulted students and teachers on over 180 occasions, breaking into or shelling 298 schools and destroying 282. Eight out of the eleven Palestinian universities came under direct attack, and a further 97 schools were vandalised or bulldozed. In addition, 43 schools were taken for use as military bases. Save the Children documented how the Israeli army wounded, disabled, and killed hundreds of students and teachers, including killing 132 students and injuring another 2,500 on their way to and from school.

The assaults undermined an education system once known for top literacy rates, a range of tertiary educational institutes and enrolment, and a high degree of equality between boys and girls, rural and urban, refugee and non-refugee, and high and low income. Students became jumpy at the sound of sirens and military vehicles, had difficulty concentrating, and reported increased bed-wetting, insomnia, stuttering, and refusing to sleep alone in their rooms. They requested frequent breaks, thinking that each moment of quiet outside might indicate the call of a curfew and the need to rush home. Exam pass-rates dropped uncharacteristically, by over a third in some subjects.

Children began postponing higher education, and the United Nations warned in 2004 that "a decade of efforts" was "under serious threat". The problems of teacher access from movement restrictions became problems of educational quality: shift teaching, missed teaching days, overcrowded classrooms, and time pressure to complete the syllabus all led to reduced feedback for students, and reduced time spent on non-compulsory subjects like art and physical education – the very subjects that could have developed children's and youths' self-confidence, expression, and resilience to the harsh conditions of military occupation.

Exhausted parents and teachers tried to shield students from the realities of economic collapse under movement restrictions, ongoing human insecurity, and the shrinking of geographic space available to them. But students were aware that field trips became scarcer,

*Figure 8.1*   Palestinians play football in the shadow of the wall, Jerusalem, 2004. The sun sets earlier, as the wall raises the horizon by 8 to 11 metres. The wall dwarfs the players, and even the car, confined to the dust below. Aside from dispossession and impoverishment, the Wall is a psychological assault on people of all ages, including youth and children. Decades of movement restrictions take their toll and are seen by Palestinians as a policy of induced transfer. (Gustaf Hansson)

and closer to home – public gardens or a book fair nearby – rather than a nature reserve or neighbouring city. Their environments were increasingly limited, confined to a village, neighbourhood, or refugee camp.

Palestinian leaders in education grew concerned as to how children who only ever lived within a confined space would be as adults in an increasingly globalising world. "Do they realise", asked one policy worker, "this isn't normal?"[26]

Nearly half the Palestinian population in the West Bank and Gaza Strip are children;[27] the toll of decades of movement restrictions, culminating in the physical and highly visible barriers of the wall, is evident not only in measurements like exam results, but also in the everyday inability to concentrate, focus, and feel at peace and secure in one's own school, travels, and home.

## 8.2  LOOKING FORWARD

### Resisting Induced Transfer

I think their aim is to emigrate us voluntarily from our land.[28]

The larger effect of quarantining the Palestinian population is to make life socially and economically unbearable and cause their emigration, mainly to Jordan.[29]

By adapting to constantly shifting rules and orders, and steadfastly refusing to concede that the possibility for normalcy in daily life has been removed, Palestinians express a steadfastness, commonly referred to as *sumud*.

We Palestinians have learned to lose without being defeated.[30]

Acknowledged as a trait common to Arab political struggle and daily life,[31] *sumud* is not unlike Scott's description of resistance among Indonesians: "So long as we confine our conception of *the political* to activity that is openly declared", he explains, "we are driven to conclude that subordinate groups essentially lack a political life, or that what political life they do have is restricted to those exceptional moments of popular explosion".[32] *Sumud* is a non-violent policy of dissidence, described by Edward Said as "a way of turning presence into small-scale obduracy",[33] in which sheer presence constitutes resistance; it contradicts "the natural behavior expected ... exodus and leaving".[34]

The internationalisation of the term *sumud* is attributed to Shehadeh, who explains that, faced with the two options of "mute submission" or "blind hate", he would choose the third: *sumud*.[35] This he defines – as paraphrased by Audeh – as "the art of hanging on at all costs and against all odds, a mental and spiritual state of being that thousands of Palestinians have learned is not easy to master".[36] Since its internationalisation in the 1970s and 1980s, the concept of *sumud* has been absorbed into studies by others, such as American psychologists examining Iraqi prisoners of war.[37] Examples and anecdotes of *sumud* abound amongst the interviews conducted for this book. For instance, one of our interviewees, Hind, speaks of a checkpoint that she passes through daily, and at which a particular soldier inspects her pregnant belly daily:

> Our feelings are strange. Me and her [the Israeli soldier] have been living together for so long, maybe the smallest thing would make us happy. But they pressured us so much. You feel you have no space. Sometimes you feel you cannot do anything. Your most beautiful years – your years go – you wonder what will happen when we get older. Have you ever felt you do not want to leave the bed? I feel that everyday.[38]

While she describes her daily wish to give up, she also makes it clear in the interview that she stays and continues by personal decision, not by a lack of choice. To Hind, to climb out of bed and to be searched every day on the way to work, and to work through the day, and then pass through the same checkpoint to go home – this is *sumud*.

Expressions of *sumud* take on greater significance when considered as part of a collective strategy that transcends the fragmenting, individualising effects of the restrictions on mobility. One of our interviewees, Hani Amer, lives in a house surrounded on all sides by walls and fences. People in difficult conditions like Hani Amer often refer to their children, their families, and all people suffering collectively, as reasons for staying in place. Given that the Israeli regime is so constantly involved with fragmenting Palestinian life, this act of renewing collectivity and asserting togetherness is itself strongly political.[39] As Taraki and Giacaman observe:

> Under the stifling regime of closure, separation, and fragmentation (especially in the West Bank), Palestinians have lost their mobility, the one dynamic factor in urban transformation in the Arab

region. If these Israeli policies continue, Palestinian society will be locked into localisms of a kind not observed anywhere else in the region today.[40]

Building and maintaining community through daily acts of adaptation is a form of opposing this kind of deliberate fragmentation. Anthropologist Rema Hammami reveals, in particularly eloquent fashion, how staying-in-place informs an essential part of collective identity, and thus how refusing to be moved is much more than an individual act:

> In terms of the society's self-image, this is a society that for more than fifty years has lived in a constant state of dispossession. [It is] an incremental dispossession: it goes on, and on, and on. And the society is extremely strong in terms of survival, in terms of survival strategies. It's very proud of that as well.
>
> I mean, I think the self-image that most Palestinians have – we all have of ourselves – is that, "We are constant losers. We're just people, and we just lose all the time. And we lose, but you know what? At the end of the day, they are not going to win. Because we're stubborn. We're stubborn bastards, right. I got nowhere else to go. This is my home. They can do what the hell they want. But I'm staying".[41]

Amid the current research on health – and mental health specifically – a strong argument emerges that although the individual is affected and although the system of identity documentation (and wider military occupation) is individualising, nevertheless a positive approach to tackling these issues would involve addressing them as collective problems. According to an international group of health professionals, mental health in the context of occupation is not simply a series of isolated and extreme incidences, it requires recognition "of collective violation" and "traumatic contexts".[42]

Thus, addressing stress through community work is an important form of resistance, against not only injustice itself, but also the reproduced exclusions and individualisation that can result from such injustice. Although *sumud* has yet to find its way into most (non-military) writing today about resistance, its concepts are often described without being given the name "sumud". Within a context of exclusion, numerous groups aim to create "open and plural forms of identity"[43] – a resistance to an externally imposed identification and limitation.

Resisting Movement Restrictions

> I expected from the beginning that I would be arrested, that I
> would be punished for what I am doing. But I do not care, I am
> Palestinian and I want to liberate my country. I will practice what
> I believe in: nonviolent resistance. I will bear the consequences
> of my actions. If every Palestinian were to be afraid, we would
> not continue. We would not have our freedom.[44]

In addition to staying-in-place, a second form of *sumud* is resistance
to the logistics of the administration of the ID/checkpoint/pass
system – active circumvention of the mobility restrictions through
ingenuity or loopholes in the system. This may take the form
of "sneaking" through or around checkpoints (or historically,
post-1948, "sneaking" home), using "false" documents, or other
adaptations that, on an individual level, make the restrictions less
effective. Attempts to circumvent checkpoints and to evade the
ascribed categories of IDs are commonplace. People take advantage
of "the social and economic assumptions held by the Israeli soldiers
and in doing so avoid having their legal status checked".[45] This
latter point is confirmed by the simple linguistic trick employed by
one man we interviewed:

> I worked in Tel Aviv for a long time – nobody thought I was
> Palestinian. I did not use the letters ha and hu, I used kh. [The
> letters ha and hu are rarely used in Hebrew, and are often replaced
> by the letter kh.] I used to speak Hebrew better than my [Jewish]
> manager, a Moroccan guy. I could pick up the language quickly.[46]

Yet another means of asserting *sumud* is refusing to be disrupted
by the occupation regime. In the following example, drawn from
the same interview, what is desired is the disruption of the smooth
running of the Israeli apparatus and the frustration of those charged
with its administration:

> One day I was going back from Tel Aviv, and a bomb was blown
> up at Erez [the main checkpoint into and out of the enclosed
> Gaza Strip]. I did not have my ID with me. The soldiers stopped
> the bus and checked IDs. They lined up the people in a cramped
> space. Because it was cramped, I was able to slip to the side, and
> lined up with the people who'd been checked. Then they gave us

all the IDs. When they distributed them, they asked if everyone had received their IDs. I said "yes".

They arrested the people they wanted to arrest. If you are suspicious, you're suspicious – according to the soldier. If he wants to take you to prison, he will take you.

I was very resilient. I never told them I had an ID card unless they actually took it from my pocket. The worst thing that could happen would be that they'd take you to prison, whether or not you had an ID card. We would try to evade them; we tried many times. At least you're creating havoc or a problem for them.[47]

The man's resourcefulness saves him from being punished for not having his pass with him (an "offence" that would have almost surely landed him in prison). His story does not stop there though; success in resistance is then defined in terms of making soldiers' harassment as costly as possible.

While this case shows that resistance within the system is possible, the power held by Israeli soldiers to coerce Palestinians remains, and arbitrary decisions to capture and abuse Palestinians continue unchecked. Steadfastness requires an occasional willingness to circumvent the arbitrary rules of the system:

I went to one Christian wedding where the bride, dressed in white, was caught at an Israeli checkpoint that would not let her through. After much arguing and shouting at the soldiers, the bride steadfastly refused to leave the car and insisted that her wedding was going on ahead.

Her driver therefore turned around and took a back route over the hills until they eventually reached the church, late and very dusty. The wedding was followed by a large party in Ramallah, where the family members congratulated everyone on getting to the wedding despite the *wada'* (situation).[48]

Here, it is the woman's *sumud* that has her refusing to back down, instead driving through the hills to find a riskier "back route" that delivers her to her wedding. While "going around" checkpoints (*liffe*) is a frequent practice, it opens "the greater risk of being shot by the Israeli military".[49] This point is confirmed by the numerous examples we cite – from the 1940s to the present – of people whose lives were endangered during simple acts of daily routine. For this reason, resistance to the mobility restrictions themselves is rarer than adaptation and staying-in-place.

Still riskier – and thus rarer – is the third level of resistance: against the system as a whole. This kind of resistance was seen, for example, when South Africans burned their passes in protest in 1907 and the 1950s. Yet to resist the *authority* of the system, and to reject the imposition of IDs and the permit regime, implies sacrifices that reverberate from the individual outward to her or his family and community. In the next two sections we consider how these sacrifices are imposed – that is, by the absence of a safety net – before returning to reviewing this third kind of resistance, as described at the beginning of the book: the freedom riders and all those who call for "freedom not permits".

### Normalcy and the Limits to Resistance

I'd like to live normally – not [especially] nice – normally.[50]

This simple wish is repeated throughout the West Bank, where the new "normal" (*'aadi*) involves dispossession, displacement, and daily harassment. The establishment of normalcy and adaptation to daily life under restrictions on movement can be seen as a political act of resistance. It is a dimension of resistance that is often missed.

In contrast with the philosophy behind blacklisting, coercion, and movement restriction, the individuals most heavily affected by such measures historically – from indigenous communities worldwide – continue to elaborate more inclusive worldviews,[51] like that of Abu Ahmed, a community leader in the Palestinian village of Budrus:

We are not against the Jewish [people or faith]. We are not against the Israelis. We are just against the occupation.

We need our freedom and [this will only be gained at the price of our hardship] through nonviolent struggle. We will not escape from the price of freedom; we have to be able to pay this price. Because we know that our right will not be given to us on a golden platter, therefore we have to struggle.[52]

Yet the struggle for freedom and normalcy also contains limitations. The kinds of adaptations that are required to cope may in fact be as socially damaging as they are liberating. Romanticising the quality of steadfastness, or *sumud*, risks glossing over the sometimes devastating individual, family, and social consequences of the coping mechanisms it requires. The costs of long-term adaptation to "normal" life under such a regime are described by Nazeeh, whose land became the site for a peaceful protest camp after he refused to make way for bulldozers and the wall:

> There is a saying in Arabic, "They live because they are not dead". This is the situation of the Palestinian people, especially in the villages where the Wall confiscated their land. I speak not only of myself, but also about those in other villages. The people of these villages are "dead", because their dignity is gone. In Palestine, land is dignity; when you lose your land, you lose your dignity. The human without dignity is a dead person; even while alive, we are dead, we are like machines walking on this earth without hope.[53]

Raja Shehadeh's *Samed: Journal of a West Bank Palestinian* contains a story in which his cousin, a Palestinian living in Jordan, comes to visit him in the West Bank. Shehadeh's cousin wears an indignant nationalism on his sleeve and makes a show of being outraged by the various visible signs of the occupation. At one point after driving past a group of Israelis working outside, he turns and questions Shehadeh. "So, a new Jewish settlement in the making! ... Why don't you do anything about them – don't you have any pride?"[54]

From Shehadeh's perspective, however, the cousin's questions are not only patronising, but also detached from and blind to the significance of the struggle of those who choose to remain in place. Shehadeh asks, "How could I tell him that seeing Palestinians in the Jordanian capital, men who have grown rich and now pay only wildly patriotic lip-service to our struggle, was more than my *sumud* in my poor and beloved land could stomach?" And, later, "Why could he not see that he, and all the others who left, are as much to blame as we *samedin* for the way things are here?"[55]

Shehadeh presents a clear view of the context for resistance, which makes rejection of the system so difficult. Palestinians who are denationalised and forced to carry passes are in a position of vulnerability; their forms of resistance through staying in place and circumventing restrictions should not be underestimated as sources of Palestinian political agency – stronger by far than any single act of traditional resistance, no matter how dramatic.

Our aim is not to paint a naïve or rosy picture of Palestinian adaptation to the regime under which they live. We suggest, rather, that this struggle for dignity and normalcy, although fraught with potentially ruinous social consequences, remains the prevalent form of resistance among Palestinians today, and indeed since the initiation of steps in the 1800s toward the outright colonialism of today.

## Denationalisation as a Shared Experience

*Wa la atawassal al-sadaqaat min baabik. Wa la asghar, amaama balaati a'taabik.*

I do not supplicate charity at your doors. Nor do I belittle myself at the footsteps of your chamber.

"ID Card", Palestinian poet Mahmoud Darwish

Palestinians from the beginning wanted the restoration of their rights, not simply aid. While Palestinians in each location were forced to cope in different ways,[56] our book brings together the one thing held in common, which is denationalisation. This explains, for instance, why Darwish's poem "ID Card", quoted here, touches all Palestinians (and all denationalised persons of every background).

Until mid-1949, "Palestinian nationality" continued to be registered in travel documents and recognised internationally; until the fateful day when Zionist leader David Ben-Gurion decided to change it. Concerned that "Israeli nationality" did not exist, he proposed "that we decide to write 'Israeli Nationality,' and then it will exist".[57]

The denationalisation of Palestinians left them stateless in a world where passports were nearly indispensable. Even for those Palestinians who later obtained Israeli citizenship, there is constant threat of a return to statelessness. Their status may be "inferior" in a state whose sovereignty was "constitutionally committed to the exclusive principle of 'only for Jews'",[58] but it remains a status, preferable to reverting to denationalisation.[59]

The indignities and harrowing obstacles that accompany a stateless travel document are infinite and can never be conveyed to other mortals ...

[Y]ou yearn for that little book, with your picture, telling all those whom it may concern to allow the bearer to pass freely without hindrance, and to assist him or her by affording him or her the protection he or she may need.[60]

When Palestinian writer Fawaz Turki was refused a permit by the UK for being "of dubious nationality", he wrote:

Her Majesty's realm did not need a permit, though, when it entered mine and robbed me of my nationality. But then there are those who need permits and those who do not. I did. And I was only asking for a permit to live in peace. I needed one, others did not.[61]

As professor and long-time spokesperson Hanan Ashrawi wrote in 2012, Palestinians need freedom, not permits:

To understand the absurdity of the occupation, we might as well ask the State of Israel how many permits it issues to its Jewish citizens during the celebration of Passover. The answer? Not a single one. [...] The disagreement over numbers will undoubtedly continue. But with its continuation, what is often overlooked is that this debate fundamentally misses the point. We should not be questioning how many permits Israel, the occupying power, does or does not issue to Christians or Muslims for their religious holidays: we should be questioning the very existence of such permits at all.[62]

She touches on a very important point made by legal experts, which is that Israel has incorporated statelessness into its structure of control:

Whereas, historically, statelessness has been seen as a "non"-status – that is, a status outside of any other legal status – Israel has internalized and "legalized" the issue, making it a recognized part of its citizenship framework.[63]

After Israel's "withdrawal" from the Gaza Strip, it retained control over the population registry – as well as that of the West Bank. Indeed, when Palestinians from overseas visit their homeland on foreign passports, Israeli officials search for each Palestinian's identity number in the population registry, and write the ID number into his or her passport. When 'Akka-born sociologist Elia Zureik arrived on his Canadian passport, Israel wrote his ID number in Hebrew into his Canadian passport, demanded he get an Israeli passport – despite having given up citizenship over 40 years earlier – and gave him an Israeli passport from Ottawa within four days of his request. When he could not recall his childhood street name at the demand of the Israeli representative in Ottawa, she pulled it up "with one click" into the population registry, leading him to conclude that, "Israel must have the most detailed information in its databases about the Palestinian people worldwide".[64]

## Resisting the Authority of the System

Resistance to the authority or legitimacy of the population registry, identity documentation, and movement restrictions, questions the legality of a system that claims not only to be legal, but even to represent the law itself. The mechanisms used to bring about the registry, IDs, and mobility restrictions are called "laws", "orders", and "regulations". At this third level of resistance, these titles are challenged, and their base claim to legitimacy is destabilised.

Some would argue that such resistance to IDs is muted by the "benefits" that IDs can offer. Sociologists emphasise that IDs enable rights and responsibilities, an "embrace" and a "grasp",[65] benefits as well as control. This is one way of looking at IDs that, it is claimed, becomes increasingly applicable with the progression of democracy and the genuine mutual benefit of state and society. In other words, when the "social contract" is one of consent, when the state is accountable to the polity, when the population in question can vote freely within an egalitarian electoral system, then IDs could provide the apparent paradoxical combination of benefit and control. But what about a military occupation and colonial legacy, a non-existent social contract, force rather than voluntary consent, a state unaccountable to a large segment of the population under its control, and a population without the right to vote? Indeed, what about a colonial state containing indigenous people whom the state rejects and wishes to "transfer" from their homes?

The case of Palestine has some commonalities with other state-controlled systems of population registration/ID around the world: denationalisation through the registry (Slovenia), documentation without citizenship (Thailand), internal movement restriction (post-revolutionary Russia and China, colonial Egypt), document retention (Iraq), exit permit requirements (Syria, Sudan), and discrimination on the basis of identity documents (Rwanda, Iraq, colonial Indonesia).[66] Yet it also has some important differences for the moment.

The "benefits" that many associate with a state and, by extension, with a state's link to individuals via population registration and identity documentation, are more aptly described as "monopolies" or "oligopolies".[67] Rather than demonstrating the people's free will and choice, or the people's power to demonstrate that choice through the capillaries of a state, IDs in Palestine demonstrate the total absence of choice for Palestinians. Coercion and collaboration, in particular, directly relate to the withholding of basic human rights; they are made possible by the amalgamation of "permissions" into one document: the identity card; and into one number: the identity number in the Population Registry.

Resisting the authority of the system – the kind of resistance of which pass-burning is but one of the many symbols and acts – is therefore perhaps the most costly, and in the case of Palestinians, one of the least recognised and thus most precarious. Any Palestinian who burns her or his ID jeopardises access to many basic freedoms, which people elsewhere in the world take for granted, and lacks recourse or an advocate. So much of Palestinian life is contained in and dictated by the identity document. It is hence almost unimaginable that an individual would risk this so-called "legal" claim to existence, in order to challenge the immense apparatus of oppression. Thus this level of resistance may in the end materialise primarily via international pressure, as in South Africa:

> [In 1991, when meeting Nelson Mandela and Walter Sisulu, Edward Said asked] "How did it happen?"
>
> They replied, "Number one, we never let go of our principles. We never changed what we were fighting for. Number two, we focused on the international dimension, because our international success in delegitimizing apartheid gave hope to the people inside to continue the struggle".[68]

The concentration of ordinary life into the hands of the state and its agents has a profound effect on the collective ability to resist. This is magnified by the absence of any international support, safeguard, or fallback for those who break free. Despite the disempowering effects of denationalisation, however, Palestinians are not immobilised, and their aims remain clear. Community leaders like Budrus villager Abu Ahmed recognise the importance of internationalising their efforts:

> Because we could not win against the occupation by ourselves alone, we have to persuade all the people around the world that we are right, that we are not terrorists, and that we are just looking for our freedom, as the French did [under occupation], as India [under colonialism], as the United States [under the British empire], as any people who are suffering from occupation in their history. All of them are struggling against occupation, and we have to struggle against occupation.

But we have to struggle in the best way. I think that the popular way and the peaceful way is the best way for our rights, if we do not want to get anyone killed from this side or that side. But also for ourselves, it's better to struggle this way.[69]

Remarkably, surmounting the restrictions on freedom are Palestinians from within, and individuals from outside the confines of the restrictions. "We expect this to be the first of many waves", said Huwaida Arraf, one of the freedom riders in 2011, "we have many more people who want to ride".[70]

# Notes

NB: URLs were last accessed in April 2012.

## CHAPTER 1

1. Kysia, R. 2008. "Freedom riders on the sea". *Electronic Intifada*, October 29.
2. *Haaretz*. 2011. "Pro-Palestinian group in the Netherlands calls for boycott of Israeli bus company"; *Haaretz*, July 16. Hadid, D. 2011. "Palestinian activists arrested on bus to Israel". *Guardian*, November 15; Al-Barghouthi, M. and Al-Saafin, D. 2011. "The freedom riders of bus 148". *Mondoweiss*, November 15.
3. Al-Barghouthi, M. and Al-Saafin, D. 2011. "The freedom riders". Hussein, S. 2011. "Palestinian 'freedom riders' arrested trying to ride bus into Jerusalem". *National Post*, November 15; Greenwood, P. 2011. "Palestinians protest 'racist' bus policy". *Guardian*, November 15; Hadid, D. 2011. "Palestinian 'freedom riders' arrested". *Yahoo News*, November 15.
4. Hadid, 2011. "Palestinian activists".
5. Hussein, 2011. "Palestinian 'freedom riders'".
6. Tilley, V. (ed.). 2009. Occupation, Colonialism, Apartheid? A Re-assessment of Israel's Practices in the Occupied Palestinian Territories Under International Law. Cape Town: Human Sciences Research Council of South Africa; Horowitz, A. 2011. "Six Palestinian freedom riders arrested traveling on Israeli-only bus". Mondoweiss, November 15; Bayoumi, M. 2004. "A bloody stupid war". Middle East Report, 231: 36–45.
7. Levinson, C. 2011. "Israel has 101 different types of permits governing Palestinian movement". *Haaretz*, December 23.
8. Nesher, T. 2012. "Border police train Israeli teens to detain Palestinian workers". *Haaretz*, January 2.
9. Ibid.
10. Issues of ideology and discourse are explored in the works of Gabi Piterberg, Oren Yiftachel, Norman Finkelstein, Gershom Gorenberg, Tom Segev, and Jonathan Cook, among numerous others. For historical examinations, see, for instance, volumes by Avi Shlaim, Eugene Rogan, Tom Segev, Samih Farsoun, and Naseer Aruri. For the 1990s, see also Weinberger, P.E. 2007. *Co-opting the PLO: A Critical Construction of the Oslo Accords, 1993–1995*. Lanham, MD: Lexington Books. Significant studies on land include: Abu Hussein, H. and McKay, F. 2003. *Access Denied: Palestinian Land Rights in Israel*. London: Zed Books; Fischbach, M.R. 2003. *Records of Dispossession: Palestinian Refugee Property and the Arab–Israeli Conflict*. New York: Columbia University Press; Khalidi, W. 1992. *All That Remains: The Palestinian Villages Occupied and Depopulated by Israel in 1948*. Beirut: Institute for Palestine Studies. Recent contributions on coexistence include those of Ali Abunimah, Udi Aloni, Susan Nathan, Michael Riordon, and Joel Kovel. On resistance,

see the writings of Omar Barghouti, the illustrated work of William Parry, and the 2002 edited collection by Jonathan Shainin and Roane Carey.

11. On health and education, see Chapters 6 and 7 of this book. Some key reports on employment, agriculture, and the economy include those of B'tselem, the World Bank, and John Dugard (in his capacity as UN Special Rapporteur), in addition to the books and articles of Avram Bornstein, Laila Farsakh, and Caroline Abu Sada, among others. On family, see: Van Esveld, Bill. 2012. *Forget About Him, He's Not Here: Israel's Control of Palestinian Residency in the West Bank and Gaza.* New York: Human Rights Watch; Ashkar, A. 2006. *Perpetual Limbo: Israel's Freeze on Unification of Palestinian Families in the Occupied Territories.* Jerusalem: B'Tselem; Makdisi, S. 2008. *Palestine Inside Out: An Everyday Occupation.* New York: W.W. Norton & Co.

12. Abu-Laban, Y., Lyon, D. and Zureik, E. (eds) 2011. *Surveillance and Control in Israel/Palestine: Population, Territory and Power.* New York: Routledge.

13. BADIL. 2003. *The Permit Maze* (Occasional Bulletin No. 12). Bethelehem: BADIL Resource Center for Palestinian Residency and Refugee Rights; Feldman, I. 2008. *Governing Gaza: Bureaucracy, Authority, and the Work of Rule, 1917–1967.* Durham, NC: Duke University Press.

14. Gordon, N. 2008. *Israel's Occupation.* Berkeley: University of California Press, p. 38.

15. Yiftachel. 2006. *Ethnocracy*, p. 52; Gordon. 2008. *Israel's Occupation*, p. 200.

16. Ophir, A., Givoni, M. and Hanafi, S. (eds) 2009. *The Power of Inclusive Exclusion: Anatomy of Israeli Rule in the Occupied Palestinian Territories.* Cambridge, MA: Zone Books, pp. 20–1.

17. Cattan, H. 1973. *Palestine and International Law: The Legal Aspects of the Arab–Israeli Conflict.* London: Longman Group, pp. 72, 88; Quigley, J.B. 2010. *The Statehood of Palestine: International Law in the Middle East Conflict.* New York: Cambridge University Press, pp. 54–5.

18. Barron, F.L. 1988. "The Indian Pass System in the Canadian West, 1882–1935." *Prairie Forum*, 13(1): 25–42, pp. 26–7.

19. Torpey, J.C. 2000. *The Invention of the Passport: Surveillance, Citizenship and the State.* Cambridge: Cambridge University Press, p. 35.

20. Davies, S. 1996. "Campaigns of opposition to ID card schemes". *Privacy International,* August 24. Accessed at http://tinyurl.com/c8wpufx; Smith, R.E. 2002. *National ID Card: A License to Live.* Providence, RI: Privacy Journal; Geisler, C. 2006. "Ownership in stateless places" in Benda-Beckmann, F.v., Benda-Beckmann, K.v. and Wiber, M.G. (eds) *Changing Properties of Property* (pp. 40–57). New York: Berghahn Books, p. 44.

21. Hayden, R.M. 1996. "Imagined communities and real victims: Self-determination and ethnic cleansing in Yugoslavia". *American Ethnologist,* 23(4): 783–801, p. 792. Torpey, J.C. 2000. *Invention of the Passport*, pp. 24, 28, 51; Mitchell, T. 1988. *Colonising Egypt.* Cambridge: Cambridge University Press, p. 167; Robinson, J. 1996. *The Power of Apartheid: State, Power and Space in South African Cities.* Oxford: Butterworth-Heinemann, p. 186; Toyota, M. 2007. "Ambivalent categories: 'Hill tribes' and 'illegal migrants' in Thailand" in Rajaram, P.K. and Grundy-Warr, C. (eds) *Borderscapes: Hidden Geographies and Insurrectionary Politics at Territory's Edge* (pp. 91–118). Minneapolis: University of Minnesota Press.

22. Hambro, L.H. 1953. "Constitutional law: Denaturalization under the Immigration and Nationality Act of 1952". *Michigan Law Review*, 51(6): 881–902; Torpey. 2000. *Invention of the Passport*, p. 125; Land-Weber, E. 2000. *To Save a Life: Stories of Holocaust Rescue*. Urbana: University of Illinois Press, p. 9; Al-Qazzaz, A. 1971. "Power elite in Iraq – 1920–1958: A study of the cabinet". *Muslim World*, 61(4): 267–83, p. 271; Fattah, I.K. 2005. "The deportations of the Fayli Kurds". *International Conference on Iraqi Refugees and Internally Displaced Persons*. Accessed at http://tinyurl.com/bv6dly7; Makiya, K. 1998. *Republic of Fear: The Politics of Modern Iraq*. Berkeley: University of California Press (under the author's pseudonym S. al-Khalil); Associated Press. 2003. "Key events in Iraq's history". *Augusta Chronicle*, September 2; Steele, J. 2004. "Iraqis rush for passports denied under Saddam". *Guardian*, August 5.

23. Kertzer, D.I. and Arel, D. (eds). 2002. *Census and Identity: The Politics of Race, Ethnicity, and Language in National Censuses*. Cambridge: Cambridge University Press, p. 2; Thierer, A. 2001. "National ID cards: New technologies, same bad idea". *TechKnowledge Newletter*, 21. Accessed at www.cato.org/tech/tk/010928-tk.html; BBC News. 2004. "Should we carry ID cards?" *BBC News*, April 30.

24. Torpey. 2000. *Invention of the Passport*, p. 7; Lyon, D. (ed.) 2003. *Surveillance As Social Sorting: Privacy, Risk, and Digital Discrimination*. London: Routledge; Anderson, B. 1991. *Imagined Communities: Reflections on the Origin and Spread of Nationalism*. London: Verso, p. 184; Tujan, A., Gaughran, A. and Mollett, H. 2004. "Development and the 'Global War on Terror'". *Race & Class*, 46(1): 53–74, p. 69.

25. Ibid, p. 71.

26. Gandy, O.H. 2003. "Data mining and surveillance in the post-9/11 environment" in Ball, K. and Webster, F. (eds) *The Intensification of Surveillance: Crime, Terrorism and Warfare in the Information Age* (pp. 26–41). London: Pluto Press, pp. 34–5.

27. Anderson. 1991. *Imagined Communities*, p. 185; Hari, J. 2007. "Inside France's secret war". *Independent*, October 5. Accessed at http://tinyurl.com/46z6mt; Uvin, P. 2002. "On counting, categorizing, and violence in Burundi and Rwanda" in Kertzer, D.I. and Arel, D. (eds) *Census and Identity: The Politics of Race, Ethnicity, and Language in National Censuses*. Cambridge: Cambridge University Press.

28. Lyon. 2003. *Surveillance*, pp. 1–2; Zureik, E. 2002. "Theorizing surveillance: The case of the workplace" in Lyon, D. (ed.) *Surveillance As Social Sorting*. London: Routledge.

29. Land-Weber. 2000. *To Save a Life*, p. 9; Aly, G. and Roth, K.H. 2004. *The Nazi Census: Identification and Control in the Third Reich*. Philadelphia, PA: Temple University Press (trans. Black, E. and Oksiloff, A.), p. 1.

30. McGreal, C. 2006. "Brothers in arms: Israel's secret pact with Pretoria". *Guardian*, February 7. Accessed at http://tinyurl.com/92n89d

31. Simon Davies of Privacy International, quoted in *Asia Sentinel*. 2004. "Indonesia to join the smart card set". *Asia Sentinel*, September 4. Accessed at http://tinyurl.com/c4pk5ss

32. FitzGerald, V. and Cuesta-Leiva, J.A. 1997. *The Economic Value of a Passport: A Model of Citizenship and the Social Dividend in a Global Economy*. Queen Elizabeth House Working Paper Series. Oxford: University of Oxford.

33. ILO. 2005. *A Global Alliance Against Forced Labor: Global Report Under the Follow-up to the ILO Declaration on Fundamental Principles and Rights at Work*. Geneva: International Labour Office (ILO), p. 49.
34. Simon Davies of Privacy International, quoted in Wang, T.A. 2002. *The Debate Over a National Identification Card*. New York: Century Foundation, p. 6.
35. ILO. 2005. *Global Alliance*, p. 49.
36. Torpey. 2000. *Invention of the Passport*, p. 164.
37. Makiya. 1998. *Republic*, p. 138.
38. ILO. 2005. *Global Alliance*, pp. 49, 51; Tyuryukanova, E. 2005. *Forced Labour in the Russian Federation Today: Irregular Migration and Trafficking in Human Beings*. Geneva: International Labour Organisation, p. 79.
39. Slater, D. 1997. "Spatial politics/social movements: Questions of (b)orders and resistance in global times" in Pile, S. and Keith, M. (eds) *Geographies of Resistance* (pp. 258–76). London: Routledge, p. 274.
40. Aly and Roth. 2004. *Nazi Census*, p. 2.
41. Land-Weber. *To Save a Life*. p. 9.
42. Torpey. 2000. *Invention of the Passport*, p. 165.
43. Torpey, J. 1997. "Revolutions and freedom of movement: An analysis of passport controls in the French, Russian, and Chinese Revolutions". *Theory and Society*, 26(6): 837–68; Smith, G.E. 1989. "Privilege and place in Soviet society" in Gregory, D. and Walford, R. (eds) *Horizons in Human Geography* (pp. 320–40). Basingstoke: Macmillan Education; Wilson, F. 1985. "Mineral wealth and rural poverty: An analysis of the economic foundations of the political boundaries in southern Africa" in Giliomee, H.B. and Schlemmer, L. (eds) *Up Against the Fences: Poverty, Passes, and Privilege in South Africa* (pp. 57–64). New York: St Martin's Press; Brown, A.P. 2004. "The immobile mass: Movement restrictions in the West Bank". *Social & Legal Studies*, 13(4): 501–21; Zolberg, A. 1978. "International migration policies in a changing world system" in McNeill, W.H. and Adams, R. (eds) *Human Migration: Patterns and Policies* (pp. 241–86). Bloomington: Indiana University Press.
44. Torpey. 2000. *Invention of the Passport*, p. 51; Mitchell. *Colonising Egypt*. p. 34.
45. Torpey. 2000. *Invention of the Passport*, p. 7.
46. ILO. 2005. *Global Alliance*, p. 9.
47. Coleman, M. 2007. "A geopolitics of engagement: Neoliberalism, the war on terrorism, and the reconfiguration of US immigration enforcement". *Geopolitics*, 12(4): 607–34; Megoran, N. 2004. "The critical geopolitics of the Uzbekistan–Kyrgyzstan Ferghana Valley boundary dispute, 1999–2000". *Political Geography*, 23: 731–64.
48. Ford, R.T. 2001. "Local racisms and the law: Introduction" in Blomley, N.K., Delaney, D. and Ford, R.T. (eds) *The Legal Geographies Reader: Law, Power, and Space* (pp. 52–3). Malden, MA: Blackwell Publishers, p. 52.
49. Van Der Stoel, M. 1996. *Situation of Human Rights in Iraq: 1996*. United Nations General Assembly Report #A/51/496.
50. Makiya. 1998. *Republic*, p. 137.
51. Van Der Stoel. 1996. *Situation*.
52. Usher, S. 2007. "Passport dilemmas beset Iraqis". *BBC News*, March 21.
53. UN News Service. 2007. "Syria: Some 5,000 Iraqis queue outside UN refugee office in Damascus to register". *UN News Service*, December 2.

54. Dugard, J. 2006. *Report of the Special Rapporteur on the Situation of Human Rights in the Palestinian Territories Occupied Since 1967* (Advance Edited Version). UN Document E/CN.4/2006/29, p. 19.
55. Bourdieu, P. 1999. "Postscript" in Bourdieu, P., Accardo, A. and Balazs, G. (eds) *The Weight of the World: Social Suffering in Contemporary Society* (pp. 627–9). Cambridge: Polity Press, p. 627; Law, L. 1997. "Dancing on the bar: Sex, money and the uneasy politics of third space" in S. Pile and M. Keith (eds) *Geographies of Resistance* (pp. 107–23). London: Routledge, p. 115.
56. Slater. 1997. "Spatial politics", p. 274.
57. Sharma, A. and Gupta, A. (eds) 2006. *The Anthropology of the State: A Reader.* Oxford: Wiley-Blackwell, p. 15.
58. Land-Weber. 2000. *To Save a Life,* pp. 16–18.
59. Orlove, B. 1993. "The ethnography of maps: The cultural and social contexts of cartographic representation in Peru". *Cartographica: The International Journal for Geographic Information and Geovisualization,* 30(1): 29–46, p. 32.
60. Ibid.
61. Robinson. 1996. *Power of Apartheid,* pp. 193, 203; Savage, M. 1984. *Pass Laws and the Disorganisation and Reorganisation of the African Population in South Africa.* Conference Proceedings of the South Africa Labour and Development Research Unit, School of Economics, University of Cape Town. Cited in Giliomee and Schlemmer. 1985. *Up Against,* p. 1.
62. Robinson. 1996. *Power of Apartheid,* p. 193.

## CHAPTER 2

1. Harvard Law School. 1929. *Nationality; Responsibility of States; Territorial Waters: Drafts of Conventions Prepared in Anticipation of the First Conference on the Codification of International Law, The Hague, 1930.* Cambridge: Harvard Law School; Harvard Law School. 1929. "The law of nationality". 1929. *American Journal of International Law,* 23 (Special Supplement 13): 40–129; Brownlie, I. 1963. "Relations of nationality in public international law". *British Yearbook of International Law,* 39: 284. UN Subcommission on Prevention of Discrimination and Protection of Minorities. 1963. *Draft Principles on Freedom and Non-discrimination in Respect of Everyone to Leave Any Country, Including His Own, and to Return to His Country. (Res. 2B(XV).* UN Document E/CN.4/846, pp. 44, 46 (paragraph II(*b*)); Wyman, D.S. 1968. *Paper Walls: America and the Refugee Crisis, 1938–1941.* Amherst: University of Massachusetts Press.
2. UNHCR. 2006. *The State of the World's Refugees: Human Displacement in the New Millennium.* Oxford: Oxford University Press, p. 112.
3. Masalha, N. 1997. *A Land Without a People: Israel, Transfer and the Palestinians 1949–96.* London: Faber and Faber Limited, pp. 61–2.
4. Zureik, E. 2011. "Colonialism, surveillance, and population control" in Zureik, E., Lyon, D. and Abu-Laban, Y. (eds) *Surveillance and Control in Israel/Palestine: Population, Territory and Power* (pp. 3–46). New York: Routledge, pp. 22, 25.
5. Cattan, H. 1973. *Palestine and International Law: The Legal Aspects of the Arab–Israeli Conflict.* London: Longman Group Ltd, p. 64; Karpat, K.H. 1978. "Ottoman population records and the census of 1881/82–1893".

*International Journal of Middle East Studies.* 9(3): 237–74, pp. 239, 243, 245–7; Karpat, K.H. 1974. "Ottoman immigration policies and settlement in Palestine" in Abu-Lughod, I. and Abu-Laban, B. (eds) *Settler Regimes in Africa and the Arab World: The Illusion of Endurance* (pp. 57–74). Wilmette, IL: The Medina University Press International, p. 74.

6. Karpat. 1978. "Ottoman", pp. 248–9, 252, 254, 256; Israel State Archives. 2010. *Genealogy: The Study of Family History.* Accessed at http://tinyurl.com/7j8v7mz.

7. Leibler, A. and Breslau, D. 2005. "The uncounted: Citizenship and exclusion in the Israeli census of 1948". *Ethnic and Racial Studies,* 28(5): 880–902, pp. 885–6; Abu-Ghazaleh, A. 1974. "The Palestinian response to Zionist settlement: A cultural dimension" in Abu-Lughod, I. and Abu-Laban, B. (eds) *Settler Regimes in Africa and the Arab World: The Illusion of Endurance* (pp. 81–93). Wilmette, IL: The Medina University Press International, p. 90; Cattan, 1973, *Palestine,* pp. 14, 16.

8. Abu-Lughod, J.L. 1971. "The demographic transformation of Palestine" in Abu-Lughod, I. (ed.) *The Transformation of Palestine: Essays on the Origin and Development of the Arab-Israeli Conflict* (pp. 139–63). Evanston: Northwestern University Press, p. 143; Leibler, A. 2007. "Establishing scientific authority: Citizenship and the first census of Israel" in Brunner, J. (ed.) *Tel Aviver Jahrbuch für Deutsche Geschichte XXXV (Tel Aviv Yearbook for German History)* (pp. 221–36). Göttingen: Wallstein Verlag, pp. 224–5; Leibler, A. 2004. "Statisticians' reason: Governmentality, modernity, national legibility". *Israel Studies,* 9(2): 121–49, p. 130.

9. Boling, G. 2001. *Palestinian Refugees and the Right of Return: An International Law Analysis* (BADIL Information and Discussion Brief No. 8). Bethlehem: BADIL Resource Center for Palestinian Residency and Refugee Rights, p. 8; Government of Palestine. 1945. "Defence (Emergency) Regulations". *The Palestine Gazette,* 1442(2): 1055–98. Masalha, N. 1997. *A Land Without a People: Israel, Transfer and the Palestinians 1949–96.* London: Faber and Faber Limited, p. 111; Gilmour, D. 1980. *Dispossessed: The Ordeal of the Palestinians 1917–1980.* London: Sidgwick & Jackson, pp. 95–6.

10. Cattan. 1973. *Palestine,* pp. 42, 74; Abu-Lughod. 1971. "Demographic", p. 156; United Nations General Assembly. 1947. *Plenary Meetings of the General Assembly, 126th Meeting,* November 28. UN Document A/PV.126; Davis, U. 1987. *Israel: An Apartheid State.* London: Zed Books, pp. 25–6.

11. Pappé, I. 2006. *The Ethnic Cleansing of Palestine.* Oxford: One World Publications, pp. 104, 109; Gilmour. 1980. *Dispossessed,* p. 93, 104; Masalha. 1997. *A Land,* p. x;. Robinson, S. 2005. *Occupied Citizens in a Liberal State: Palestinians Under Military Rule and the Colonial Formation of Israeli Society, 1948–1966.* Dissertation: Stanford University, p. 117; Rouhana, N. 1997. *Palestinian Citizens in an Ethnic Jewish State: Identities in Conflict.* New Haven: Yale University Press, pp. 81–2.

12. Boqa'i, N. 2008/9. "Palestinian internally displaced persons inside Israel: Challenging the solid structures". *Palestine–Israel Journal of Politics, Economics and Culture,* 15(4)/16(1); Al-Haj, M. 1988. "The Arab internal refugees in Israel: The emergence of a minority within the minority". *Immigrants & Minorities,* 7(2): 149–65; Rouhana. 1997. *Palestinian,* pp. 81–2.

13. Israel State Archives. 2010. *Genealogy*; Robinson. 2005. *Occupied Citizens*, p. 57; Pappé. 2006. *Ethnic Cleansing*, p. 211; Leibler. 2007. "Establishing", p. 226.

14. W.A.H. (name withheld by request). 2006. Former teacher in Tarshiha, and 78-year-old survivor of 1948 war, interview with Adah Kay, April 25, Tarshiha.

15. Robinson. 2005. *Occupied Citizens*, p. 59.

16. Cattan. 1973. *Palestine*, p. 88.

17. United Nations General Assembly. 1948. *Progress Report of the United Nations Mediator on Palestine (3rd Session)*, September 16. UN Document A/648.

18. W.A.H. 2006. Interview.

19. Leibler. 2007. "Establishing", p. 227; Robinson. 2005. *Occupied Citizens*, p. 58; Leibler. 2004. "Statisticians", p. 132.

20. Robinson. 2005. *Occupied Citizens*, pp. 57–8.

21. Leibler and Breslau. 2005. "Uncounted", pp. 893–4.

22. Peretz, D. 1995. *Palestinian Refugee Compensation* (Information Paper No. 3). Washington, DC: The Center for Policy Analysis on Palestine, p. 3.

23. Leibler. 2007. "Establishing", p. 226.

24. Peretz. 1995. *Palestinian*, p. 6; Korn, A. 2000. "Military government, political control and crime: The case of Israeli Arabs". *Crime, Law & Social Change*, 34: 159–82, p. 163 – quoting Ya'acov Shimoni, August 29, 1948, Israel State Archives (ISA), Minority Affairs Ministry Papers (MAM), Gimel/308/9; Landau, J.M. 1969. *The Arabs in Israel: A Political Study*. Oxford: Oxford University Press, p. 34.

25. Robinson. 2005. *Occupied Citizens*, pp. 51–2.

26. Leibler. 2007. "Establishing", pp. 229–30.

27. Robinson. 2005. *Occupied Citizens*, pp. 51–2; Peretz. 1995. *Palestinian*, p. 6.

28. Israel Central Bureau of Statistics. 2010. *Previous Censuses*. Accessed at http:// tinyurl.com/ccdydep; Robinson. 2005. *Occupied Citizens*, p. 59; Rouhana. 1997. *Palestinian*, pp. 50–1.

29. Robinson. 2005. *Occupied Citizens*, p. 52; Lustick, I. 1980. *Arabs in the Jewish State: Israel's Control of a National Minority*. Austin: University of Texas Press, pp. 48–9.

30. United Nations General Assembly. 1948. *Universal Declaration of Human Rights*. Accessed at www.un.org/en/documents/udhr; Robinson. 2005. *Occupied Citizens*, p. 51; Boling. 2001. *Palestinian*, p. 4.

31. Boling. 2001. *Palestinian*, p. 4.

32. Robinson. 2005. *Occupied Citizens*, p. 53; Rouhana. 1997. *Palestinian*, pp. 81–2. Leibler. 2007. "Establishing", p. 234; Korn. 2000. "Military", p. 163.

33. Kanaana, S. 2005. Professor of Anthropology, Birzeit University, interview with Adah Kay, April, Birzeit.

34. Boling. 2001. *Palestinian*, pp. 2–4.

35. G.B. (name withheld by request). 2005. Journalist, translator, and 64-year-old survivor of 1948 war, interview with Amahl Bishara, July 2, Burke, VA, USA.

36. Rouhana. 1997. *Palestinian*, pp. 81–2; Landau. 1969. *Arabs*, p. 30; Boling. 2001. *Palestinian*, p. 2; Lustick. 1980. *Arabs*, p. 61.

37. G.B. 2005. Interview.

38. W.A.H. 2006. Interview.

39. Boling. 2001. *Palestinian*, pp. 14–15.

40. Korn. 2000. "Military", p. 179.
41. Morris, B. 2004. *The Birth of the Palestinian Refugee Problem Revisited.* Cambridge: Cambridge University Press, p. 292.
42. Robinson. 2005. *Occupied Citizens*, p. 70; Gilmour. 1980. *Dispossessed*, p. 101; Masalha. 1997. *A Land*, p. 9.
43. Korn, A. 2000. "Crime and legal control: The Israeli Arab population during the military government period (1948–66)". *British Journal of Criminology*, 40: 574–93, p. 586.
44. Israel State Archives. 2010. *Genealogy;* Leibler and Breslau. 2005. "Uncounted", p. 897; Davis. 1987. *Israel*, p. 18.
45. Kamen, C.S. 2005. *The 2008 Israel Integrated Census of Population and Housing: Basic Conception and Procedure.* Tel Aviv: Israel Central Bureau of Statistics, p. 13. Boqa'i. 2008/9. "Palestinian".
46. Korn. 2000. "Military", p. 167.
47. Kamen. 2005. *2008 Israel*, p. 5; Robinson. 2005. *Occupied Citizens*, p. 59.
48. Kamen. 2005. *2008 Israel*, p. 2.
49. Leibler. 2004. "Statisticians"; p. 132. Kamen. 2005. *2008 Israel*, pp. 2, 5; Davis. 1987. *Israel*, p. 27.
50. Robinson. 2005. *Occupied Citizens*, p. 81; Davis. 1987. *Israel*, p. 27.
51. Masalha. 1997. *Land*, p. xviii.
52. Peretz. 1995. *Palestinian*, p. 5.
53. Segev, T. 1986. *1949: The First Israelis.* New York: The Free Press (trans. Weinstein, A.N.), pp. 46–7.
54. Leibler and Breslau. 2005. "Uncounted", p. 894; Robinson. 2005. *Occupied Citizens*, p. 106.
55. Segev. 1986. *1949: The First Israelis*, p. 52.
56. Robinson. 2005. *Occupied Citizens*, p. 150.
57. Segev. 1986. *1949: The First Israelis*, p. 52.
58. Boling. 2001. *Palestinian*, p. 4; Pappé. 2006. *Ethnic Cleansing*, pp. 53–4; Robinson. 2005. *Occupied Citizens*, p. 111.
59. Masalha. 1997. *Land*, p. 12.
60. Gilmour. 1980. *Dispossessed*, p. 106.
61. Robinson. 2005. *Occupied Citizens*, pp. 81–2; Contini, P. 1949. *Legal Aspects of the Problem of Compensation to Palestine Refugees*, November 22. UN Document A/AC.25/W/32. Citing a memorandum by Dr. G. Meron for the Government of Israel to the UNCCP Technical Committee (28 July 1949).
62. Robinson. 2005. *Occupied Citizens*, pp. 44–5.
63. International Committee of the Red Cross. 1949. "Article 49". *Convention (IV) Relative to the Protection of Civilian Persons in Time of War*, August 12. Geneva.
64. Boling. 2001. *Palestinian*, pp. 9–10; International Committee of the Red Cross. 1949. "Article 6" and "Article 158". *Convention (IV) Relative to the Protection of Civilian Persons in Time of War*, August 12. Geneva.
65. Contini. 1949. *Legal Aspects.*
66. Boqa'i. 2008/9. "Palestinian".
67. Korn. 2000. "Military", p. 179; Robinson. 2005. *Occupied Citizens*, p. 113.
68. Kanaana. 2005. Interview.
69. Robinson. 2005. *Occupied Citizens*, p. 115.
70. Kanaana. 2005. Interview.
71. Peretz. 1995. *Palestinian*, p. 9.

72. Robinson. 2005. *Occupied Citizens*, pp. 119, 129.
73. Ibid. pp. 120–1.
74. Kretzmer, D. 1990. *The Legal Status of the Arabs in Israel*. Boulder, CO: Westview Press, p. 36; citing Rubinstein, A. 1959. *The Constitutional Law of the State of Israel*. Jerusalem, pp. 161, 182.
75. Gilmour. 1980. *Dispossessed*, p. 92; Boqa'i. 2008/9. "Palestinian".
76. Robinson. 2005. *Occupied Citizens*, p. 126.
77. Robinson. 2005. *Occupied Citizens*, p. 140; Masalha. 1997. *A Land*, p. 11; Gilmour. 1980. *Dispossessed*, p. 105.
78. Boling. 2001. *Palestinian*, pp. 33–4; Quoting Zeltner, J. in A.B. v. M.B. 1951. 17 *Israel Law Reports* 110, Tel Aviv District Court, April 6.
79. Akram, S. 2000. *Protection and its Applicability to the Palestinian Refugee Case*. (BADIL Information and Discussion Brief No. 4). Bethlehem: BADIL Resource Center for Palestinian Residency and Refugee Rights, pp. 3–4.
80. Boqa'i. 2008/9. "Palestinian".
81. State of Israel. 1952. "Nationality Law (5712)". *Israel Official Gazette*, 93: 22; Rouhana. 1997. *Palestinian*, pp. 50–1; citing Halabi, U. 1987. *Discrimination on the Basis of National Affiliation in Israeli Legislation*. Master's thesis, Hebrew University Law School, Jerusalem; Robinson. 2005. *Occupied Citizens*, p. 176.
82. Rouhana. 1997. *Palestinian*, pp. 50–1; citing Halabi. 1987. *Discrimination*.
83. Robinson. 2005. *Occupied Citizens*, p. 175.
84. Ibid. p. 176.
85. Masalha. 1997. *Land*, pp. 3–4; Korn. 2000. "Military", p. 164; Korn. 2000. "Crime", pp. 582–3.
86. Landau. 1969. *Arabs*, p. 30.
87. Korn. 2000. "Military", p. 179; citing Israel State Archives. Police Ministry Papers. Gimel/6839.
88. Masalha. 1997. *Land*, p. 7; Leibler. 2007. "Establishing", pp. 223, 235; Korn. 2000. "Military", p. 163; Davis. 1987. *Israel*, p. 36.
89. Robinson. 2005. *Occupied Citizens*, p. 129.
90. United Nations Human Rights Committee. 1999. *General Comment No. 27: Freedom of Movement (Art. 12)*. UN Document CCPR/C/21/Rev.1/Add.9.
91. Korn. 2000. "Crime", p. 583; Rouhana. 1997. *Palestinian*, pp. 50–1; citing Halabi. 1987. *Discrimination*.
92. Robinson. 2005. *Occupied Citizens*, p. 128; Abu-Lughod, 1971, "Demographic", pp. 161–3.
93. Masalha. 1997. *Land*, pp. 112, 123.
94. Leibler, A.E. 2011. "'You must know your stock': Census as surveillance practice in 1948 and 1967" in Zureik, E., Lyon, D. and Abu-Laban, Y. (eds) *Surveillance and Control in Israel/Palestine: Population, Territory and Power* (pp. 239–56). New York: Routledge, p. 242.
95. Al-Haq. 1989. *Nation Under Siege*. Ramallah: Al-Haq, p. 336; Maksidi, S. 2008. *Palestine Inside Out: An Everyday Occupation*. New York: W.W. Norton & Co. Inc., p. 77.
96. Dodd, P. and Barakat, H. 1968. *River Without Bridges: A Study of the Exodus of the 1967 Palestinian Arab Refugees*. Beirut: Institute for Palestine Studies, pp. 5, 35; Schiff, B.N. 1995. *Refugees unto the Third Generation: UN Aid to Palestinians*. Syracuse: Syracuse University Press, pp. 52, 68, 187, 302.
97. Abu-Lughod. 1971. "Demographic", p. 163.

98. Masalha. 1997. *Land*, p. 111.
99. Gilmour. 1980. *Dispossessed*, p. 102–3, 107.
100. Rouhana. 1997. *Palestinian*, pp. 81–2; Robinson. 2005. *Occupied Citizens*, p. 179; Davis. 1987. *Israel*, p. 38.
101. United Nations General Assembly. 2008. *The Syrian Golan*. UN Document A/RES/62/85.
102. Masalha. 1997. *Land*, p. 120.
103. Leibler. 2007. "Establishing", p. 236.
104. Elazar, D.J. 1987. *Backing into a Jewish Majority in Israel*. Jerusalem: Jerusalem Center for Public Affairs.
105. Elazar. 1987. *Backing*.
106. Israel Central Bureau of Statistics. 2010. *Previous Censuses*.
107. Hass, A. 2005. "Go study in Australia?" *Ha'aretz*, December 14.
108. Zureik, E. 2001. "Constructing Palestine through surveillance practices". *British Journal of Middle Eastern Studies*, 28(2): 205–27.
109. Boling. 2001. *Palestinian*, pp. 5–6.
110. Cattan. 1973. *Palestine*, p. 72.

## CHAPTER 3

1. Karpat, K.H. 1978. "Ottoman population records and the census of 1881/82–1893". *International Journal of Middle East Studies*. 9(3): 237–74, pp. 248, 253.
2. Fischbach, M.R. 2011. "British and Zionist data gathering on Palestinian Arab landownership and population during the Mandate" in Zureik, E., Lyon, D. and Abu-Laban, Y. (eds) *Surveillance and Control in Israel/Palestine: Population, Territory and Power* (pp. 297–312). New York: Routledge, p. 302–4; Elazar, D.J. 1995. *Albert Elazar: A Personal Memoir of My Father*. Jerusalem: Jerusalem Center for Public Affairs.
3. Tegart, C.A. 1920–42. *Sir Charles Tegart Collection*. Archived documents, GB165-0281, St. Antony's College Middle East Centre Archives, University of Oxford; Abu-Ghazaleh, A. 1974. "The Palestinian response to Zionist settlement: A cultural dimension" in Abu-Lughod, I. and Abu-Laban, B. (eds) *Settler Regimes in Africa and the Arab World: The Illusion of Endurance* (pp. 81–93). Wilmette, IL: The Medina University Press International, p. 89; Cohen, H. 2011. "The matrix of surveillance in times of national conflict: The Israeli–Palestinian case" in Zureik, E., Lyon, D. and Abu-Laban, Y. (eds) *Surveillance and Control in Israel/Palestine: Population, Territory and Power* (pp. 99–112). New York: Routledge, p. 101.
4. Segev, T. 1986. *1949: The First Israelis*. New York: The Free Press (trans. Weinstein, A.N.), p. 50; quoting *Hapraklit* (The Lawyer), February 1946, pp. 58–64.
5. Pappé, I. 2006. *The Ethnic Cleansing of Palestine*. Oxford: One World Publications, pp. 53, 267.
6. Pappé. 2006. *Ethnic Cleansing*, p. 20; Fischbach. 2011. "British", p. 305.
7. Cohen. 2011. "Matrix", p. 101; Finkelstein, N. G. 2003. *Image and Reality of the Israel-Palestine Conflict* (2nd ed.). London: Verso, p. 15; Freedman, R.O. 2003. "Classical Zionism is still relevant". *Israel Studies Forum*. 19(1): 89–97, pp. 93–4; Lustick, I. 2003. "Zionist ideology and its discontents: A research note". *Israel Studies Forum*. 19(1): 98–103, p. 100; Yuval-Davis, N.

2003. "Conclusion" in Nimni, E. (ed.) *The Challenge of Post-Zionism* (pp. 182–96). London: Zed Books; Abu-Lughod, J.L. 1971. "The demographic transformation of Palestine" in Abu-Lughod, I. (ed.) *The Transformation of Palestine: Essays on the Origin and Development of the Arab-Israeli Conflict* (pp. 139–63). Evanston: Northwestern University Press, p. 151; Miller, R. 2000. *Divided Against Zion: Anti-Zionist Opposition in Britain to a Jewish State in Palestine, 1945–1948.* London: Frank Cass.

8. Allon, Y. 1970. *The Making of Israel's Army.* London: Vallentine Mitchell, p. 7; Yiftachel, O. 2006. *Ethnocracy: Land and Identity Politics in Israel/ Palestine.* Philadelphia: University of Pennsylvania Press, p. 54.

9. Gorny, Y. 1987. *Zionism and the Arabs, 1882–1948: A Study of Ideology.* Oxford: Clarendon Press, pp. 13, 26; Berkowitz, M. 2005. "Rejecting Zion, embracing the Orient: The life and death of Jacob Israel De Haan" in Kalmar, I.D. and Penslar, D.J. (eds) *Orientalism and the Jews* (pp. 109–24). Hanover and London: Brandeis University Press; Cohen. 2011. "Matrix", p. 100.

10. The following section draws from: Pappé. 2006. *Ethnic Cleansing*, pp. 19, 21–2, 28, 53, 171.

11. Ibid. p. 53.

12. Ibid. p. 200.

13. Ibid. p. 190.

14. Morris, B. 2004. *The Birth of the Palestinian Refugee Problem Revisited.* Cambridge: Cambridge University Press, p. 482.

15. Pappé. 2006. *Ethnic Cleansing*, p. 190.

16. Morris. 2004. *Birth,* pp. 149–50.

17. Boqa'i, N. 2006. *Returning to Kafr Bir'im.* Bethlehem: BADIL Resource Center for Palestinian Residency and Refugee Rights, pp. 23, 25.

18. Pappé. 2006. *Ethnic Cleansing*, p. 189.

19. Lustick, I. 1980. *Arabs in the Jewish State: Israel's Control of a National Minority.* Austin: University of Texas Press, p. 192.

20. Pappé. 2006. *Ethnic Cleansing*, pp. 64, 200.

21. Palumbo, M. 1991. *The Palestinian Catastrophe.* New York: Faber and Faber, pp. 171–2; Robinson, S. 2006. *A History of Israeli Citizenship from the Margins.* Lecture delivered at Rice University, Houston, Texas, October 24, p. 13.

22. Pappé. 2006. *Ethnic Cleansing*, pp. 211, 213; Lustick. 1980. *Arabs,* p. 26; Robinson, S. 2005. *Occupied Citizens in a Liberal State: Palestinians Under Military Rule and the Colonial Formation of Israeli Society, 1948–1966.* Dissertation: Stanford University, pp. 113, 118.

23. Fischbach. 2011. "British", pp. 309–10; Israel State Archives. 2010. *Genealogy: The Study of Family History.* Accessed at http://tinyurl.com/7j8v7mz; Zureik, E. 2011. "Colonialism, surveillance, and population control" in Zureik, E., Lyon, D. and Abu-Laban, Y. (eds) *Surveillance and Control in Israel/Palestine: Population, Territory and Power* (pp. 3–46). New York: Routledge, p. 10; Black, I. and Morris, B. 1991. *Israel's Secret Wars: A History of Israel's Intelligence Services.* New York: Grove Weidenfeld, p. 129.

24. Kretzmer, D. 1990. *The Legal Status of the Arabs in Israel.* Boulder, CO: Westview Press, p. 136; Robinson. 2006. *History,* p. 4; Landau, J.M. 1969. *The Arabs in Israel: A Political Study.* Oxford: Oxford University Press, p. 94; Gilmour, D. 1980. *Dispossessed: The Ordeal of the Palestinians 1917–1980.*

London: Sidgwick & Jackson, p. 95; Jiryis, S. 1968. *The Arabs in Israel*. Beirut: Institute for Palestine Studies, p. 25; Lustick. 1980. *Arabs*, p. 194.

25. Schoenman, R. 1988. *The Hidden History of Zionism*. San Francisco: Socialist Action Books, p. 52; Lustick, 1980. *Arabs*. p. 193; Boqa'i, N. 2008/9. "Palestinian internally displaced persons inside Israel: Challenging the solid structures". *Palestine–Israel Journal of Politics, Economics and Culture*, 15(4)/16(1); Cohen. 2011. "Matrix", p. 104.
26. Lustick. 1980. *Arabs*, p.193.
27. Cohen. 2011. "Matrix", p. 104.
28. Lustick. 1980. *Arabs*, p. 193.
29. Korn, A. 2000. "Military government, political control and crime: The case of Israeli Arabs". *Crime, Law & Social Change*, 34: 159–82, p. 169.
30. Robinson. 2005. *Occupied Citizens*, p. 131.
31. Schoenman. 1988. *Hidden*, p. 29.
32. Robinson. 2005. *Occupied Citizens*, p. 131.
33. Lustick. 1980. *Arabs*, p. 193; Cohen. 2011. "Matrix", p. 103.
34. Robinson. 2005. *Occupied Citizens*, p. 152.
35. Lustick. 1980. *Arabs*, pp. 54–5.
36. Quoted in Lustick. 1980. *Arabs*, p. 25.
37. Robinson. 2005. *Occupied Citizens*, p. 55.
38. Leibler, A. and Breslau, D. 2005. "The uncounted: Citizenship and exclusion in the Israeli census of 1948". *Ethnic and Racial Studies*, 28(5): 880–902, p. 894.
39. Zureik. 2011. "Colonialism", pp. 18–9.
40. Cook, J. 2006. *Blood and Religion: The Unmasking of the Jewish and Democratic State*. London: Pluto Press, pp. 100–1.
41. Robinson. 2005. *Occupied Citizens*, p. 111.
42. Quigley, J. 1990. *Palestine and Israel: A Challenge to Justice*. Durham: Duke University Press, p. 134.
43. Robinson. 2005. *Occupied Citizens*, p. 103.
44. Halabi, U. 2011. "Legal analysis and critique of some surveillance methods used by Israel". in Zureik, E., Lyon, D. and Abu-Laban, Y. (eds) *Surveillance and Control in Israel/Palestine: Population, Territory and Power* (pp. 199–218). New York: Routledge, p. 206.
45. Robinson. 2005. *Occupied Citizens*, p. 103.
46. Halabi. 2011. "Legal", p. 205; Davis, U. 1987. *Israel: An Apartheid State*. London: Zed Books, p. 61.
47. Halabi. 2011. "Legal", p. 206; Cook. 2006. *Blood*, pp. 15–6; Quigley. 1990. *Palestine*, p. 126.
48. Robinson. 2005. *Occupied Citizens*, p. 149.
49. Black and Morris. 1991. *Israel's Secret*, p. 129; United Nations Security Council. 1953. *The Palestine Question*, November 16. UN Document S/636/Rev.1.
50. United Nations Security Council. 1953. *The Palestine Question*, October 27. UN Document S/PV.630.
51. United Nations Security Council, 1953, *Palestine Question*, November 16.
52. Cohen. 2011. "Matrix", p. 105.
53. Halabi. 2011. "Legal", p. 207.
54. Cook. 2006. *Blood*, pp. 142–3.
55. Quigley. 1990. *Palestine*, p. 181.

56. Al-Haq. 1989. *Nation Under Siege*. Ramallah: Al-Haq, p. 323.

57. Hass, A. 2005. "You exist if the Israeli computer says so". *Ha'aretz*, September 28.

58. Quigley. 1990. *Palestine*, p. 136.

59. Quigley. 1990. *Palestine*, pp. 129; Cook. 2006. *Blood*, pp. 15–6; Rouhana, N. 1997. *Palestinian Citizens in an Ethnic Jewish State: Identities in Conflict*. New Haven: Yale University Press, p. 220.

60. Cohen. 2011. "Matrix", p. 105.

61. Quigley. 1990. *Palestine*, pp. 201–2.

62. Turki, F. 1974. *The Disinherited: Journal of a Palestinian Exile*. New York: Monthly Review Press, pp. 123–4.

63. Quigley. 1990. *Palestine*, p. 146; Halabi. 2011. "Legal", p. 206; Zureik. 2011. "Colonialism", p. 21.

64. Quigley. 1990. *Palestine*, pp. 201–2.

65. Ibid. pp. 201–2.

66. Be'er, Y. and Abdel-Jawad, S. 1994. *Collaborators in the Occupied Territories: Human Rights Abuses and Violations*. Jerusalem: B'Tselem, p. 59; Zureik. 2011. "Colonialism", p. 19; Merriman, R. 2006. "Portraits of Palestinian resistance: Introduction". *Electronic Intifada*, June 8.

67. Quigley. 1990. *Palestine*, pp. 204–5.

68. Benvenisti, M. 1987. *1987 Report*. Jerusalem: West Bank Database Project, p. 35.

69. Ibid. p. 35.

70. Cohen. 2011. "Matrix", p. 109.

71. Al-Haq. 1989. *Nation*, p. 323.

72. Hass, A. 2002. "Israel's closure policy: An ineffective strategy of containment and repression". *Journal of Palestine Studies*, 31(3): 5–20.

73. Al-Haq. 1989. *Nation*.

74. Ibid. p. 329.

75. Kelly, T. 2006. "Documented lives: Fear and the uncertainties of law during the second Palestinian Intifada". *Journal of the Royal Anthropological Institute*, 12: 89–107.

76. Dugard, J. 2007. *Implementation of General Assembly Resolution 60/251*, January 29. UN Document A/HRC/4/17.

77. B'Tselem and Hamoked. 2007. *Absolute Prohibition: The Torture and Ill-treatment of Palestinian Detainees*. Jerusalem: B'Tselem and Hamoked.

78. Halabi. 2011. "Legal", p. 206.

79. Cook. 2006. *Blood*, pp. 62–3.

80. Ibid. pp. 40, 44.

81. Halabi. 2011. "Legal", p. 206; Zureik. 2011. "Colonialism", p. 21.

82. Cook. 2006. *Blood*, pp. 98, 100–1.

83. Ibid. pp. 97–8, 134.

84. Halabi. 2011. "Legal", pp. 208–10, 212.

85. B'Tselem. 2012. *Statistics*. Accessed at http://old.btselem.org/statistics/english

86. Denes, N. 2011. "From tanks to wheelchairs: Unmanned aerial vehicles, Zionist battlefield experiences, and the transparence of the civilian" in Zureik, E., Lyon, D. and Abu-Laban, Y. (eds) *Surveillance and Control in Israel/Palestine: Population, Territory and Power* (pp. 171–98). New York: Routledge, p. 185.

87. Cook, C., Hanieh, A. and Kay, A. 2004. *Stolen Youth*. London: Pluto Press, p. 61.
88. Dalrymple, J. 2000. "Newly published SS handbook gives blueprint for Nazi Britain". *Independent*, March 3.
89. 1945. "Nazi's black list discovered in Berlin". *Guardian*, September 14.

## CHAPTER 4

1. Korn, A. 2000. "Military government, political control and crime: The case of Israeli Arabs". *Crime, Law & Social Change*, 34: 159–82, pp. 168–9.
2. Robinson, S. 2005. *Occupied Citizens in a Liberal State: Palestinians Under Military Rule and the Colonial Formation of Israeli Society, 1948–1966*. Dissertation: Stanford University, pp. 4, 39.
3. Karpat, K.H. 1978. "Ottoman population records and the census of 1881/82–1893". *International Journal of Middle East Studies*. 9(3): 237–74, pp. 245, 255.
4. Ibid. pp. 252–3.
5. Ibid. p. 256.
6. Robinson. 2005. *Occupied Citizens*, p. 40.
7. Robinson, S. 2006. *A History of Israeli Citizenship from the Margins*. Lecture delivered at Rice University, Houston, Texas, October 24, p. 4. Robinson. 2005. *Occupied Citizens*, p. 61.
8. Robinson. 2005. *Occupied* Citizens, p. 60. Quoting Hanna Ibrahim, a villager from Bi'na (Acre district).
9. Ibid. pp. 65–6.
10. Segev, T. 1986. *1949: The First Israelis*. New York: The Free Press (trans. Weinstein, A.N.), p. 52.
11. Robinson. 2006. *History*, p. 4.
12. Pappé, I. 2006. *The Ethnic Cleansing of Palestine*. Oxford: One World Publications, p. 53.
13. Robinson. 2006. *History*, p. 6.
14. Ibid. p. 125.
15. Ibid. p. 73.
16. Ibid. p. 120.
17. Ibid. pp. 178–9.
18. Ibid. pp. 91–2.
19. Quoted in Segev. 1986. *1949: The First Israelis*, p. 65.
20. Lustick, I. 1980. *Arabs in the Jewish State: Israel's Control of a National Minority*. Austin: University of Texas Press, p. 146; Cohen, H. 2011. "The matrix of surveillance in times of national conflict: The Israeli–Palestinian case" in Zureik, E., Lyon, D. and Abu-Laban, Y. (eds) *Surveillance and Control in Israel/Palestine: Population, Territory and Power* (pp. 99–112). New York: Routledge, pp. 103–4.
21. Quoted in Jiryis, S. 1968. *The Arabs in Israel*. Beirut: Institute for Palestine Studies, p. 20.
22. Lustick. 1980. *Arabs*, p. 84.
23. Korn. 2000. "Military, p. 175; Lustick. 1980. *Arabs*, p. 146.
24. Landau, J.M. 1969. *The Arabs in Israel: A Political Study*. London: Oxford University Press, pp. 2–3.

25. Gilmour, D. 1980. *Dispossessed. The Ordeal of the Palestinians 1917–1980.* London: Sidgwick & Jackson, p. 93.
26. Pappé. 2006. *Ethnic Cleansing*, p. 201.
27. Israel State Archives. 2010. *Genealogy: The Study of Family History.* Accessed at http://tinyurl.com/7j8v7mz
28. Leibler, A. 2007. "Establishing scientific authority: Citizenship and the first census of Israel" in Brunner, J. (ed.) *Tel Aviver Jahrbuch für Deutsche Geschichte XXXV (Tel Aviv Yearbook for German History)* (pp. 221–36). Göttingen: Wallstein Verlag, p. 224.
29. Robinson. 2006. *History*, p. 11.
30. Segev. 1986. *1949: the First Israelis*, p. 52.
31. Lustick. 1980. *Arabs*, p. 204.
32. Robinson. 2006. *History*, p. 11.
33. Robinson. 2005. *Occupied Citizens*, pp. 158–9.
34. Robinson. 2006. *History*, p. 10.
35. Robinson. 2005. *Occupied Citizens*, p. 151.
36. Kanaana, S. 2005. Professor of Anthropology, Birzeit University, interview with Adah Kay, April, Birzeit.
37. Boqa'i, N. 2008/9. "Palestinian internally displaced persons inside Israel: Challenging the solid structures". *Palestine–Israel Journal of Politics, Economics and Culture*, 15(4)/16(1).
38. Korn. 2000. "Military", p. 174.
39. Lustick. 1980. *Arabs*, pp. 195–6.
40. Robinson. 2005. *Occupied Citizens*, p. 136; Boqa'i. 2008/9. "Palestinian".
41. Robinson. 2005. *Occupied Citizens*, pp. 64–5.
42. Quoted in Quigley, J. 1990. *Palestine and Israel: A Challenge to Justice.* Durham: Duke University Press, pp. 131–2.
43. Robinson. 2005. *Occupied Citizens*, p. 127.
44. Lustick. 1980. *Arabs*, pp. 195–6.
45. Quigley. 1990. *Palestine*, p. 132.
46. Korn. 2000. "Military", p. 169.
47. Quigley. 1990. *Palestine*, p. 133.
48. Schölch, A. (ed.) 1983. *Palestinians over the Green Line.* London: Ithaca Press, pp. 19–20.
49. Kirschbaum, D.A. 2007. "Israeli emergency regulations and the defense (emergency) regulations of 1945". *Israeli Law Resource Center.* Accessed at http://tinyurl.com/7hz2c2q
50. Zureik, E. 2011. "Colonialism, surveillance, and population control" in Zureik, E., Lyon, D. and Abu-Laban, Y. (eds) *Surveillance and Control in Israel/Palestine: Population, Territory and Power* (pp. 3–46). New York: Routledge, p. 16.
51. Be'er, Y. and Abdel-Jawad, S. 1994. *Collaborators in the Occupied Territories: Human Rights Abuses and Violations.* Jerusalem: B'Tselem, p. 26.
52. Ibid. p. 79.
53. Ibid. p. 77.
54. Ibid. p. 78.
55. Ibid. p. 79.
56. Ibid. p. 26.
57. Schoenman, R. 1988. *The Hidden History of Zionism.* San Francisco: Socialist Action Books, p. 50.

58. Al-Haq. 1989. *Nation under siege*. Ramallah: Al-Haq, p. 336.
59. Be'er and Abdel-Jawad. 1994. *Collaborators*, p. 26.
60. Schoenman. 1988. *Hidden*, p. 17.
61. Al-Haq. 1989. *Nation*, p. 336.
62. Ibid. p. 336.
63. A.O. (name withheld by request). 2007. Municipal engineer, interview with Nadia Abu-Zahra, March 7, by telephone from Oxford, UK.
64. Cook, C., Hanieh, A. and Kay, A. 2004. *Stolen Youth*. London: Pluto Press, p. 58.
65. A.O. 2007. Interview.
66. B'Tselem. 2003. *Zeita: Border Police Officer Forces Man from 'Attil to Commit Sexual Act with Donkey*. Accessed at http://tinyurl.com/6yzg43h
67. B'Tselem. 2006. *Israeli Soldiers Use Khaled al-Kafarneh as Human Shield: Beit Hanuna July 2006*. Accessed at http://tinyurl.com/66d6tpc
68. Pappé. 2006. *Ethnic Cleansing*, pp. 20, 267.
69. Ibid. pp. 133–5.
70. Robinson. 2006. *History*, p. 9.
71. Sa'di. 2011. "Ominous designs: Israel's strategies and tactics of controlling the Palestinians during the first two decades" in Zureik, E., Lyon, D. and Abu-Laban, Y. (eds) *Surveillance and Control in Israel/Palestine: Population, Territory and Power* (pp. 83–98). New York: Routledge, p. 90. Quoting Arab Affairs Committee, 1958, *Protocol of Meeting of the Arab Affairs Committee*, January 30, Labor Party Archive, Files 7/32 (Hebrew), p. 4.
72. Be'er and Abdel-Jawad. 1994. *Collaborators*, p. 32.
73. Sa'di. 2011. "Ominous", p. 90.
74. Robinson. 2006. *History*, p. 9.
75. Robinson. 2005. *Occupied Citizens*, p. 127.
76. Robinson. 2006. *History*, p. 8.
77. Robinson. 2005. *Occupied Citizens*, pp. 121–2.
78. Korn. 2000. "Military", p. 169.
79. Kanaana. 2005. Interview.
80. Korn. 2000. "Military", p. 180.
81. Kanaana. 2005. interview.
82. Be'er and Abdel-Jawad. 1994. *Collaborators*, pp. 33–4.
83. Robinson. 2006. *History*, p. 9.
84. Be'er and Abdel-Jawad. 1994. *Collaborators*, p. 32.
85. Korn, 2000. "Military". p. 170.
86. Kanaana. 2005. Interview.
87. A.G. (name withheld by request). 2006. 74-year old survivor of 1948 war, interview with Adah Kay, June 18, Shafa 'Amr.
88. Robinson. 2006. *History*, p. 12.
89. Kanaana. 2005. Interview.
90. Robinson. 2006. *History*, p. 5.
91. Kanaana. 2005. Interview.
92. Quigley. 1990. *Palestine*, p. 108.
93. Cohen. 2011. "Matrix", p. 105.
94. Schoenman. 1988. *Hidden*, p. 76.
95. Cook, J. 2006. *Blood and Religion: The Unmasking of the Jewish and Democratic State*. London: Pluto Press, p. 7.
96. Korn. 2000. "Military", p. 169.

97. Be'er and Abdel-Jawad. 1994. *Collaborators*, pp. 34–5.
98. Mishal Shikhter, head of the Military Government, in the January 30, 1958 meeting of Mapai's Committee for Arab Affairs. Quoted in: Sa'di. 2011. "Ominous", p. 93.
99. Zureik. 2011. "Colonialism", p. 22.
100. Sa'di. 2011. "Ominous", p. 90.
101. Dakkak, I. 1983. "Survey of the attitudes of Palestinian wage-earners on both sides of the 1949 Armistice line" in Schölch, A. (ed.) *Palestinians over the Green Line* (pp. 117–46). London: Ithaca Press, p. 138.
102. Be'er and Abdel-Jawad. 1994. *Collaborators*, pp. 33–4.
103. Ibid. pp. 35–6.
104. Ibid. p. 35.
105. A.G. 2006. Interview.
106. Be'er and Abdel-Jawad. 1994. *Collaborators*, pp. 27–8.
107. Kanaana. 2005. Interview.
108. Ibid.
109. Korn. 2000. "Military", p. 168.
110. Sa'di. 2011. "Ominous", p. 89.
111. Robinson. 2006. *History*, p. 10.
112. Robinson. 2005. *Occupied Citizens*, p. 142.
113. Y.S.O. (name withheld by request). 2006. Former vice-principal of Tarshiha High School, and 75-year-old survivor of 1948 war, interview with Adah Kay, April, Tarshiha.
114. Segev. 1986. *1949: the First Israelis*, p. 65.
115. Cohen. 2011. "Matrix", p. 106; Segev. 1986. *1949: the First Israelis*, p. 65.
116. Quoted in Abu-Zahra, N. 2007. "Population control for resource appropriation" in Cowen, D. and Gilbert, E. (eds) *War, Citizenship, Territory* (pp. 303–26). Aldershot: Ashgate Publishing Ltd., p. 321.
117. International Committee of the Red Cross. 1949. "Article 51". *Convention (IV) Relative to the Protection of Civilian Persons in Time of War*, August 12. Geneva.

## CHAPTER 5

1. Karpat, K.H. 1978. "Ottoman population records and the census of 1881/82–1893". *International Journal of Middle East Studies*. 9(3): 237–74, pp. 244, 253.
2. Schoenman, R. 1988. *The Hidden History of Zionism*. San Francisco: Socialist Action Books, pp. 53–4.
3. Quigley, J. 1990. *Palestine and Israel: A Challenge to Justice*. Durham: Duke University Press, pp. 106–7.
4. Kanaana, S. 2005. Professor of Anthropology, Birzeit University, interview with Adah Kay, April, Birzeit.
5. Pappé, I. 2006. *The Ethnic Cleansing of Palestine*. Oxford: One World Publications, p. 201.
6. Gilmour, D. 1980. *Dispossessed: The Ordeal of the Palestinians 1917–1980*. London: Sidgwick & Jackson, p. 104.
7. In the words of Ben Gurion, "the military regime came into existence to protect the right of Jewish settlement in all parts of the state." Quoted in Quigley. 1990. *Palestine*, p. 19.

8. *Maariv* newspaper, December 29, 1961, quoted in Jiryis, S. 1968. *The Arabs in Israel*. Beirut: Institute for Palestine Studies, p. 53; Gilmour. 1980. *Dispossessed*, p. 95; Boqa'i, N. 2008/9. "Palestinian internally displaced persons Inside Israel: Challenging the solid structures". *Palestine–Israel Journal of Politics, Economics and Culture*, 15(4)/16(1).

9. Peretz, D. 1995. *Palestinian Refugee Compensation* (Information Paper No. 3). Washington, DC: The Center for Policy Analysis on Palestine, p. 19.

10. Segev, T. 1986. *1949: The First Israelis*. New York: The Free Press (trans. Weinstein, A.N.), p. 79.

11. Quoted in Peretz. 1995. *Palestinian*, p. 6.

12. Ibid. pp. 4–6.

13. Sa'di, "Ominous designs: Israel's strategies and tactics of controlling the Palestinians during the first two decades" in Zureik, E., Lyon, D. and Abu-Laban, Y. (eds) *Surveillance and Control in Israel/Palestine: Population, Territory and Power* (pp. 83–98). New York: Routledge, p. 87; Gilmour. 1980. *Dispossessed*, p. 93.

14. Leibler, A. and Breslau, D. 2005. "The uncounted: Citizenship and exclusion in the Israeli census of 1948". *Ethnic and Racial Studies*, 28(5): 880–902, p. 896; Sa'di. 2011. "Ominous", p. 85; Davis, U. 1987. *Israel: An Apartheid State*. London: Zed Books, p. 38; Korn, A. 2000. "Crime and legal control: The Israeli Arab population during the military government period (1948–66)". *British Journal of Criminology*, 40: 574–93, p. 582; Robinson, S. 2005. *Occupied Citizens in a Liberal State: Palestinians Under Military Rule and the Colonial Formation of Israeli Society, 1948–1966*. Dissertation: Stanford University, pp. 43, 64.

15. Peretz. 1995. *Palestinian*, p. 6.

16. Y.S.O. (name withheld by request). 2006. Former vice-principal of Tarshiha High School, and 75-year-old survivor of 1948 war, interview with Adah Kay, April, Tarshiha.

17. Peretz. 1995. *Palestinian*, pp. 7, 10.

18. Kimmerling, B. 2002. "Jurisdiction in an immigrant–settler society: The 'Jewish and democratic state'". *Comparative Political Studies*, 35(10): 1119; Boqa'i. 2008/9. "Palestinian".

19. Korn. 2000. "Military", p. 174.

20. Gilmour. 1980. *Dispossessed*, pp. 102, 106; Korn, A. 2000. "Military government, political control and crime: The case of Israeli Arabs". *Crime, Law & Social Change*, 34: 159–82, p. 173; Rouhana, N. 1997. *Palestinian Citizens in an Ethnic Jewish State: Identities in Conflict*. New Haven: Yale University Press, pp. 81–2; Peretz. 1995. *Palestinian*, p. 7.

21. Gilmour. 1980. *Dispossessed*, p. 104; Quigley. 1990. *Palestine*, p. 97.

22. Peretz. 1995. *Palestinian*, pp. 6–7; Korn. 2000. "Military", pp. 168, 174; Masalha, N. 2003. *The Politics of Denial: Israel and the Palestinian Refugee Problem*. London: Pluto Press, p. 39.

23. G.B. (name withheld by request). 2005. Journalist, translator, and 64-year-old survivor of 1948 war, interview with Amahl Bishara, July 2, Burke, VA, USA.

24. Korn, 2000. "Military", p. 174; Pappé. 2006. *Ethnic Cleansing*, p. 159.

25. Boqa'i. 2008/9. "Palestinian".

26. Boqa'i, N. 2006. *Returning to Kafr Bir'im*. Bethlehem: BADIL Resource Center for Palestinian Residency and Refugee Rights.

27. Ibid. p. 23.

28. Ibid. p. 31.
29. Morris, B. 2004. *The Birth of the Palestinian Refugee Problem Revisited.* Cambridge: Cambridge University Press, p. 313.
30. Boqa'i. 2006. *Returning*, p. 35.
31. Ibid. p. 36.
32. Ibid. p. 39.
33. Ibid. p. 67.
34. Quoted in Segev. 1986. *1949: The First Israelis*, pp. 48–9.
35. Korn. 2000. "Military", p. 181.
36. Quigley. 1990. *Palestine*, pp. 106–7; Korn. 2000. "Military", pp. 164–5, 171; Gilmour. 1980. *Dispossessed*, p. 95.
37. Masalha. 2003. *Politics*, p. 149.
38. Korn. 2000. "Military", p. 165.
39. Kanaana. 2005. interview.
40. Korn. 2000. "Military", pp. 164–5.
41. Quigley. 1990. *Palestine*, pp. 106–7; Gilmour. 1980. *Dispossessed*, p. 105.
42. Korn. 2000. "Military", p. 165. Citing her interview with Benjamin Lobetkin, July 1, 1993.
43. Kanaana. 2005. interview.
44. W.A.H. (name withheld by request). 2006. Former teacher in Tarshiha, and 78-year-old survivor of 1948 war, interview with Adah Kay, April 25, Tarshiha.
45. Korn. 2000. "Crime", p. 575; Jiryis. 1968. *Arabs*, pp. 27–8.
46. Kanaana. 2005. Interview.
47. Jiryis. 1968. *Arabs,* pp. 27–8; Korn. 2000. "Military", p. 176.
48. Kanaana. 2005. Interview.
49. Jiryis. 1968. *Arabs*, pp. 27–8.
50. Korn. 2000. "Military", p. 181.
51. Pappé. 2006. *Ethnic Cleansing*, p. 54; Gilmour. 1980. *Dispossessed*, p. 108; Lustick, I. 1980. *Arabs in the Jewish State: Israel's Control of a National Minority.* Austin: University of Texas Press, p. 47.
52. Y.S.O. 2006. Interview.
53. Gilmour. 1980. *Dispossessed*, p. 98.
54. Rouhana. 1997. *Palestinian*, pp. 81–2; Y.S.O. 2006. Interview; Lustick. 1980. *Arabs*, p. 124.
55. W.A.H. 2006. Interview.
56. Lustick. 1980. *Arabs*, p. 124.
57. Pappé. 2006. *Ethnic Cleansing*, p. 193.
58. Boqa'i. 2008/9. "Palestinian".
59. W.A.H. 2006. Interview.
60. Korn. 2000. "Military", p. 166.
61. Ibid.
62. Quoted in Pappé. 2006. *Ethnic Cleansing*, p. 54.
63. Gilmour. 1980. *Dispossessed*, pp. 97–8.
64. W.A.H. 2006. Interview.
65. Y.S.O. 2006. Interview; Gilmour. 1980. *Dispossessed*, p. 99.
66. Israeli writer Aharon Cohen, quoted in Gilmour. 1980. *Dispossessed*, pp. 97–8.
67. Korn. 2000. "Military", p. 165.
68. Leibler, A. 2007. "Establishing scientific authority: Citizenship and the first census of Israel" in, Brunner, J. (ed.). *Tel Aviver Jahrbuch für deutsche*

*Geschichte XXXV, (Tel Aviv Yearbook for German History)* (pp. 221–36). Göttingen: Wallstein Verlag, p. 227

69. From the court records, cited in Jiryis. 1968. *Arabs*, pp. 97–109.
70. From the court records, cited in Schoenman. 1988. *Hidden*, pp. 24–5; Jiryis. 1968. *Arabs*, pp. 97–109.
71. Korn. 2000. "Military", pp. 165–6; Korn, A. 2004. "Political control and crime: The use of defense (emergency) regulations during the military government". *Adalah's Review*, 4: 23–32, p. 26; Jiryis, 1968, *Arabs*, p. 22; Lustick, 1980, *Arabs*, pp. 127–8.
72. Sa'di. 2011. "Ominous", p. 86.
73. Gilmour. 1980. *Dispossessed*, p. 99.
74. Quigley. 1990. *Palestine*, p. 112.
75. Sa'di. 2011. "Ominous", p. 87; citing Melman, Y. and Raviv, D. 1988. "A final solution to the Palestinian problem?" *Guardian Weekly,* February 21, 19; Masalha, N. 2001. *Ariel Sharon: A Political Profile.* London: Council for the Advancement of Arab–British Understanding.
76. Gilmour. 1980. *Dispossessed*, p. 100.
77. Sa'di. 2011. "Ominous", pp. 95–6; Segev, T. *1967: Israel, the War, and the Year that Transformed the Middle East.* London: Little, Brown, p. 534.
78. Korn. 2000. "Military", p. 177; Halabi, U. 2011. "Legal analysis and critique of some surveillance methods used by Israel" in Zureik, E., Lyon, D. and Abu-Laban, Y. (eds) *Surveillance and Control in Israel/Palestine: Population, Territory and Power* (pp. 199–218). New York: Routledge, pp. 206–12.
79. Rouhana. 1997. *Palestinian*, p. 92; citing Lewin-Epstein, N. and Semyonov, M. 1993. *The Arab Minority in Israel's Economy: Patterns of Ethnic Inequality.* Boulder, CO: Westview Press; Gilmour. 1980. *Dispossessed*, p. 101.
80. Wiemer, R. 1983. "Zionism and the Arabs after the establishment of the state of Israel" in Schölch, A. (ed.) *Palestinians over the Green Line* (pp. 26–63). London: Ithaca Press, p. 56; Abu-Zahra, N. 2007. "Population control for resource appropriation" in Cowen, D. and Gilbert, E. (eds) *War, Citizenship, Territory* (pp. 303–26). Aldershot: Ashgate Publishing Ltd, pp. 308–9.
81. Al-Haq. 1989. *Nation Under Siege.* Ramallah: Al-Haq p. 323.
82. Al-Haq. 1989. *Nation*, p. 323; El Fassed, A. 2007. "Abbas' Village League". *Electronic Intifada*, September 10.
83. Al-Haq. 2002. *Death Traps: Israel's Use of Force at Checkpoints in the West Bank.* Ramallah: Al-Haq.
84. Hass, A. 2005. "Gaza after the pullout: Israeli control over the population registry means continued control over Gaza Strip". *Haaretz*, September 26.
85. Hass, A. 2010. "IDF order will enable mass deportation from West Bank". *Haaretz*, April 11.
86. Quigley. 1990. *Palestine*, p. 204.
87. Rabah, J. and Fairweather, N. 1995. *Israeli Military Orders in the Occupied Palestinian West Bank: 1967–1992.* Jerusalem: Jerusalem Media and Communications Center, pp. 5, 11; Dugard. J. 2004. *Question of the Violation of Human Rights in the Occupied Arab Territories, Including Palestine.* Special Rapporteur Report to the United Nations Economic and Social Council Commission on Human Rights, September 8. UN Document E/CN.4/2004/6; World Bank. 2010. *Checkpoints and Barriers: Searching for Livelihoods in the West Bank and Gaza, Gender Dimensions of Economic Collapse.* Washington, DC: World Bank, p. 113.

88.  Rabah and Fairweather. 1995. *Israeli*, pp. 5, 11; Abu-Zahra, N. 2008. "Identity cards and coercion" in Pain, R. and Smith, S.J. (eds) Fear: Critical Geopolitics and Everyday Life (pp. 175–92). Aldershot: Ashgate Publishing Ltd, p. 186.

89.  Shalabi, N. 2005. Landowner and community leader, interview with Nadia Abu-Zahra and Olof Sjölund, March 20, Mas'ha (Arabic, trans. Tuqan Tuqan).

90.  World Bank. 2008. *West Bank and Gaza: The Economic Effects of Restricted Access to Land in the West Bank*. Washington, DC: World Bank; Peretz. 1995. *Palestinian*, p. 10; Sudilovsky, J. 2011. "Absentee landowners? West Bank landowners can't get to their land". *Catholic News Service*, December 30.

91.  Quigley. 1990. *Palestine*, p. 204.

92.  Al-Khasawneh, A.H. 1994. *The Human Rights Dimensions of Population Transfer, Including the Implantation of Settlers*. Special Rapporteur Progress Report to the United Nations Subcommission on Prevention of Discrimination and Protection of Minorities, June 30, UN Document E/CN.4/Sub.2/1994/18.

93.  Turki, F. 1974. "Alienation of the Palestinian in the Arab world" in Abu-Lughod, I. and Abu-Laban, B. (eds) *Settler Regimes in Africa and the Arab World: The Illusion of Endurance* (pp. 119–24). Wilmette, IL: The Medina University Press International, p. 119.

94.  Qumsiyeh, M. 2004. *Sharing the Land of Canaan: Human Rights and the Israeli–Palestinian Struggle*. London: Pluto Press, p. 7.

95.  Cattan, H. 1973. *Palestine and International Law: The Legal Aspects of the Arab–Israeli Conflict*. London: Longman Group, p. 81.

96.  UN OCHA. 2011. "Palestinian communities affected by the Barrier" in *Humanitarian Atlas*. Jerusalem: United Nations Office for the Coordination of Humanitarian Affairs (UN OCHA), p. 24.

97.  Palestinian Central Bureau of Statistics (PCBS). 2011. *Palestinians at the End of 2011*. Accessed at http://tinyurl.com/84lpw3n

98.  The term "ghetto" was used by newly arrived Zionists to describe the situation of urban Palestinians. Writing about the deliberate replacement of indigenous Palestinian place names with Hebrew ones, Israeli Foreign Affairs official Alexander Dotan stated in 1952, "[A] Hebrew name has not been found yet for 'Ajami', and some new [Jewish] immigrants still incorrectly call the Arab neighbourhood within it the 'Ghetto' or 'Arab Ghetto'". Quoted in Piterberg, G. 2001. "Erasures". *New Left Review*, 10: 31–46, p. 46.

99.  Halabi. 2011. "Legal", p. 207.

100.  Galili, L. 2003. "Every prison has a door". *Ha'aretz*, August 29.

101.  Shah, S. 1997–98. "On the road to apartheid: The bypass road network in the West Bank". *Columbia Human Rights Law Review*, 29: 221–90, p. 223; B'Tselem. 2004. *Forbidden Roads: Israel's Discriminatory Road Regime in the West Bank*. Jerusalem: B'Tselem, p. 6; Tilley, V. (ed.). 2009. *Occupation, Colonialism, Apartheid? A Re-assessment of Israel's Practices in the Occupied Palestinian Territories Under International Law*. Cape Town: Human Sciences Research Council of South Africa, p. 197.

102.  Shah. 1997–98. "On the road", pp. 223, 225.

103.  NAD-NSU. 2002. *Israeli and Palestinian Security-Controlled Areas* [map]. Ramallah: Negotiations Support Unit, Negotiations Affairs Department (NAD-NSU), Palestinian Liberation Organisation.

104. Foundation for Middle East Peace. 1996. "Road map for IDF redeployment: The West Bank". *Settlement Report*, 6(2).
105. Al-Haq. 2002. *Death*.
106. PASSIA. 2001. *Sovereign Areas According to the Sharon Proposal* [map]. Jerusalem: Palestinian Academic Society for the Study of International Affairs (PASSIA). Palestinian Grassroots Anti-apartheid Wall Campaign; PASSIA. 2004. *Facilitating Disengagement: Israel's West Bank Road Plan* [map]. Jerusalem: Palestinian Grassroots Anti-apartheid Wall Campaign. Palestinian Grassroots Anti-apartheid Wall Campaign; PASSIA. 2006. *The Occupation's "Convergence Plan" Settlement Evacuation Plan* [map]. Jerusalem: Palestinian Grassroots Anti-apartheid Wall Campaign.
107. B'Tselem. 2004. *Forbidden Roads: Israel's Discriminatory Road Regime in the West Bank*. Jerusalem: B'Tselem; Palestinian Grassroots Anti-apartheid Wall Campaign. 2010. *Wall Fact Sheet*. Accessed at www.stopthewall.org/downloads/pdf/2010wallfactsheet.pdf
108. Applied Research Institute of Jerusalem. 2006. *Limiting the Access of Palestinians on Bypass Roads*. Accessed at www.poica.org/editor/case_studies/view.php?recordID=821. UN OCHA. 2011. *Special Focus: August 2011: West Bank Movement and Access Update*. Jerusalem: United Nations Office for the Coordination of Humanitarian Affairs (UN OCHA).
109. Palestinian Grassroots Anti-apartheid Wall Campaign. 2010. *Wall Fact Sheet*.
110. BBC News. 2010. "West Bank mosque 'set alight by Jewish settlers'". *BBC News*, October 4; Palestinian Grassroots Anti-apartheid Wall Campaign. 2010. *Wall Fact Sheet*.
111. Cartographer and planner Jan de Jong, quoted in van der Tol, J. 2010. "Dutch expert maps Israeli land grab". *Radio Netherlands Worldwide*, September 30.
112. UN OCHA. 2011. *Special Focus: July 2011: Barrier Update*. Jerusalem: United Nations Office for the Coordination of Humanitarian Affairs (UN OCHA).
113. Palestinian Grassroots Anti-apartheid Wall Campaign. 2003. *The Wall in the West Bank* [map]. Accessed at http://tinyurl.com/cbtf6uj; B'Tselem. 2011. *The Separation Barrier*. Accessed at www.btselem.org/separation_barrier; Palestinian Grassroots Anti-apartheid Wall Campaign. 2007. *Palestinian Towns and Villages: Between Isolation and Expulsion*. Jerusalem: Palestinian Grassroots Anti-apartheid Wall Campaign, pp. 26–30.
114. UN OCHA. 2011. "Palestinian communities", p. 24; Palestinian Grassroots Anti-apartheid Wall Campaign. 2007. *Palestinian Towns*, pp. 6, 8, 17, 36; B'tselem. 2010. *The Separation Barrier: Statistics*, January 1. Accessed at www.btselem.org/separation_barrier/statistics
115. Palestinian Grassroots Anti-apartheid Wall Campaign. 2007. *Palestinian Towns*, p. 26.
116. United Nations World Food Programme and Food and Agriculture Organization. 2009. *Occupied Palestinian Territory: Food Security and Vulnerability Analysis Report (A Synthesis of Recent Surveys and Studies)*. Rome: WFP and FAO, p. ix; Palestinian Grassroots Anti-apartheid Wall Campaign. 2010. *Wall Fact Sheet*.
117. B'Tselem. 2011. *Checkpoints, Physical Obstructions, and Forbidden Roads*. Accessed at http://tinyurl.com/6hz4wrp
118. Palestinian Grassroots Anti-apartheid Wall Campaign. 2007. *Palestinian Towns*, p. 31.

119. Cook, J. 2006. *Blood and Religion: The Unmasking of the Jewish and Democratic State*. London: Pluto Press, p. 29; Palestinian Grassroots Anti-apartheid Wall Campaign. 2010. *Wall Fact Sheet*; Zureik, E. 2011. "Colonialism, surveillance, and population control" in Zureik, E., Lyon, D. and Abu-Laban, Y. (eds) *Surveillance and Control in Israel/Palestine: Population, Territory and Power* (pp. 3–46). New York: Routledge, p. 31.
120. Ziv, H. 2004. *The Bureaucracy of Occupation*. Tel Aviv: Machsom Watch and Physicians for Human Rights – Israel, (trans. Weingarten, S.), p. 8.
121. UN OCHA. 2011. "Palestinian communities", p. 24; UN OCHA. 2011. *Special Focus: July*.
122. Cook. 2006. *Blood*, p. 152.
123. Gazit, N. 2009. "Social agency, spatial practices, and power: The micro-foundations of fragmented sovereignty in the occupied territories". *International Journal of Politics, Culture, and Society*, 22: 83–103, p. 95.
124. Ibid. p. 96.
125. Human Rights Watch. 2011. *Israel: New Commander Should Protect Palestinians from Settler Violence*. Accessed at http://tinyurl.com/7f9j97o; B'Tselem. 2011. *Violence by Settlers*. Accessed at http://tinyurl.com/6joulhc; Munayyer, Y. 2012. *When Settlers Attack*. Washington, DC: The Palestine Center, p. i.
126. Human Rights Watch. 2011. *Israel*.
127. Fathallah Abu Rida, quoted in Human Rights Watch. 2011. *Israel*.
128. Amer, H. 2005. Landowner and community leader, interview with Nadia Abu-Zahra, March, Mas'ha [Arabic, trans. Ramzi Azbarga].
129. Halabi. 2011. "Legal", p. 216.

## CHAPTER 6

1. Medicks, O. 2003. Volunteer with Gush Shalom, interview with Monalisa Sundbom and Olof Sjölund, June 7, Mas'ha.
2. UN OCHA. 2003. *Consolidated Appeals Process, Occupied Palestinian Territory 2004*. Geneva: United Nations Office for the Coordination of Humanitarian Affairs (UN OCHA), p. 18.
3. UN OCHA. 2005. *Review of the Humanitarian Situation in the Occupied Palestinian Territory for 2004*. Geneva: United Nations Office for the Coordination of Humanitarian Affairs (UN OCHA); World Bank. 2004. *Four Years: Intifada, Closures and Palestinian Economic Crisis: An Assessment*. Washington, DC: World Bank, p. 46; World Health Organization. 2009. *Health Conditions in the Occupied Palestinian Territory, Including East Jerusalem, and in the Occupied Syrian Golan*. UN Document A62/INF. DOC./2.
4. Batniji, R., Rabai'a, Y., Nguyen-Gillham, V., Giacaman, R., Sarraj, E., Punamali, R-L., Saab, H. and Boyce, W. 2009. "Health as human security in the occupied Palestinian territory". *Lancet*, 373(9666): 1133–43, p. 1139.
5. Mash'al, J. 2005. General Director, Palestine Medical Relief Society (PMRS), interview with Adah Kay, March 16, Ramallah.
6. International Commission of Jurists (ICJ) 1997. *Maastricht Guidelines on Violations of Economic, Social and Cultural Rights*. January 26, 1997, Maastricht. Available at: www.unhcr.org/refworld/docid/48abd5730. html. Adopted by the participants of an expert seminar, organized by the

International Commission of Jurists, the Maastricht Centre for Human Rights and the Urban Morgan Institute for Human Rights (Maastricht, January 22–27, 1997), on the occasion of the 10th anniversary of the Limburg Principles.

7. Mash'al. 2005. Interview.
8. Palestinian Grassroots Anti-apartheid Wall Campaign. 2007. *Palestinian Towns and Villages: Between Isolation and Expulsion*. Jerusalem: Palestinian Grassroots Anti-apartheid Wall Campaign, p. 6.
9. Scaafi, M. 2005. Director of Emergency Services, Palestine Medical Relief Society (PMRS), interview with Adah Kay, May, Ramallah.
10. Jubran, J. 2005. Programme Manager, Health Research Department, HDIP (Health, Development, Information and Policy Institute), interview with Adah Kay, March 8, Ramallah.
11. Ziv, H. 2003. *At Israel's Will: The Permit Policy in the West Bank*. Tel Aviv: Physicians for Human Rights – Israel, p. 7.
12. Giacaman, R., Khatib, R., Shabaneh, L., Ramlawi, A., Sabri, B., Sabatinelli, G., Khawaja, M. and Laurance, T. 2009. "Health status and health services in the occupied Palestinian territory". *Lancet*, 373(9666): 837–49, p. 845.
13. Jubran. 2005. Interview.
14. Jubran, J. 2005. *Health and Segregation II: The Impact of the Israeli Separation Wall on Access to Health Care Services: An Updated Research:* Ramallah: Health, Development, Information and Policy Institute, pp. 45–9.
15. Mash'al. 2005. Interview.
16. Husseini, A., Abu-Rmeileh, N.M.E., Mikki, N., Ramahi, T.M., Abu Ghosh, H., Khalili, M., Bjertness, E., Holmboe-Ottesen, G. and Jervell, J. 2009. "Cardiovascular diseases, diabetes mellitus, and cancer in the occupied Palestinian territory". *Lancet*, 373(9668) : 1041–9, p. 1042; Mashal, J. and Jubran, J. 2005. *Health Development Under Uncertainty: The Palestinian Health Care System*. Ramallah: Health, Development, Information and Policy Institute.
17. Mataria, A., Khatib, R., Donaldson, C., Bossert, T., Hunter, D.J., Alsayed, F. and Moatti, J-P. 2009. "The health-care system: An assessment and reform agenda". *Lancet*, 373(9670): 1207–17, p. 1209.
18. Euro-Mid. 2011. *Restricted Hopes: Report of Euro-Mediterranean Observatory for Human Rights (Euro-Mid): On the Breach of West Bank Palestinians' Right to Travel by Israeli Authorities*. Geneva: Euro-Mediterranean Observatory for Human Rights, p. 24.
19. Ibid. p. 4.
20. World Health Organization. 2006. *Health*, p. 4.
21. A. (name withheld by request). 2006. Orthopaedic/traumatology specialist, interview with Adah Kay, April 7, Marda (Arabic, trans. F.A. – name withheld by request).
22. Christian Aid. 2004. *Facts on the Ground: The End of the Two-State Solution?* London: Christian Aid, p. 36.
23. Mashal and Jubran. 2005. *Health*, p. 30; Scaafi, M. 2005. Director of Emergency Services, Palestine Medical Relief Society (PMRS), interview with Adah Kay, May, Ramallah.
24. Khatib, R. and Daoud, A. 2002. *The Impact of the Israeli Military Invasion of the West Bank on Pharmaceutical Supply and Availability*. Ramallah: Institute of Community and Public Health, Birzeit University; Khatib, R. and Halileh, S.

2002. *The Impact of Israeli Incursion, Siege and Closure on the Immunization Program in the West Bank*. Ramallah: Institute of Community and Public Health, Birzeit University.

25. Izzat, N. 2004. Landowner and farmer, interview with Nadia Abu-Zahra and Gustaf Hansson, July 11, Jayyous (Arabic, trans. Nadia Abu-Zahra).

26. Khatib and Daoud. 2002. *Impact*.

27. Abdul Rahim, H.F., Wick, L, Halileh. S., Hassan-Bitar, S., Chekir, H., Watt, G. and Khawaja, M. 2009. "Maternal and child health in the occupied Palestinian territory". *Lancet*, 373(9667): 967–77.

28. Khatib and Halileh. 2002. *Impact*.

29. Médecins du Monde. 2005. *The Ultimate Barrier: Impact of the Wall on the Palestinian Health Care System*. Paris: Médecins du Monde, p. 11.

30. Quoted in Médecins du Monde. 2005. *Ultimate*, p. 11.

31. Survey conducted by the Palestinian Ministry of Health with UNICEF support, 2003.

32. B'Tselem. 2002. Wounded in the Field: Impeding Medical Treatment and Firing at Ambulances by IDF Soldiers in the Occupied Territories. Accessed at http://tinyurl.com/5tf3lmh

33. World Health Organization. 2006. *Health*; Mashal and Jubran. 2005. *Health*, p. 26; B'Tselem. 2003. *Harm to Medical Personnel: The Delay, Abuse and Humiliation of Medical Personnel by Israeli Security Forces*. Accessed at http://tinyurl.com/48bzfl3; Ziv, H. 2002. *A Legacy of Injustice: A Critique of Israeli Approaches to the Right to Health of Palestinians in the Occupied Territories*. Tel Aviv: Physicians for Human Rights – Israel; Lotze, M. 2004. *Medicine Under Siege: Israeli Attacks upon the Palestinian Medical Establishment During the Second Intifada*. Ramallah: Al-Haq.

34. Quoted in Médecins du Monde. 2005. *Ultimate*, p. 11.

35. A. 2006 Interview.

36. Quoted in Médecins du Monde. 2005. *Ultimate*, p. 11.

37. Batniji et al. 2009. "Health", p. 1140.

38. Scaafi. 2005. interview.

39. Wick, L., Mikki, N., Giacaman, R. and Abdul Rahim, H. 2005. "Childbirth in Palestine". *International Journal of Gynaecology and Obstetrics*, 89(2): 174–8; McDowall, D. and Bell, W. 2003. *Losing Ground: Israel, Poverty and the Palestinians*. London: Christian Aid, p. 39; UN OCHA. 2005. *Review*; Baha Arafah, D. 2005. *Beyond "Life or Death": Palestinian Emergency Medical Transport Under Long-Term Closure in the West Bank*. Boston, MA: Harvard University.

40. World Health Organization. 2002. *Health Conditions of and Assistance to the Arab Population in the Occupied Arab Territories including Palestine: Supplementary Report by the Secretariat*. UN Document A55/33 Add.1, p. 2.

41. Médecins du Monde. 2005. *Ultimate*, pp. 13–4.

42. United Nations General Assembly. 2005. *The Issue of Palestinian Pregnant Women Giving Birth at Israeli Checkpoints*. Report of the United Nations High Commissioner for Human Rights. UN Document A/60/324; Abdul Rahim et al. 2009. "Maternal", p. 973; Wick, L. and Mikki, N. 2004. *Childbirth in Palestine: Reported Practices and Evidence Based Guidelines*. Ramallah: Institute of Community and Public Health, Birzeit University.

43. United Nations General Assembly. 2005. *Israeli Practices Affecting the Human Rights of the Palestinian People in the Occupied Palestinian Territory,*

*Including East Jerusalem, Note by the Secretary-General*, August 18. UN Document A/60/271.

44. United Nations General Assembly. 2006. *Implementation of General Assembly Resolution 60/251 of 15 March 2006 entitled "Human Rights Council"*, November 16. UN Document A/HRC/3/1/Add.1.

45. Amnesty International. 2005. *Israel: Conflict, Occupation and Patriarchy: Women Carry the Burden*. London: Amnesty International.

46. Al-Haq. 2004. *In Focus: Medical Restrictions*. Accessed at http://tinyurl.com/3fggfue; Mashal and Jubran. 2005. *Health*, p. 29; World Health Organization. 2003. "Health sector bi-weekly report". *Health in Forum News*, 2(8), cited in Lotze. 2004. *Medicine*, p. 28.

47. J.A.H. (name withheld by request). 2006. Police officer and dialysis patient, interview with Adah Kay, April 7, Marda (Arabic, trans. F.A. – name withheld by request).

48. Quoted in Baha Arafah. 2005. *Beyond*, p. 67.

49. Scaafi. 2005. interview.

50. Ibid.

51. Rytter, M.J.H., Kjældgaard, A-L., Brønnum-Hansen, H. and Helweg-Larsen, K. 2006. "Effects of armed conflict on access to emergency health care in Palestinian West Bank: Systematic collection of data in emergency departments". *British Medical Journal*, 332(7550): 1122–4.

52. Ibid. p. 1123.

53. Batniji et al. 2009. "Health", p. 1139.

54. Scaafi. 2005. Interview.

55. Ibid.

56. Mash'al. 2005. Interview.

57. Jubran. 2005. *Health*, pp. 26–7.

58. Ziv. 2002. *Legacy*, p. 37.

## CHAPTER 7

1. K.T. (name withheld by request). 2005. Programme Manager, Advocacy Unit, National Plan of Action for Children, Palestinian Authority, interview with Adah Kay, February 26, Ramallah.

2. UNICEF. 2004. *UNICEF Humanitarian Action, Occupied Palestinian Territory, Donor Update, June 7*. New York: United Nations Children's Fund (UNICEF).

3. Palestinian Monitoring Group. 2005. *Trend Analysis: Education Under Occupation: Disruptions to Palestinian Education Stemming from Israeli Military and Settler Activity, 01 September 2003 – 30 June 2005*. Ramallah: Negotiations Affairs Department, Palestinian Liberation Organisation, p. 5.

4. Nicolai, S. 2007. *Fragmented Foundations: Education and Chronic Crisis in the Occupied Palestinian Territory*. Paris: UNESCO International Institute for Educational Planning and Save the Children UK, p. 113.

5. Hammami, R. 2005. Professor, Women's Studies Institute, Birzeit University, interview with Monalisa Sundbom, March, Jerusalem.

6. UNICEF. 2002. "Thousands of Palestinian children denied access to schools", October 2. Accessed at http://tinyurl.com/3flkqm2; Birzeit University, Palestinian Ministry of Planning and UNDP. 2005. *Palestine Human Development Report 2004*. Ramallah and Gaza: Birzeit University, Palestinian

Ministry of Planning and United Nations Development Program (UNDP); Right to Education Monitor. 2004. *Barriers to Education: The Israeli Military Obstruction of Access to Schools and Universities in the West Bank and Gaza Strip*. Ramallah: Birzeit University, p. 12.

7. UN OCHA. 2003. *Consolidated Appeals Process, Occupied Palestinian Territory 2004*. Geneva: United Nations Office for the Coordination of Humanitarian Affairs (UN OCHA), p. 19.
8. Ibid. p. 19.
9. Palestinian Monitoring Group. 2005. *Trend*.
10. UNICEF. 2004. *UNICEF*.
11. Right to Education Monitor. 2004. *Barriers to Education: The Israeli Military Obstruction of Access to Schools and Universities in the West Bank and Gaza Strip*. Ramallah: Birzeit University, p. 4; Palestinian Monitoring Group. 2005. *Trend*, p. 6.
12. N. (name withheld by request). 2005. Teacher, United Nations Relief and Works Agency for Palestine Refugees (UNRWA) School in Aida Refugee Camp, interview with Adah Kay, April, Bethlehem (Arabic, trans. F.A. – name withheld by request).
13. Ibid.
14. Ibid.
15. M.B. (name withheld by request). 2005. Head, Education Programme, United Nations Relief and Works Agency for Palestine Refugees (UNRWA), interview with Adah Kay, March 22, East Jerusalem.
16. M.B. 2005. Interview.
17. Ibid.
18. Ibid.
19. Ibid.
20. R.H. (name withheld by request). 2005. Head Teacher, United Nations Relief and Works Agency for Palestine Refugees (UNRWA) Girls' Secondary School in al-Am'ari Refugee Camp, interview with Adah Kay, March 30, Ramallah.
21. N. 2005. Interview.
22. R.H. 2005. Interview.
23. M.B. 2005. Interview.
24. UN OCHA. 2003. *Consolidated*.
25. Villalobos, M. 2004. *Report of the UN Special Rapporteur on the Right to Education*, December 17. UN Document E/CN.4/2005.
26. Article 26 of the Universal Declaration of Human Rights 1948, and Articles 28 and 29 of the 1989 UN Convention on the Rights of the Child (CRC). Article 3 of the 1989 UN Convention on the Rights of the Child (CRC).
27. Nicolai. 2007. *Fragmented*, pp. 31, 36–7.
28. Y.A.F. (name withheld by request). 2005. Mayor, Deir Ballout village, interview with Adah Kay, May, Deir Ballout (Arabic, trans. F.A. – name withheld by request).
29. Y.A.F. 2005. interview.
30. UNICEF. 2002. "Thousands".
31. Al-Haq. 2005. *Palestinian Education under Israeli Occupation*. Stockholm: Conference on International Law in the Shadow of Israeli Occupation (April 12), p. 4.
32. Helou, J. 2005. Director, Tamer Institute, interview with Adah Kay, February 21, Ramallah.

33. K.T. (name withheld by request). 2005. Programme Manager, Advocacy Unit, National Plan of Action for Children, Palestinian Authority, interview with Adah Kay, February 26, Ramallah.

34. C. (name withheld by request). 2006. British theatre director and international volunteer, interview with Nadia Abu-Zahra, August, by telephone from London, UK.

35. Palestinian Monitoring Group. 2005. *Trend*, p. 6.

36. Birzeit University, Palestinian Ministry of Planning and UNDP. 2005. *Palestine*; Palestinian Ministry of Education and Higher Education (MOEHE). 2005. *Assessment 10: The Effect of the Israeli Occupation on Education 28/9/2000 – 14/6/2004*. Ramallah: MOEHE.

37. I.B. (name withheld by request). 2005. Coordinator, English Department, Open University of Jerusalem, interview with Adah Kay, June, Ramallah.

38. Ibid.

39. Save the Children. 2003. *Growing Up Under Curfew: Safeguarding the Basic Rights of Palestinian Children*. London: Save the Children Sweden and Save the Children UK; Palestinian Ministry of Education reports within Palestinian Monitoring Group. 2005. *Trend*, p. 4.

40. World Bank. 2006. *West Bank and Gaza Education Sector Analysis: Impressive Achievements Under Harsh Conditions and the Way Forward to Consolidate a Quality Education System*. Accessed at http://tinyurl.com/7fy8czt; Palestinian Central Bureau of Statistics (PCBS), UNICEF and UNFPA. 2003. *Youth Survey*. Cited in Birzeit University, 2005, *Barriers to Education Fact Sheet*, accessed at http://tinyurl.com/cb4rr54

41. Birzeit University. 2005. *Barriers*.

42. Palestinian Monitoring Group. 2005. *Trend*.

43. World Bank. 2006. *West Bank*.

44. UN OCHA. 2003. *Consolidated*.

45. Giacaman, R., Abdullah, A., Abu Safieh, R. and Shamieh, L. 2002. *Schooling at Gunpoint: Palestinian Children's Learning Environment in War-like Conditions*. Ramallah: Institute of Community and Public Health, Birzeit University.

46. Save the Children. 2003. *Growing*.

47. Palestinian Monitoring Group. 2005. *Trend*, p. 8.

48. Ibid. p. 8.

49. Right to Education Monitor. 2004. *Barriers to Education: The Israeli Military Obstruction of Access to Schools and Universities in the West Bank and Gaza Strip*. Ramallah: Birzeit University, p. 9.

50. UN OCHA. 2003. *Consolidated*.

51. UN OCHA. 2003. *Consolidated*.

52. Giacaman et al. 2002. *Schooling*.

53. R.H.. 2005. interview.

54. UNICEF, WFP, WHO, UNRWA, FAO, OCHA, UNIFEM, UNFPA, UNDP and UNESCO. 2004. "UN bodies concerned about safe access for 60,000 Palestinian school students to Tawjihi exam sites", June 7. Accessed at http://tinyurl.com/7mr2vzf

55. Helou. 2005. Interview.

56. R.H. 2005. Interview.

57. R.M. (name withheld by request). 2005. School Counsellor, United Nations Relief and Works Agency for Palestine Refugees (UNRWA) Girls' Secondary

School in al-Am'ari Refugee Camp, interview with Adah Kay, March 30, Ramallah.
58. D.M. (name withheld by request). 2005. Director, Planning Unit, National Plan of Action for Children, Palestinian Authority, interview with Adah Kay, February 26, Ramallah.

## CHAPTER 8

1. Cook, C., Hanieh, A. and Kay, A. 2004. *Stolen Youth*. London: Pluto Press, p. 58; Amnesty International. 2002. *Israel and the Occupied Territories: Mass Detention in Cruel, Inhuman and Degrading Conditions*. London: Amnesty International.
2. Montell, J. 2002. "Operation Defensive Shield: The propaganda war and the reality." *Tikkun Magazine*, July/August. Accessed at www.tikkun.org/article. php/jul2002_montell
3. Amnesty International. 2002. *Israel and the Occupied Territories*.
4. Amnesty International. 2002. *Israel/Occupied Territories: Amnesty International Calls for a Commission of Inquiry into Mass Arbitrary Detention of Palestinians*. London: Amnesty International.
5. Farah, J.K. 2003. "Commentary: A West Bank music education". *Musicworks Magazine*, 88.
6. 'Awni Sa'id, from al-Am'ari refugee camp in Ramallah, quoted in Amnesty International. 2002. *Israel/Occupied Territories*.
7. See also Chapter 3 of this book.
8. Dugard, J. 2003. *Report of the United Nations Special Rapporteur of the Commission on Human Rights*, September 8. UN Document E/CN.4/2004/6.
9. Israel Ministry of Foreign Affairs. 2008. *Israel's Disengagement Plan: Selected Documents*. Accessed at http://tinyurl.com/43l87
10. Roy, S. 2002. "Living with the Holocaust". *Journal of Palestine Studies*, 32(1): 5–12, 11–12.
11. Pappé, I. 2006. *The Ethnic Cleansing of Palestine*. Oxford: One World Publications, p. 56.
12. Boqa'i, N. 2006. *Returning to Kafr Bir'im*. Bethlehem: BADIL Resource Center for Palestinian Residency and Refugee Rights, pp. 23, 25.
13. Benvenisti, M. 1987. *1987 Report*. Jerusalem: West Bank Database Project, p. 35.
14. Davis, U. 1987. *Israel: An Apartheid State*. London: Zed Books, p. 38.
15. Yehoshua Palmon, quoted in Sa'di, A. 2011. *The Role of Social Sorting and Categorization Under Exceptionalism in Controlling a National Minority: The Palestinians in Israel*. Working Paper V: The New Transparency: Surveillance and Social Sorting. Kingston, ON: Surveillance Studies Centre, Queen's University, p. 4.
16. Levy, G. 2007. "Using children as human shields". *Haaretz*, March 22; B'Tselem. 2007. *Human Shields: State Response*. Accessed at http://tinyurl. com/6u666bp
17. Palestinian Central Bureau of Statistics (PCBS). 2011. *Palestinians at the End of 2011*. Accessed at http://tinyurl.com/84lpw3n
18. Robinson, S. 2005. *Occupied Citizens in a Liberal State: Palestinians Under Military Rule and the Colonial Formation of Israeli Society, 1948–1966*. Dissertation: Stanford University, p. 52.

19. Kanaana, S. 2005. Professor of Anthropology, Birzeit University, interview with Adah Kay, April, Birzeit.

20. Quoted in Pappé. 2006. *Ethnic Cleansing*, p. 54.

21. From the court records, cited in Jiryis. 1968. *Arabs*, pp. 97–109.

22. Sa'di. 2011. "Ominous designs: Israel's strategies and tactics of controlling the Palestinians during the first two decades" in Zureik, E., Lyon, D. and Abu-Laban, Y. (eds) *Surveillance and Control in Israel/Palestine: Population, Territory and Power* (pp. 83–98). New York: Routledge, p. 95.

23. Human Rights Watch. 2012. *Forget About Him, He's Not Here: Israel's Control of Palestinian Residency in the West Bank and Gaza*. New York: Human Rights Watch, p. 3.

24. Palestinian Grassroots Anti-apartheid Wall Campaign. 2010. *Wall Fact Sheet*. Accessed at www.stopthewall.org/downloads/pdf/2010wallfactsheet.pdf

25. A. (name withheld by request). 2006. Orthopaedic/traumatology specialist, interview with Adah Kay, April 7, Marda (Arabic, trans. F.A. – name withheld by request).

26. D.M. (name withheld by request). 2005. Director, Planning Unit, National Plan of Action for Children, Palestinian Authority, interview with Adah Kay, February 26, Ramallah.

27. Palestinian Central Bureau of Statistics (PCBS). 2007. *Palestine in Figures 2006*. Ramallah: PCBS.

28. Morrar, A. 2004. Landowner and community leader, interview with Maj Greitz and Olof Sjölund, June 26, Budrus [Arabic, trans. Tuqan Tuqan].

29. Zureik, E. 2011. "Colonialism, surveillance, and population control" in Zureik, E., Lyon, D. and Abu-Laban, Y. (eds) *Surveillance and Control in Israel/Palestine: Population, Territory and Power* (pp. 3–46). New York: Routledge, p. 27.

30. Hammami, R. 2005. Professor, Women's Studies Institute, Birzeit University, interview with Monalisa Sundbom, March, Jerusalem.

31. MacCoun, R.J., Kier, E. and Belkin, A. 2006. "Does social cohesion determine motivation in combat? An old question with an old answer". *Armed Forces & Society*, 32: 646–54, p. 648; Wong, L., Kolditz, T.A., Millen, R.A. and Potter, T.M. 2003. *Why They Fight: Combat Motivation in the Iraq War*. Carlisle, PA: Strategic Studies Institute, US Army War College, pp. 5, 6, 27.

32. Scott, J. 1997. "The infrapolitics of subordinate groups" in Rahnema, M. and Bawtree, V. (eds) *The Post-Development Reader* (pp. 311–28). London: Zed Books, p. 323.

33. Said, E.W. and Mohr, J. 1999. *After the Last Sky: Palestinian Lives*. New York: Columbia University Press, p. 100.

34. Cited in Latendresse, A. 1995. *Jerusalem: Palestinian Dynamics of Resistance and Urban Change, 1967–94*. Jerusalem: Palestinian Academic Society for the Study of International Affairs, p. 9.

35. Shehadeh, R. 1982. *The Third Way: A Journal of Life in the West Bank*. London: Quartet Books; Shehadeh, R. 1984. *Samed: Journal of a West Bank Palestinian*. New York: Franklin Watts.

36. Audeh, N. 1983. "Review: Steadfastness. Reviewed Work(s): The third way: A journal of life in the West Bank by Raja Shehadeh", *Journal of Palestine Studies*, 12: 76–9, p. 77.

37. Griffith, J. 2007. "Further considerations concerning the cohesion–performance relation in military settings", *Armed Forces & Society*, 34: 138–47, pp. 139–40.
38. Salameh, H. 2004. Accountant, interview with Nadia Abu-Zahra, June 26, Jerusalem.
39. Amer, H. 2005. Landowner and community leader, interview with Nadia Abu-Zahra, March, Mas'ha (Arabic, trans. Ramzi Azbarga).
40. Taraki, L. and Giacaman, R. 2006. "Modernity aborted and reborn: Ways of being urban in Palestine". In Taraki, L. (ed.) *Living Palestine: Family Survival, Resistance, and Mobility Under Occupation* (pp. 1–51). Syracuse, NY: Syracuse University Press, p. 32.
41. Hammami. 2005. interview.
42. Giacaman, R., Shannon, H., Saab, H., Arya, N. and Boyce, W. 2006. "Individual and collective exposure to political violence: Palestinian adolescents coping with conflict", *European Journal of Public Health*, 17(4): 361–8, pp. 363–4.
43. Featherstone, D. 2005. "Towards the relational construction of militant particularisms: Or why the geographies of past struggles matter for resistance to neoliberal globalisation", *Antipode*, 27: 250–71, pp. 265–6.
44. Ibid. pp. 265–6.
45. Kelly, T. 2006. "Documented lives: Fear and the uncertainties of law during the second Palestinian intifada", *Journal of the Royal Anthropological Institute*, 12: 89–107, p. 97.
46. A.O. (name withheld by request). 2007. Municipal engineer, interview with Nadia Abu-Zahra, March 7, by telephone from Oxford, UK.
47. Ibid.
48. Kelly, T. 2008. 'The attractions of accountancy: Living an ordinary life during the second Palestinian intifada". *Ethnography* 9(3): 351–76, p. 366.
49. Kelly. 2006. "Documented", p. 102.
50. Salameh. 2004. Interview.
51. Panel discussion in 2005 Borderland Studies Conference, Albuquerque, US.
52. Morrar. 2004. Interview.
53. Shalabi, N. 2005. Landowner and community leader, interview with Nadia Abu-Zahra and Olof Sjölund, March 20, Mas'ha (Arabic, trans. Tuqan Tuqan).
54. Shehadeh. 1984. *Samed*, p. 9.
55. Ibid. pp. 8–9.
56. Said, E. 1979 [1992]. *The Question of Palestine* (2nd ed.). New York: Vintage Books, pp. 116–7; Sa'di, A.H. and Abu-Lughod, L. 2007. *Nakba: Palestine, 1948, and the Claims of Memory*. New York: Columbia University Press, p. 183.
57. Robinson, S. 2006. *A History of Israeli Citizenship from the Margins*. Lecture delivered at Rice University, Houston, Texas, October 24, p. 1.
58. Davis, U. 1987. *Israel: An Apartheid State*. London: Zed Books, p. 60.
59. Cook, J. 2006. *Blood and Religion: The Unmasking of the Jewish and Democratic State*. London: Pluto Press, p. 28.
60. Turki, F. 1974. *The Disinherited: Journal of a Palestinian Exile*. New York: Monthly Review Press, p. 84.
61. Ibid. p. 94.

62. Ashrawi, H. 2012. "Palestinians need freedom in Jerusalem, not Israeli permits". *Haaretz*, April 11.
63. Jefferis, D.C. 2012 (forthcoming). "Institutionalizing statelessness: The revocation of residency rights of Palestinians in East Jerusalem". *International Journal of Refugee Law*, p. 2 (of 28).
64. Zureik, E. 2004. "Israel and me: Enigmas of departure". *openDemocracy.net*. Accessed at www.opendemocracy.net/arts-multiculturalism/article_2033.jsp
65. Torpey, J.C. 2000. *The Invention of the Passport: Surveillance, Citizenship and the State*. Cambridge: Cambridge University Press, p. 11.
66. Zorn, J. 2009. "A case for Slovene nationalism: Initial citizenship rules and the Erasure". *Nations and Nationalism*, 15(2): 280–98; Toyota, M. 2005. "Subjects of the state without citizenship: The case of 'hill tribes' in Thailand" in Kymlicka, W. and He, B. (eds) *Multiculturalism in Asia: Theoretical Perspectives* (pp. 110–35). Oxford: Oxford University Press; Torpey, J. 1997. "Revolutions and freedom of movement: An analysis of passport controls in the French, Russian, and Chinese revolutions". *Theory and Society*, 26(6): 837–68; Mitchell, T. 1988. *Colonising Egypt*. Cambridge: Cambridge University Press; Makiya, K. 1998. *Republic of Fear: The Politics of Modern Iraq*. Berkeley: University of California Press (under the author's pseudonym S. al-Khalil), p. 137; Steele, J. 2004. "Iraqis rush for passports denied under Saddam". *Guardian*, August 5; Ghadry, F.N. 2005. "Syrian reform: What lies beneath". *Middle East Quarterly*, 12(1): 61–70; de Mabior, J.G. 2003. *Laws of the New Sudan*. Accessed at http://tinyurl.com/7e3jse5; Uvin, P. 2002. "On counting, categorizing, and violence in Burundi and Rwanda" in Kertzer, D.I. and Arel, D. (eds) *Census and Identity: The Politics of Race, Ethnicity, and Language in National Censuses* (pp. 148–75). Cambridge: University of Cambridge Press; Fattah, I.K. 2005. "The deportations of the Fayli Kurds". *International Conference on Iraqi Refugees and Internally Displaced Persons*. Accessed at http://tinyurl.com/bv6dly7; Anderson, B. 1991. *Imagined Communities: Reflections on the Origin and Spread of Nationalism*. London: Verso, p. 185.
67. Torpey. 2000. *Invention*, p. 7; Lyon, D. 2009. *Identifying Citizens: ID Cards as Surveillance*. Oxford: Polity Press, p. 68.
68. Said, E.W. and Rabbani, M. 1995. "Symbols versus substance: A year after the Declaration of Principles", *Journal of Palestine Studies*, 24: 60–72, p. 71.
69. Morrar. 2004. Interview.
70. Hussein, S. 2011. "Palestinian 'freedom riders' arrested trying to ride bus into Jerusalem". *National Post*, November 15.

# Index

*Compiled by Sue Carlton*

Page numbers in **bold** refer to illustrations

Karm'iel 107, 165
Karpat, Kamal 67–8
Koenig Report (1974) 107
Kollek, Teddy 75
Korn, Alina 103

land
    expropriation/confiscation 26, 27–8,
        **36**, 75–6, 94–5, 96
    importance of 19
Land Party (*el-Ard*) 53
Lavi, Shlomo 34
Law of Entry (1952) 42, 43, 162
Law of Nationality (1952) 41, 162
Law of Return (1950) 39–40, 41, 162
Law to Prevent Infiltration (1954) 71, 77
Lebanon 26, 30, 38, 50
    armistice agreement with Israel 34,
        111
Lehavot Haviva kibbutz 96
Little Triangle 29, 35, 70, 93, 164
Lyon, David 4

Maastricht Guidelines 123
Machnes, Gad 25, 48
McMahon–Hussein Correspondence
    (1915–18) 22
Maguire, Mairead 1
Majd al-Kurum 31, 52
al-Majdal 31–2, 40, 71
Mandela, Nelson 182
Markovsky, Emmanuel 35
marriage 41, 56, 63, 73, 74
massacres 31, 57, 98, 106
Médecins du Monde 129, 131, 134
military courts 59, 72, 73, 103
military orders 44, 58, 61, 109–10, 115,
    166
mobile workers 76, 108, 166
movement restriction 2–4, 6, 18–19, 60,
    61, 92–121, 164–7
    and access to health care 122–37,
        167–9
    and criminalisation of Palestinians
        102–3
    and education 142–52, 154–9,
        169–70, 171
    enforcement 102–3
    and ID (identity documentation)
        12–17, 93
    maps of 111–14, **112**, **113**, 115
    psychological effects 111
    resistance to 175–7
    *see also* checkpoints; ID; pass system
*mukhtars* (village leaders) 74–5, 77–8,
    89–90

Musam, R. 22–4
*musta'ribeen* 59

Nahaf 74
Nahmani, Yosef 42
Naqab 29, 93, 94, 106, 164
    Bedouin 24–5, 40, 42
National Forestry Centre, Peru 17
nationality 43, 46, 57
    and ID cards 58, 62–3, 108
    Israeli 58, 179
    Palestinian 5, 45, 57, 162, 179–80
Nazi regime
    and blacklisting 65
    use of IDs/registration 7–8, 9, **9**,
        11–12, 16, 20
normalcy, struggle for 177–9
Nu'man 117, 118, 140

Oslo Accords 60, 61, 92, 114–15, 118

Palestine
    administrative divisions (Oslo
        Accords) 92, 114–15, 118
    Christian communities 56, 57, 58
    Jewish colonies **113**, 116, 118
        *see also* Israel, expansion/settlement
        policy
    labelled as empty country 21
    recognition in 1919 22
Palestine Monitoring Group 142
Palestine Order-in-Council (1937) 8, 53,
    68, 93
Palestinian Authority National Plan for
    Children 158
Palestinian Red Crescent Society (PRCS)
    131
Palmon, Yehoshua 25, 34, 35, 40, 99
    and blacklisting 48, 51, 54, 56, 69, 98
    and temporary residence permits 70,
        84, 98
Pappé, Ilan 50, 52
pass system 92, 100–2, 119, 165, 175
    history of 5–6
    punishment for violations 166
    *see also* permissions
pass-burning 177, 182
passports 7–8, 11–16, 47, 53, 57, 60–1,
    71, 73, 87, 179, 180
    and finger prints 63
    and markings 16
    *see also* ID
People's Guard 25
permanent residency, applications for
    38–40

Milton Keynes UK
Ingram Content Group UK Ltd.
UKHW011810181023
430868UK00006B/61